Merchants and Gentry in North-East England 1650-1830

The Carrs and the Ellisons

Merchants and Gentry in North-East England 1650-1830

The Carrs and the Ellisons

A. W. Purdue

**University of
Sunderland Press**

© A. W. Purdue

ISBN 1873757085

First published 1999

Published in Great Britain by
University of Sunderland Press
The Teleport
Doxford International
Sunderland
SR3 3XD

Tel: 0191 5252400
Fax: 0191 5201815

British Cataloguing-in-Publications Data
A catalogue record for this book is available from the British Library

Printed in Great Britain by Athenaeum Press, Gateshead

The Author

Bill Purdue is Senior Lecturer in History at the Open University. His publications include *The Second World War* (1999) and, with co-author, John Golby, *The Civilisation of the Crowd, Popular Culture in England 1750-1900* (1984 and 1999), *The Making of the Modern Christmas* (1986) s *The Monarchy and the British People* (1988).

Contents

Illustrations

1. Hebburn Hall by Tom Finch for South Tyneside Public Libraries (the church was built on to the hall in the 19th C)

2. General Cuthbert Ellison (1698-1785)

3. Henry Ellison (1699-1775) (by Pompeo Batoni)

4. Gateshead Park House (by W. H. Knowles) (Gateshead Public Library)

5. Cuthbert Ellison (1773-1860) by John Hopper

6. Dunston Hill (by Harriet Carr)

7. Ralph Carr (1711-1806)

8. Hanover Square by W H Knowles (Gateshead Public Library)

9. Hedgeley Hall in 1892 by Thomas Hope McLachlan

10. Newcastle upon Tyne 1827 (from Dunston Hill) by J. W. Carmichael

11. Cross House by W H Knowles (Gateshead Public Library)

12. Annabella Carr (1763-1822); John Carr (1764-1817); Ralph Carr (1768-1837); Harriet Carr (1771-1848) (by Harriet Cheney née Carr)

Acknowledgments

My first acknowledgment must be to Sir Ralph Carr-Ellison, who suggested to me the idea of a book based on his family papers. His advice and encouragement have been indispensable and his patience inexhaustible during the many years of my research. I have enjoyed his warm hospitality at Hedgeley Hall and Beanley Hall, while working on the papers in his personal possession. Few historians can have worked in such a pleasant environment as the study at Hedgeley, nor experienced such a kind reception as I received from Sir Ralph, the late Lady Mary Carr-Ellison, and John and Catherine Carr-Ellison.

The late Colonel H. R. Carr and the Rt. Hon. Lord Carr of Hadley gave generously with their time and provided me with valuable information.

Fellow historians have been generous with their advice. My friend and mentor, Professor Norman McCord, has read through many drafts of this work, pointed me to new sources and in general made available to me his great command of the history of the North East. Another good friend, Professor Jeremy Black, has given generously of his time and his expertise and has been a great source of encouragement. Among the many other historians to which I am indebted are Dr Joyce Ellis , Professor Esmond Wright, and Dr Tony Barrow.

All historians are aware of how dependent they are on the work of librarians and archivists and the time that is saved by their advice. The indexing done some years ago by Frank Manders at Gateshead Central Library and Robin Gard at the Northumberland Record Office, on, respectively, the Ellison and the Carr-Ellison papers constitute invaluable guides to bulky collections of documents, while the assistance given by their successors, Annette Burton and then Sally Bird and the staff at the NRO and by Eileen Carnaffin and her staff at Gateshead Central Library has been unstinting. The local history librarians at South Tyneside Central Library were also most helpful.

I must thank both the Arts Faculty and the North Region of the Open University for their support in terms of periods of research leave.

Dr Peter Rushton brought both his historical expertise and an academic editor's eye to my manuscript on behalf of Sunderland University Press, while Andrea Murphy and Moira Page of Business Education Publishers saw the book through to publication with care and professionalism. I thank them both.

My wife, Marie, and daughter, Jessica, have put up with my long periods of seclusion in my study and my absorption in the North East of the eighteenth century and I am grateful for their support.

Introduction

The history of the Carr and Ellison families is entwined with that of the North East of England. During the period 1650 to 1830, they played a prominent part in the economic, political and social life of the region. The Carr and Ellison Papers cast considerable light on the development of the dynamic pre-industrial economy, upon the social structure of Newcastle and the counties of Northumberland and Durham, upon the exercise of patronage and influence and upon the manners and mores of polite and gentry society.

The sources available to the historian are often arbitrary and this is especially so when it comes to the letters, the diaries, the estate papers and the business records of individual families. That we have such extensive records for the Carr and Ellison families is due in large part to two remarkable men, who kept almost everything, the letters they received, copies of many letters they sent, their bills, their accounts and even their jottings, and to their descendents who treasured these collections. The kernels of the Carr-Ellison Papers at the Northumberland Record office and of the Ellison papers at Gateshead Public Library are the private papers of, respectively, Ralph Carr (1711-1806) and Henry Ellison (1699-1775), though both collections comprise much of value from before and after their lifetimes. To have family papers from one generation is perhaps an encouragement to subsequent generations to retain theirs and the Carr-Ellison Papers continue into the twentieth century.

These papers together with the Cotesworth papers (Gateshead Public Library) and other papers in the possession of Sir Ralph Carr-Ellison, Lord Lieutenant of Tyne and Wear, to which I have been privileged to have had access, constitute an invaluable resource. They enable us to follow the progress of two families from their mercantile success in the seventeenth century to their solid gentry and landowning status in the nineteenth, during which century the main line of the Ellisons died out and the then head of the Carr family, Ralph Carr, succeeding to the entailed Ellison estates in 1870, changed his name to Carr-Ellison.

By the nineteenth century members of the Carr family were already conscious of their family history and the wealth of papers that enabled it to be traced in some detail from the early eighteenth century. Mrs Caroline Twistleton, a granddaughter of the merchant, Ralph Carr, produced an unpublished manuscript based on her childhood recollections of holidays at her grandfather's house of Dunston Hill and the information gleaned from conversations with her older relatives as well as upon study of the family records. Colonel R.E.Carr and C.E.Carr produced the three volume history of *The Family of Carr* (1893-99), a remarkable work of genealogical and historical research. This book is greatly indebted to what must be one of the most well-researched family histories of its period and which will remain *the* history of the Carr family. The present author asserts only that his aims and preoccupations are different to those of the family historians.

Modern historians have made more use of the Ellison than the Carr-Ellison Papers. Edward Hughes, in one of the best books written on North East history, *North Country life in the Eighteenth Century. The North East 1700-1750* (1952) referred extensively to the Ellison Papers and others have followed his lead. Extracts from the Ellison Papers have been edited and published by Edward Hughes ("The Correspondence of Colonel Robert Ellison", *Archaeologia Aeliana*, 4th series Vol.xxx1) and Joyce Ellis, the historian of William Cotesworth, ("The Letters of Henry Liddell to William Cotesworth", *The Surtees Society*, Vol.cxcv11). Dr Ellis has used the Carr-Ellison as well as the Ellison and Cotesworth Papers in her many publications on the early eighteenth century economy while the American historian, William I. Roberts, III, quarried the Carr-Ellison Papers for his assessment of Ralph Carr's involvement in the American colonial trade ("Ralph Carr: A Newcastle Merchant and the American Colonial Trade", *Business History Review*, 1968). For the most part, however, the Ellison Papers, especially those for the later years of the eighteenth century and for the early nineteenth century, have been little used, while the Carr-Ellison Papers have been neglected and surprisingly little attention has been paid to that great North East merchant, Ralph Carr.

The Ellison Papers and the Carr-Ellison Papers are the main primary sources on which this book relies. Each collection is voluminous and contains information on economic, social and political aspects of the families' history and that of the North East. Essentially these papers begin in the 1720s and 1730s, but I considered that, to provide a proper context for the position of the Ellisons and Carrs in the early eighteenth century, it was important to demonstrate how they established themselves in the society of Newcastle and Tyneside from the mid-seventeenth century. The first chapters of both sections 1 and 2 are dependent, therefore, upon secondary sources and printed primary sources.

Chapters 3 and 4 of Section 2 contain material which I have already published in the form of articles in academic journals: "An Oxford College, Two parishes and a Tithe -Farmer: The modernisation of Tithe Collection", *Rural* History (1997) 8,1;

and "John and Harriet Carr: a Brother and Sister from the North East on the Grand Tour", *Northern History* (1994) Vol. xxx.

The aim of this book is to set the history of the Carrs and Ellisons against the development of the region on which they had such an influence. The families were linked in their generations with the economic, social and political history of Tyneside and the North East.

Regions, unlike counties, are contestable entities with ragged boundaries but the North East is usually taken as, before the late twentieth century, the two counties of Durham and Northumberland and part of north Yorkshire. The context for this study is essentially the centre and north of the region. Its *de facto* capital was Newcastle upon Tyne, a county in its own right since 1400, which dominated not only the lower reaches of the Tyne, but all of Northumberland, for which it was the county town, and most of Durham. As such it was a region of many contrasts, both in terms of natural resources, which varied from a fertile coastal plain, intersected by river valleys, to rugged uplands, and its human settlement.

When Macaulay, writing in the early nineteenth century and concerned to depict the backwardness of England in the seventeenth century as a foil to the progressive and dynamic country of his own day, sought for the very epitome of wildness and lawlessness, he selected Northumberland. There, he suggested, "the traces left by ages of slaughter and pillage were still distinctly perceptible, many miles south of the Tweed, in the face of the country and in the lawless manners of the people".[1] Macaulay both exaggerated and generalised for there was a world of difference between areas of Northumberland, between, for instance, the upper reaches of the North Tyne valley and the secure and relatively tranquil lower Tyne. The architecture of the early decades of the century gives us some idea of such differences: Denton Hall, just outside Newcastle, is a Jacobean mansion built without any provision for defence, while, even at Chipchase Castle on the North Tyne, the Heron family felt secure enough to build a mansion on to their tower house; by contrast fortified farmhouses, such as that at Woodhouses in the foothills of the Cheviots, were still being built in the same period. There was, however, evidence enough for Macaulay's selective picture. The Union of the Crowns of 1603 did, within a decade, put an end to full-scale border raids but, as one historian has put it, did not "transform the people of the border area into paragons of industry and orderliness".[2]

Durham was odd geographically and unique politically. The county palatine included three outposts, which today are in Northumberland: Norham, Islandshire and Bedlingtonshire. Until the reign of Henry VIII, the Prince Bishops had exercised the rights of the crown within their domains and the powers of the bishops remained considerable, while the landholding and wealth of the diocese continued to be enormous until the nineteenth century. Among Durham's many anachronisms, neither the city nor county sent MPs to parliament until the Interregnum after which there was a hiatus, during which Bishop Cosin contested such a slight to his authority, until parliamentary representation began again in 1675.

The concentrated county, though not its northern outposts, had for long been more secure and settled than Northumberland to which its many unfortified Elizabethan mansions bear witness. It had, save for Newcastle, larger towns, including the sea ports of Sunderland and Hartlepool, while even its rugged uplands had a law and order unknown to the border areas of Northumberland. Its agriculture was more prosperous and its trades more varied and dynamic than were those of its neighbouring county. Yet it, like its neighbour, looked for leadership and wealth to a town on the north bank of the river Tyne, Newcastle.

The town of Newcastle prided itself on a very different image to that of its county, Northumberland. Its first history, Gray's *Choragraphia,* was published in 1649 and the author waxed eloquent in declaiming its prosperity and progress. Its development in recent decades had, he believed, amply justified its description by that founding father of the historical discipline, William Camden:

> *Camden calls Newcastle* Ocellus, *the eye of the north, the harth that warmeth the south parts of the kingdom with fire- an Egypt to all the shires of the north, in time of famine, for bread.*[3]

This description points to three reasons for the town's importance: its military significance because of its strategic position on the lowest convenient crossing of the Tyne and proximity to the Scottish border; the vital nature of its coal trade to the nation; and its role as the granary and financial centre for the surrounding countryside.

There were not only economic connections between Newcastle and its rural hinterland but strong social links. The worlds of the rural gentry and yeomen and that of the burghers of Newcastle were linked socially and by kinship. In the commercial world of the town the younger sons of gentry and yeomen could hope to prosper via apprenticeships to the merchant elite, the members of the Merchant Adventurers' Company, while urban fortunes would be invested in the landowning which proffered both security and status.

A free borough from a very early date, Newcastle was granted successive royal charters from 1175. The charter granted by King John in 1216 gave privileges to a Gild Merchant, which effectively became the town's government before its supremacy was challenged by the craft guilds. Although the later mediaeval period saw power in the town gradually shift from merchants to craftsmen, the formation of the Company of Merchant Adventurers in 1512 heralded a swing back to merchant control. During the sixteenth and seventeenth centuries, the wealthiest and most politically influential men in Newcastle were those merchant adventurers who were also hostmen, the company which controlled the coal trade.

The expansion of the North-East economy during the period 1650 to 1830 is well known but has often been treated as a prelude to and preparation for the industrial economy which came to characterise the region in the late nineteenth century, rather than being seen in its own right as an expansive and prosperous economy. The central features of the region's increasing prosperity during these years were the extraction and export of its mineral resources and the late flowering of its agricultural potential in the novel context of social and political stability.

If by industry is meant manufacturing, then, despite the existence of Crowley and Co., one of the biggest iron manufacturers in Britain, this was not an industrial economy. Those economic activities which have often been seen as harbingers of the later nineteenth century economy, ship-building, glass-making and the iron industry, were at best junior partners in an economy dominated by mining and agriculture together with trade and shipping.

The experience of Newcastle as a long-standing trading centre and of the Tyne as the conduit for the import and export of goods was essential to the prosperity of the hinterland. The hegemony of the coal trade from late Elizabethan times overlaid a previous economic order in which it had been wool rather than coal which had made merchant fortunes in Newcastle and the town had the institutions and experience to develop the burgeoning coal trade.

The economic and social relationships between Newcastle, the trading centre and *de facto* capital of the region, and the essentially rural counties of Northumberland and Durham, were crucial to the region's development. Newcastle strove, largely successfully, to maintain its claim to control all trade in or out of the Tyne and the trade in coal linked landowners, merchants and shipowners. The younger sons of gentry and yeomen sought their fortunes via Newcastle apprenticeships, while well-to-do merchants purchased estates in the adjacent counties.

The town was also the social centre of the region. During the eighteenth century, as it expanded away from the riverside, it acquired the amenities for a polite society: fine squares of houses, shops, theatres and an assembly room. Here was a social and cultural life in which the wealthier citizens of the town mixed with the gentry families who maintained town houses.

Both the Carr and Ellison families made their early economic progress in the mercantile world of Newcastle and, though they were by the late eighteenth century considerable landowners and part of a national as well as a provincial elite, they maintained their links with Newcastle, its business world, its society and its politics.

A particular emphasis is placed in this study upon the question of social mobility and upon relations between merchants and gentry. The degree of social mobility in England during the period covered by this book has for long been a vexed question amongst historians. In *An Open Elite? England 1540-1880* (1984), Lawrence and Jeanne C. Fawtier Stone have argued, taking Nortumberland as one of their case studies, that the English landed elite was not open to penetration from rich newcomers from below. It will be argued in the following pages that there was in fact considerable social mobility and that well-to-do merchants found little difficulty in attaining gentry status. Indeed the evidence seems to suggest no great gulf between land and commerce. Such was the economic dynamism of Newcastle and Tyneside, that, not only did new money come out of town and old families dispatch younger sons into town, but wealthy families were reluctant to leave behind the source of their wealth and occupied for several generations an intermediate position of merchant-gentry or gentrified merchants before becoming purely landed. The fact that coal came from landed estates was one important determinant of social familiarity between gentry (and even aristocracy) and trade. The social standing of the principal shippers of Newcastle, members of the Merchant Adventurers Company, was another.

Successful merchants in the seventeenth century looked more to Durham than to Northumberland when they sought to invest urban wealth in land. There is evidence enough for social mobility in Northumberland and the Stones' thesis of a closed Northumbrian elite does little justice to the Ridleys, Blacketts and Allgoods, who established themselves on broad acres in the eighteenth century, nor to the many families, such as the Strakers and Claytons, who did so in the nineteenth. Save for the close neighbourhood of Newcastle, neither communications nor availability of estates made Northumberland so suitable for such purchases as Durham which was, much earlier, a county marked by the ease with which new money was able to acquire land and social acceptance in county society. A recent study has demonstrated just how much mobility there was in and out of the landed elite in that county.[4]

The Carr and Ellison Papers give us considerable information about the social and family lives of the North-East elite in this period. Housing, manners, domestic arrangements and cultural interests changed from the rough and ready standards of the early eighteenth century, not just in step with those of the nation, but at a jump, as a provincial elite caught up with London and south-country ways. Just as country houses replaced old fortified houses, so a provincial social and cultural life followed a southern pattern while retaining its internal idiosyncrasies. Richer and longer established families like the Ellisons forged firm links with London society, sent their children to southern public schools, purchased military commissions for their sons and maintained houses in London. More newly arrived families like the Carrs were not far behind them.

Marriages have always been alliances of economic import and means of advancement but this was especially true in the late seventeenth and eighteenth centuries due to the demographic crisis that affected all sections of English society.[5] Amongst the landed elite the failure to produce male heirs had serious consequences for the descent of property which continued until the late nineteenth century. The strategy often adopted to circumvent the absence of male heirs was inter-familial inheritance and frequently the hyphenation of names.[6] In such circumstances marriage to an heiress was an increasing means of economic and social advancement. That marriages had a strong element of economic and social alliance did not exclude affection and even love. It had never done so but this period has been seen as one in which, from the top of society downwards, affection in marriage increased.[7] The growth of sensiblity made, not only for sensitive relationships between the sexes, but for a more indulgent attitude towards children.

All such developments can be found in the history of the Carrs and Ellisons, but the lives of the family members, if comfortable and generally prosperous, were confined by the worries and fears about money and health that are the constant lot of mankind. Debts were a perennial problem, even to the Ellisons with their substantial assets, while the emergence of a proto-professional corps of doctors did little to temper the pain and discomfort of ill-health.

A natural corollary of economic and social position was political influence and power and the Ellisons in particular played a role in the parliamentary representation of the region from Robert Ellison's time as MP for Newcastle during the Civil War to Cuthbert Ellison's eighteen years in the same position from 1812 to 1830. But behind the protagonists at election time lay the web of patronage, loyalties and inter-dependence, which all merchants and country gentlemen were part of. A position of influence had to be maintained, even if its base was wealth and possessions, and involved time-consuming public office, whether as justice of the peace, sheriff or deputy-lieutenant, and the support of charities.

The Carrs and Ellisons contributed to the economic, social and political development and history of Tyneside and the North-East and prospered as the region did. Their wealth grew and their estates expanded with the region but, just as the region was no closed or introverted economy or society but enjoyed intimate links with London and, via its trading links, with Europe and even North America, so Carrs and Ellisons were at home in the capital and travelled extensively abroad as traders, soldiers and tourists. They were part of a responsible and hard-working elite, which valued money which had come by effort and perseverance, though also by advantageous marriages, and which, as it slowly exchanged civic for county offices, leavened patronage with public spirit.

The history of the two families, the Ellisons of Hebburn Hall and the Carrs of Dunston Hill, thus provide us with examples of economic advancement and social mobility. Both families came initially from Northumberland, though the Ellison origins are somewhat obscure, both flourished in the commercial world of Newcastle and both in time acquired country seats in County Durham close to Tyneside.

At the beginning of this account in the mid-seventeenth century, the Ellisons were already well established as Newcastle merchants, while, although Carrs abounded in mercantile circles, our branch of the Carrs had for generations inhabited the smaller world of Hexham and Hexhamshire. Their respective stations and the very different societies they inhabited at this time point to the considerable contrast between parts of rural Northumberland and the bustling commercial town only twenty miles away.

The young John Carr's journey to Newcastle to become an apprentice to the Merchant Adventurers' Company in 1655 brought him onto the lower rungs of Newcastle society at a time when the Ellisons were moving into the inner merchant elite. By 1830 both families were firmly within the ranks of the landed gentry. What follows is the history of a gradual transition.

References

1.   T. B. Macaulay. *The History of England from the Accession of James 11,* vol.1 (Everyman Edition 1919) p.221.

2.   Norman McCord, *North East England* (1979) p.14.

3.   W. Gray, *Chorographia or A Survey of Newcastle upon Tyne,* (First published 1649; refs. to 1883 edition) p.91.

4.   W. Gray, *Chorographia or A Survey of Newcastle upon Tyne,* (First published 1649; refs. to 1883 edition) p.91.

5. S. Halliday, "Social Mobility, Demographic Change and the Landed Elite of County Durham, 1610-1819: an open or shut case?", *Northern History*, vol.xxx, 1994.

6. See E. A. Wrigley and R. S. Schofield, *The Population History of England 1541-1871* (1981) pp.162-70.

7. See L. Stone, *The Family, Sex and Marriage in England 1500-1800* (1977) and L. Stone and J. C. F.Stone, *An Open Elite? England 1540-1880* (1984) pp. 105-142.

8. Stone, *The Family, Sex and Marriage*.

Merchants and Gentry in North-East England 1650-1830

The Carrs and the Ellisons

Part I

The Ellisons of Hebburn Hall

Chapter 1

Ocellus

Nay more than fo, men fay it doth, dull mettals change to gold,
To fay therefore it is a god, our alchymifts are bold.

John Johnson

Newcastle, with over 10,000 inhabitants, was in the mid-seventeenth century one of the largest provincial cities in England. From the viewpoint of London, which it provided with coal, it was probably the most important.

It was as the centre of the coal trade that the town was increasingly known to the world and it was upon that trade that its wealth and prosperity had come to be based. Its first historian, William Gray, described the extent of the employment it created:

> *Many thousand people are employed in this trade of coales - many live by*
> *working them in the pits - many by conveying them in wagons and waines*
> *to the river Tine; many men are employed in conveying the coales in*
> *keeles from the stathes aboard the ships....this great trade hath made this*
> *towne to flourish in all trade.[1]*

The coal trade was by the mid-seventeenth the leading sector of the Newcastle economy, a trade which, rather than diminishing other trades, enriched and expanded them. Its leadership was a relatively recent development, with the shipment of coal out of the Tyne accelerating sharply from the late years of Elizabeth's reign, and its dominance overlaid a previous economic order. During the late mediaeval period, it had been wool rather than coal that had made merchant fortunes when Newcastle had been one of the ten staple towns after the staple of wool had been removed from Calais in 1353; then the houses and warehouses of the wool merchants had stood in the Cloth Market, the centre of commerce and the home of mayors and aldermen.

The grip of the coal trade on the civic life of Newcastle was firm but informal. As Roger Howell, the leading authority on Newcastle during the period of the Civil

War, has shown[2], the trade affiliations of those admitted as freemen in the first sixty years of the seventeenth century seem to show a town without any dominant trade or industry with scarcely a mention of the coal trade. The clothing trades had the greater share of admissions in the early decades, giving way to the maritime trades towards mid-century, yet no trade gained more than thirty percent of admissions. But, as Howell has demonstrated, this is misleading in that the dominant trade, the coal trade, is not overtly represented in these lists but is there, nevertheless, because the hostmen, who dealt with the export of coal, were generally also members of another company, the most important hostmen usually being members of the Mercers' Company, one of the three companies which made up the Merchant Adventurers. The coal trade was both ubiquitous and yet inseparable from other trades because, as a newcomer, it had to fit in with and work within an existing economic and political order, while, as it was a risky trade, it was unwise to be solely dependent upon it. Real power in Newcastle lay in the hands of hostmen who belonged to one of the three companies or mysteries who made up the Merchant Adventurers' Company.

One man's monopoly is, no doubt, another's cooperative enterprise and both terms could be used to describe the merchant guilds of Newcastle and, indeed, the town itself from mediaeval times until the eighteenth century. Merchant guilds developed in Newcastle, as elsewhere in England, during the second half of the eleventh century as those burgesses who were shopkeepers or warehousemen got together to protect by union their rights and privileges as traders. They sought exemption from tolls and taxes in their own towns and other towns in which they did business, the imposition of taxes upon others and a monopoly of trade for members of the guild as opposed to other inhabitants.

The charter granted by King John to Newcastle in 1216 gave the merchant guild such special privilege and protection. Its members were to be exempt from tolls and dues in all his seaports and they had the right to reparations for any tolls and customs wrongly exacted from them, which they could extract by distraining the goods in Newcastle belonging to those who violated their privileges. The historian of the Newcastle Merchant Adventurers, F.W. Dendy, concluded that, "Within a century after the gild merchant in Newcastle, its members had evidently formed an exclusive class" and "...a distinction had grown up between the burgesses generally and the burgesses who were merchants".[3]

From mediaeval times until the early nineteenth century, the history of Newcastle was in large part that of the rise and fall of layers of monopolistic influence and power. In the first place there was Newcastle's claim to control all trades into and out of the Tyne; on this all citizens of Newcastle could unite. Then there was the distinction within Newcastle between the rights of the burgesses as opposed to other inhabitants. Although a burgess may originally have been simply a citizen of the town and a man could become a free burgess or freeman without belonging to any trade or craft guild, it became the norm that only members of companies were free burgesses. If all companies had privileges and especially the twelve leading companies or mysteries, which provided the members of the Common Council, then the merchant companies, who fiercely preserved their sole right to trade against the craft guilds and who generally occupied the top positions in civic government, were by far the best situated. It must be noted, however, that even the Newcastle Merchant Adventurers had themselves to bend the knee and make payments, not only to kings and central government, but, in the sixteenth and sevententh centuries, to the London Company of Merchant Adventurers, as did other Newcastle companies, such as the Silversmiths who had to recognise the superior authority of the London Silversmiths.

Newcastle was perpetually concerned to preserve its control of the entire river to a point well above the town against the claims of the Bishop of Durham and the prior of Tynemouth before the Reformation and the traders of other riparian towns after it. The celebrated campaign by Ralph Gardiner of North Shields against Newcastle's control of the river was the latest episode in a long war.[4] Within Newcastle, the three companies which made up the Merchant Adventurers (the Boothmen, the Mercers and the Drapers) strove to maintain their privileges against the craft guilds while, as we shall see, even in the inner circle of power of Hostmen and Merchant Adventurers, there was an established oligarchy and its rivals.

One family which had firmly and rapidly established itself in the mercantile and civic life of the town was the Ellison family. The Ellisons had been in Newcastle for about a century and a half by 1650. Before this they had probably been yeomen at Hawkwell near Stamfordham, a village eight miles north-west of Newcastle, where the Elysons had a share in the fields..[5]

Welford comments that:

> It is a noticeable circumstance that the Ellisons make their appearance in Newcastle history all of a sudden as it were. The books of the company of Merchant Adventurers of Newcastle contain entries of the apprenticeships of John and Cuthbert Ellison, dated respectively 1523 and 1524; the books of Trinity House show that in the last named year "Sir" Robert Ellison was chaplain and John Ellison an alderman of the fraternity. Six years later, Robert Ellison occurs in the Merchants' books as entering upon his apprenticeship. Thus in the space of seven years, we have evidence of five Ellisons living in Newcastle, of whom no previous notice

*occurs- a chaplain, an elder brother of the Trinity House, and three
young men just commencing life as merchant adventurers.*[6]

In the course of his career the first Cuthbert Ellison held the offices of Sheriff and
Governor of the Merchant Adventurers and was Mayor in 1549 and 1554. While
Governor of the Merchant Adventurers, he issued a bye-law regulating the dress
and conduct of apprentices. The rowdy and bawdy behaviour of apprentices was a
perennial problem in most towns and the periodic reactions of authority were
sometimes warranted, but often no more than the intrinsic irritation of the middle-
aged with the high spirits of the young. It would appear from the preamble to
Ellison's bye-law that the behaviour of the Newcastle apprentices had given more
than the usual cause for scandal:

> *...what dyseng cardeng and mummying! what typling, daunseng, and
> brasenge of harlots;.what garded cotes, jagged hose lyned with silk, and
> cut shoes! what use of gitternes by night! what wearynge of berds! what
> daggers ys by them worne crosse overthwarte their backs, that theise
> theire doings are more cumlye and decent for raging ruffians than
> seemlie for honest apprentizes.*[7]

If these were Cuthbert Ellison's words, he had certainly a turn of phrase and one
wonders whether he had heard John Knox preach in Newcastle five years
previously.

Cuthbert's will of February 1556 reveals him to have been a man of wealth and
property: houses in the Bigg Market, the Windaes, Middle Street and Gowler
Rawe; land at Bamburgh; leases on farmland and mills at Heworth; and a half share
in a salt-pan.

This first Cutbert Ellison's son and grandson, both also called Cuthbert, were
members of the Merchant Adventurers' Company. Though neither held his high
offices nor wielded his influence, they consolidated the family's position in
Newcastle he had so effectively established. The landholding at Heworth referred to
in the grandfather's will was retained and extended. A lease of 1632 details tracts of
land at Heworth and on the foreshore at Jarrow leased by the children of the third
Cuthbert Ellison, then minors; the banks of the lower Tyne were already becoming
valuable as the coal trade increased and colliers needed to discharge their ballast on
ballast-shores.

By the mid-seventeenth century, the Ellison's were well established as members of
Newcastle's elite. Christopher, Robert and Benjamin Ellison, the sons of the third

Cuthbert, were all Merchant Adventurers and, if not perhaps members of the inner circle that had its grip on the town's government, part of the wider oligarchy.

The tendency for power and wealth in Newcastle to pass into the hands of a small number of related families was assisted by several factors. These included the relative independence of the town from local aristocratic influence and the nature of its constitution, which was complex and cumbersome in its electoral process and designed to ensure continuity and the concentration of power in a few hands. Newcastle had been administratively separate from Northumberland since 1400 and had a social and economic order largely independent of aristocratic or gentry influence. As Howell has argued:

> *Newcastle was not dominated by a powerful local family or even by a complex of local gentry families ...Those members of the local gentry who exercised influence in Newcastle politics, like the Liddells and the Maddisons, owed their landed position in the county to their trading connections in the town rather than their town power to their local influence.*[8]

The strengthening of the position of a governing clique was not unwelcome to Tudor and Stuart sovereigns who sought, as had their mediaeval predecessors, to work through the governing bodies of towns, and found it easier to do so in conjunction with established oligarchies, rather than with the whole community of burgesses.

Although the Reformation removed some ecclesiastical opposition to Newcastle's power (the Prior of Tynemouth for instance), the new men, who took over church lands and were eager to exploit mineral wealth, were, if not themselves Newcastle merchants, just as much a threat to the town's domination of the river and the coal trade; but that domination held for the time being and was indeed increased by a charter of 1600 and by the so-called "Grand Lease".

The Grand Lease demonstrates the difficulties, which faced even a powerful man who dared to take on the Newcastle oligarchy and break into its coal trade. In 1577 Thomas Sutton, Surveyor of the Ordnance in the North, was granted by Queen Elizabeth the lease of all the coalmines in the Bishop of Durham's manor of Gateshead and Whickham for 79 years. He wished to work the coalmines himself but, as he was not a freeman of Newcastle, he was excluded from the local market. In 1583 he sold the lease, which had by then been extended to 99 years, to two Newcastle merchants, Henry Anderson and William Selby. The acquisition of the lease put Anderson and Selby and other hostmen who were their associates in a wonderful position at a time when the demand for coal was growing apace.

The inner ring which dominated Newcastle was not composed of all hostmen (it was in fact not difficult to become a member of this new company which did not rank among the mysteries) but just those who were also powerful merchants. After an analysis of office holding in the town, Howell concluded that it was not the Hostmen alone, but those coal-traders who were also Merchant Adventurers, and particularly mercers, who formed the inner ring.[9] The Common Council of the town was very similar in composition to the governing body of the Merchant Adventurers, while those who held the major offices of Mayor, Sheriff or Member of Parliament were nearly always Merchant Adventurers and Hostmen and usually mercers:

> To be a Hostman without at the same time being a member of the Merchant Adventurers was of small avail....The inner ring which dominated the town was largely composed of the men who held membership in both companies, such as Sir George Selby, Sir Henry Anderson and Leonard Carr.[10]

An inner circle of power will always be faced with problems and threats to its position: divisions within the inner circle, jealousy from the outer circle and the ambitions of those without. But within Newcastle, opponents of those in power had to be very careful that their opposition was not made use of by those who were enemies to the position of the town itself. Few in Newcastle would have wanted to see the town's control of the river and the coal-trade brought to an end. What was to alter the situation and give an opportunity to wealthy and ambitious men, Merchant Adventurers but outside the inner ring, was the internecine conflict known as the English Civil War or Great Rebellion.

Newcastle and the Civil War

Historians have, of late, become sceptical as to the accuracy of the term, "English Civil War", arguing that "English" does scant justice to the Scottish and Irish dimensions of events and that, within England, much account needs to be taken of provincial and county issues.[11] What occurred, it has been argued, was, "military failure and collapse in the face of a Scots rebellion and invasion".[12] Such revisionism also rejects explanations which see the war as either about clear cut constitutional divisions or as a social conflict between specific classes or strata.

Newcastle felt the full force of Scotland's involvement, being occupied by Leslie's army in 1640-41 and then besieged and taken in 1644. With the fortunes of war and the twists of national politics, factions in Newcastle had their hour and rose and fell. What is clear is that such factions had more to do with a struggle for power and position within the town and with an attempt to usurp the position of the existing elite by those who were just outside it than with conflict between distinct social groups or classes. What did correspond, albeit imperfectly, for there were some puritans within the old inner circle, to factions in Newcastle was religion and the new oligarchy, which took over in 1645, was a puritan one. Those disenfranchised for their royalism in 1645, men like Sir John Marley, Sir George Baker, Sir Nicholas Cole, Sir James Liddell and Sir Ralph Bowes, were overwhelmingly hostmen, mercers and, from a puritan viewpoint, delinquents. The new men who took over were headed by Henry Dawson and included Thomas Bonner and William Johnson; all were merchants, but outside the inner ring, and puritans, and they cooperated with more established Newcastle figures such as John Blakiston, Henry Warmouth and Sir Lionel Maddison, who were associated with the parliamentary and puritan cause.

But, despite war and religion, life goes on. The attitude to the civil war amongst the majority of Newcastle burgesses and the wider body of inhabitants was that it was a terrible disruption to their innocent pursuit of wealth and the making of livings. Yet, it also provided opportunities:

> More often than not ...the bulk of the population shifted and turned in their loyalties as the military situation demanded and ...used the political troubles of the time to work out local rivalries.[13]

Among those who prospered in these "interesting times" was the head of the Ellison family, Robert Ellison (1614-78). He had by 1643 become a supporter of the parliamentary cause and was forced to leave Newcastle. A Resolution of the Common Council of September 1643 declared that:

> Whereas out of disaffection to his majesty and the present government Robert Ellison merchant [and others] have withdrawn themselves and most part of their estates, out of Newcastle and have refused to hold with our sovereign lord the king against all persons, to live and die according to the oath they took when they were made free burgesses and have been incendiaries and have treated with men of another nation to invade their kingdom and possess themselves of this town - ordered that they be disenfranchised.[14]

He played a prominent role after the town's capture by the Scots when there was a purge of Marley and other royalists .

In December 1644 the House of Commons passed a series of resolutions affecting Newcastle. The Mayor, Sheriff, Recorder, Collector of Customs and several aldermen were dismissed; the duties of the Sheriff, the royalist James Cole, were to be taken over by Robert Ellison. At the same time a committee of fourteen was appointed to sequestrate the estates of "delinquents" and Robert Ellison was a member. In May 1645 The Commons issued further orders confirming the dismissal of delinquents from office and castigating the "malignant and wicked party, ill-affected to the King and Parliament, and the true Protestant religion". Henry Lawson, Henry Dawson, Thomas Legard, John Cosin and Thomas Bonner were made aldermen and Ellison was made sheriff. By June Ellison was, along with the Town Clerk, issuing decrees concerning the management of the coalmines belonging to delinquents. He was in a powerful position for his brief was a wide one and he was entitled to make decisions in the light of, "the best management of the State".[15]

Robert Ellison, despite his high standing in the eyes of Parliament, was not a member of the puritan faction led by Henry Dawson and, unlike most of that clique, he can not be seen as an outsider to the old oligarchy as were the Dawsons, Bonners and Johnsons. Ellison was both a hostman and a mercer while he was related to the Selby family and to the Carrs of Newcastle who were influential in the inner ring. His position was unusual and in the long run advantagous for he seems to have retained the confidence of much of the old elite as the best custodian of their interests in unpropitious times and to have been less identified with the puritan faction than other established figures like Warmouth and Maddison. At the same time, as a parliamentarian, he was in a position to benefit from the turmoil of the times.

His differences with the puritan faction can be seen in the parliamentary election of 1647 when he and Henry Warmouth contested the seat left vacant by the removal of Sir Henry Anderson, a moderate reformer opposed to royal policies when elected in 1640, but who had later rallied to the king's forces. A new member for Newcastle was therefore required to join the remaining sitting member, John Blackiston, soon to gain notoriety as a regicide. Both Warmouth and Ellison were strong parliamentarians and the fierceness of the election contest points to to the rivalry of factions based on internal Newcastle interests and issues being at least as important as national politics. Warmouth was supported by such leading members of the puritan faction as Henry and George Dawson and Thomas Bonner, while among Ellison's backers were Robert Carr and Robert Anderson who belonged to well-established Newcastle families. Although Warmouth was the son of a mayor and was himself an alderman and former sheriff, Ellison had the closer connections with the old oligarchy and in the election we can, perhaps, see the hostmen-mercer establishment backing a moderate parliamentarian as the best bet to keep the temporarily dominant new men of the extreme puritan faction at bay.

Some 700 freemen turned out to vote and the mayor, Henry Dawson, together with the sheriff and most of the aldermen, considered that Warmouth was the winner. That judgement was fiercely denied by Ellison's supporters and, although Warmouth was temporarly allowed to take his seat, a House of Commons committee eventually decided that his election was illegal. Ellison won the subsequent contest against a new opponent, Thomas Ledgard, a prominent member of the Dawson circle. Despite further objections on the grounds of unfair pratices, Robert Ellison's election was allowed to stand.[16]

Essentially a moderate parliamentarian, who supported reconciliation with the king, Robert Ellison was among those MPs who were forcibly excluded from the Commons by Colonel Pride on 6 December 1648. Unlike his fellow MP for Newcastle, Blackiston, he thus bore no responsibility for the king's death and was indeed opposed to it.

The election dispute in Newcastle reveals that there were factions within the ranks of the parliamentary supporters but this did not rule out cooperation on a number of fronts. There was much to play for. Political power and personal economic advantage have rarely, if ever, been entirely separate and seventeenth century mores took a realistic view of their connection. Royalists, now dispossessed of their political positions, could expect to pay a price in terms of sequestrations, while, conversely, the new men installed in political office could hope to improve their political fortunes.

Local committees were set up to sequestrate the estates of those who had espoused the royalist cause and were in the terminology of the time "delinquents". This was of course a national issue but very important in a region where royalism was strong and had made its mark with the stout defence of Newcastle in 1644 and where there were perpetual rumours and fears of royalist plotting. But, as ever, local rivalries and ties complicated the issues. On Newcastle's committee sat men like John Blackiston, all three Dawsons (Henry, George and William), Thomas Bonner and Thomas Ledgard. This was not a body likely to deal lightly with men who were not only royalists but members of the Newcastle establishment that the sequestrators dearly wished to replace. Yet, although the committee could be harsh enough and one of its victims, Sir Thomas Riddell, was only cleared of his delinquency on payment of £4,000, the control of the chief delinquents, such as Sir Thomas Liddell, Sir Francis Anderson, and even Sir Thomas Riddell and Marley himself, over the key to power and wealth on Tyneside, the coal trade, was left largely intact.

Among the reasons for this was the great difficulty in establishing, amidst the complex pattern of ownership and occupation of estates and mines on Tyneside, who exactly owned what. Then there was the fact that many families had members on both sides of the political cum religious divide and, when it came to family as opposed to ideological interests, family loyalties often won out and relatives would be protected and estates and assets transferred to other parties. Above all, it was important to protect the coal trade and Newcastle's domination of it; the existing owners had the wealth and experience to run it.

There were threats to the position of Newcastle and its merchant elite, which made for a certain unity in the town. The Council of Trade, set up in 1650, was perceived by the Merchant Adventurers of York, Hull, Newcastle and Leeds as London dominated and as challenging the privileges of northern towns. The northern Merchant Adventurers were therefore concerned to petition for the same protection as Londoners for their trades, for the right of non-Londoners to join the Greenland and Muscovy Companies, and for the regulation and enforcement of apprenticeships. Their opinion was that "Trade bee not left loose but may be regulated by companies". The Newcastle Merchant adventurers and the town as a whole were, as usual, fighting on two fronts in this period: against the engrossing of London and against the challenge from other interests on the Tyne; a report of the Council of 26 September 1651 condemned Newcastle Corporation's assertion of its privileges over navigation in the river so that it could extort dues from shipping and its harassment of craftsmen at North Shields. The Navigation Act of 1651 posed new problems, hindering imports from Holland and making Newcastle merchants pay high prices for colonial and staple goods at London.[17]

These troubled times were not favourable to allowing the all important coal trade to fall into inexperienced hands. New men did not therefore take over the trade, though the Dawson clique seem to have attempted to do so, becoming hostmen and making determined efforts to gain control. The records of the Hostmen's Company show, however, that the main trade stayed in established hands. Some new men with political clout did get in but only to the fringes of the trade. Thomas Bonner acquired the ballast shores at St. Anthony's and Byker and was able to exploit their leases while Robert Ellison did the same thing at Hebburn. The two acted together in impropriating the tithes of Jarrow church.

Bourne in his *History of Newcastle* relates:

> But after the death of King Charles 1, Thomas Bonner and Robert Ellison
> got in to be magistrates; and these men having gotten wealth and
> increase by the Rebellion, did purchase Jarrow; and what could not be
> done before in a lawful time, they did bring to pass in this unlawful
> juncture, building a shore and casting ballast, to the great detriment of
> the River. And having the Town at Command, Mr Bonner bought St.

Anthony's, and Robert Ellison bought Hebburn, and there they both built shores, and got the allowance of the Common Council when they were beyond resisting: and since that Mr Carr [Ralph Carr of Cocken], a man that deserved well of his present Majesty [CharlesII], and the Town hath procured that his brother Ellison (for old Ellison's son married his sister) should have liberty to erect his shore to a great length, and which in time will utterly overthrow our navigation, for they will dam out the indraught- which makes rivers far off the Sea to be walled out; it will go by and not come in: and some Ancient and discreet mariners of ships have said they have not left a berth to save our ships in, when any land-flood or storm happens in the River.[18]

Robert Ellison's acquisition of the Hebburn estate together with Hebburn Hall was an important step in the rise of the Ellison family. After four generations as Newcastle merchants, the Ellisons could now be said to have acquired a sort of gentry status although the bulk of their income came from trade. Hebburn Hall was to be the family seat until the nineteenth century and it still remains in the ownership of the Carr-Ellison family. According to Mackenzie and Ross, "the old mansion house at Hebburn was strongly built, as if for defence, like the Border towers".[19] It had previously belonged to the fiercely Catholic Hodgson family, which had in its chief branch terminated in an heiress, who had married Francis Carr of Cocken, who sold the estate to Robert Ellison. Francis Carr was later to sell the Cocken estate to Sir Ralph Carr of the long-established Newcastle merchant family, who was to be MP for Newcastle in the 'seventies and 'eighties and whose sister, Jane, married Robert Ellison's son, Cuthbert,

Roger Howell, though he considers that affairs were on the whole carried out efficiently and conscientiously under the puritan corporation, does refer to some corruption within the norms of the age: "The amount of money that Alderman Henry Rawling made out of ballast shores is rather suspicious, and there is some doubt too about the lands that Thomas Bonner and Robert Ellison purchased for themselves while holding town office". But, as Howell points out, the merchants of Elizabeth's reign had done much the same thing with the Grand Lease.[20] There can be little doubt, however, that the leading puritans enriched themselves during the Interregnum. William Johnson, mayor of Newcastle in 1653-54, bought an estate and substantial mansion at Kibblesworth and the Bonners also acquired land there.

But if the fortunes of the puritan faction were at their zenith in the mid-1650s, a reckoning was to come with the restoration. Newcastle had sent a loyal address to Oliver Cromwell in 1654 and then condolences to Richard Cromwell on news of his father's death in 1658. As late as 1659 petitions to Parliament, which was then considering a bill for the better government of the towm, still protested loyalty to the Commonwealth. Royalist feeling was, however, increasingly evident in the autumn of 1659 and the position of the puritan faction was becoming uncomfortable.

Thomas Bonner had just been elected mayor for the third time. He and the Dawsons had for some years managed mayoral elections so as to keep the office within their circle, but this year the times were a changing: Commonwealth generals rushed hither and thither (both Monck and Lambert were to be at Newcastle during the winter) and emissaries were crossing to the king in Holland, while, in Newcastle, Marley was back. That pillar of puritan rectitude, Ambrose Barnes, saw the way things were going and resigned his position as alderman in September. Bonner, the "miracle of the age", as Barnes had called him, had resigned the lucrative position of Steward of the manor and lordship of Gateshead and Whickham a few days earlier. Barnes's hagiographical biographer described the sorry scene when:

> The worthy Mayor of Newcastle making scruple to surrender the staff to Sir John Marlow (sic), who was thought a fit person to succeed him, was so pusht and bruized in the Spittal, that he was caryed out in his chair half dead, such was the violence of the faction.[21]

Robert Ellison was in a more advantageous position. He was able to return to parliament when, under General Monck's protection, the excluded MPs of 1648 took their seats once more in February 1660. He went on to serve in the Convention Parliament (April-December 1660), which resolved in favour of government by king, Lords and Commons and agreed to the king's unconditional return. As one of those who had assisted in the peaceful restoration of the monarchy, Ellison's position was fairly secure.

With the proclamation of the king in June 1660, the population of Newcastle, which had so roundly cursed Sir John Marley for bringing the Scots upon the town, sought credit for having been continuously, if often discreetly, loyal to the royalist cause and the stout defence against the Scots became a proud boast. Not surprisingly, back came the old guard of aldermen, Sir James Clavering, Sir Francis Liddell, Henry Maddison and Cuthbert Carr, and out went the new, George Dawson, Christopher Nicholson, Henry Rawling, William Johnson and Peter Sanderson.[22]

All in all, it was a pretty modest reckoning, as indeed the penalties paid by the royalists had been modest enough. John Blackiston, the regicide MP, was dead but his wife forfeited her estate. Otherwise most of the men who had governed Newcastle during the Interregnum lost office but little else, though those who refused to embrace the broad church that was Anglicanism would find their religious practices for the time being outside the law. Perhaps the former moderation begat the latter. Perhaps it was felt the puritan corporation had governed Newcastle efficiently and had not been unpopular.

References

1.   Gray, *Chorographia,* p.84.

2.   Roger Howell Jr., *Newcastle -upon-Tyne and the Puritan Revolution* (1967). This chapter is greatly indebted to Howell's interpretation of events in Newcastle during the Civil War, which it follows closely. See also Professor Howell's, "Newcastle and the Nation: the seventeenth century experience" in *Archaeologia Aeliana.*

3.   J. R. Boyle and F. W. Dendy, (eds.) "Extracts from the Records of the Merchant Adventurers of Newcastle", Vol. I (1895), *Surtees Society,* Vol. XCIII.

4.   Gardiner, who was not a freeman of Newcastle and who was in business as a brewer and coal shipper at North Shields, fought a long legal battle against the monopolies of Newcastle. Arrested and imprisoned, he escaped in 1653 and took his case to London where he petitioned parliament without success. His *England's Grievance Discovered* (1655) recounts his struggle against Newcastle's control over the Tyne.

5.   The ancestry of the Ellisons has not been traced very far back. Such excellent historians as Hodgson and Surtees, respectively the historians of Northumberland and Durham, concluded that the Ellison pedigree could only be definitely traced to Cuthbert Ellison of Newcastle who was born in the early sixteenth century. Welford mentions one "Rob fil Elye" listed in the pipe rolls of the reign of Henry III. R.Welford, *Men of Mark 'twixt Tyne and Tweed* (1895) p.145. The Northumberland County History mentions a Thomas Elyson who appears in the "Black Book of Hexham" as a Priory tenant in 1479 and a John Ellison, Vicar of Cholerton in 1485. *Northumberland County History*, Vol III p.148 and Vol. IV p.267.

6.   Welford, *ibid,* p.145.

7.   An Acte for the Apparel of Apprentices, 14 Nov. 1554. Boyle and Dendy, *Records of Merchant Adventurers,* Vol. I pp.20-22.

8.   Howell, *Newcastle and the Puritan Revolution*, p.28.

9.   *Ibid*, p.45.

10. *Ibid*, p.47.

11. See,for instance,A. J. Fletcher,*The Outbreak of the English Civil War* (1981) and C. Russell (ed.)*The Origins of the English Civil War(1975).*

12. J. C. D.Clark,*Revolution and Rebellion.State and Society in England in the seventeenth and eighteenth centuries* (1986) p.54.

13. Howell, *Newcastle and the Puritan Revolution*, pp.342-343.

14. Alfred J. Ellison, *Ellison Portraits 1510-1936*, typed manuscript 1936, p. 45, South Tyneside Central Library.

15. Richard Welford, biographical article on Robert Ellison in *Newcastle Weekly Chronicle,* 16 May 1891.

16. See Howell, *Newcastle and the Puritan Revolution,* pp. 182-184.

17. J. P. Cooper, "Social and Economic Policies under the Commonwealth" in *The Interregnum. The Quest for Settlement* (1972), G.E.Alymer (ed.) p. 137.

18. Henry Bourne, *History of Newcastle* (1736) p.173.

19. E. Mackenzie and E. Ross, *An Historical, Topographical, and Descriptive View of the County Palatinate of Durham (1834)* vol. I, p.15.

20. Howell, *Newcastle and the Puritan Revolution*, pp.213-214.

21. W. H. D.Longstaffe, *Memoirs of Ambrose Barnes,* Surtees Society vol., MDCCCLXVI, 1867, p.173.

22. Howell, *Newcastle and the Puritan Revolution*, p.186.

Chapter 2

Hebburn Hall

Hebburn Hall by Tom Finch for South Tyneside Public Libraries
(the church was built on to the hall in the 19th C)

About four hundred years ago there stood upon the spot upon which Hebburn Hall now stands a great stone tower, with walls that were three and a half feet thick, and small window openings, and most probably with but one low narrow doorway. Who placed it their no one knows; but it was built in a manner that tells us that the people who lived in it had to make good their own safety...From its summit they could see Jarrow Monastery to which the manor belonged, and Monkton (the birthplace of the Venerable Bede), and Sheriff Hill, Gateshead, and the Tyne flowing placidly through the adjacent lands.

F. R. Wilson 1887

The Ellisons seem to have survived the Restoration easily enough. They were well connected, had friends across the political divide and had not been extreme puritans. Robert Ellison retained Hebburn Hall and the Hebburn estate, together with the lucrative ballast shores, hung on to his share of the land at Jarrow he and Bonner had acquired, and continued as the impropriator of the Jarrow tithes. Two years before his death in 1678, he was made Governor of the Merchant Adventurers' Company. He died at the age of 64, leaving numerous children (he and his first wife, Elizabeth Gray, were said to have produced twenty-two).

If the Ellisons, in Welford's phrase, entered Newcastle history, "all of a sudden", they also took over much of the south bank of the river Tyne pretty quickly. As we have seen, the family had already by the time of the Civil War interests in land at Jarrow, but by 1660 Robert Ellison had become the major landowner of the area. Succeeding generations expanded the Ellison estates and if, in 1790, the then head of the family, Henry Ellison (1734-95), had climbed on the roof of the newly rebuilt Hebburn Hall much of the land he could have seen, from Gateshead to Jarrow, would have been his.

On Robert Ellison's death in 1678, his eldest son Cuthbert (1638-85)[1] came into a mixed inheritance, which bestrode the worlds of agriculture and commerce and the status of merchant and country gentleman. The Elizabethan mansion, Hebburn Hall, surrounded by its park, looked over fields and trees to a River Tyne that from a distance appeared serene. A closer inspection, however, would have revealed the bustle of the river traffic, ships dumping their ballast on Hebburn shore and a colliery extracting the coal from the Hebburn Vale seam. The great town a few miles up river could not be ignored and Cuthbert Ellison Esq. of Hebburn Hall was a Merchant Adventurer and Hostman of Newcastle. The town would for another century or more remain within its ancient walls but its power and influence were felt to the mouth of the river. The Ellisons were ensconced at Hebburn because of their position in Newcastle and, like many rising families on Tyneside, were to preserve their urban and commercial connections and for long be both merchants and gentry.

Durham, as we have seen, appears to have been a county marked by social mobility into the elite and its necessary corollary, a rapid turnover in the ownership of estates. A great deal of land had been disposed of by the crown since the early sixteenth century both after the dissolution of the monasteries and after the sequestration of estates: the Cocken estate had, for instance, been granted by Henry VIII to John Hilton of Newcastle from whom it had passed by descent and then mortgage to Cuthbert Ellison's brother-in-law, Ralph Carr; while the extensive lands taken from the Earl of Westmorland after the 1569 rebellion had found a number of new buyers. The research of S.J.Halliday has found 173 incomers who acquired Durham estates in the period 1610-1815. Such incomers included: men from gentry families, either landed already or younger sons; professional men, mainly lawyers; and merchants, 36 of them. Such categories were unlikely to have been mutually exclusive for sons of gentry became lawyers, while, as we have seen, younger sons of gentry sought entry to Newcastle apprenticeships. The arrival of Newcastle merchants at Hebburn Hall was, therefore, hardly unusual and, indeed, the Ellison's predecessors, the Hodgsons, had made their money out of the coal trade.[2]

Cuthbert Ellison, who, as we have seen, had married Jane Carr, daughter of William Carr of Newcastle and the sister of Sir Ralph Carr (three times mayor of Newcastle; MP for the town in 1679, 1680 and 1688-9; and, from 1665, owner of the Cocken estate) [3] was not to enjoy his inheritance for long. He died in London in 1685 at the age of forty-six, a first sign of the metropolitan connections that were to be characteristic of the Ellisons. He was succeeded by his son Robert.

Marriages have for long been, *inter alia,* economic alliances and a significant path to economic and social advance for those who married into the right family. At the least, a good marriage produced influential relatives. The Ellison fortunes were to owe much to advantageous marriages. As Cuthbert married Jane Carr, so their son Robert married Elizabeth Liddell, daughter of Sir Henry Liddell, Bt. of Ravensworth Castle. The family was thus allied with one of the rising and most prosperous and influential families of the North. Three of Elizabeth's brothers were Members of Parliament and, in the next generation, Sir Henry Liddell, the fourth baronet, was, in 1747, to be ennobled as the first Baron Ravensworth. Henry Liddell and George Liddell were both brilliant businessmen, who were among the select group who really understood and were able, to some degree, to manipulate the North-East economy. Nor was the Liddells' a merely local purchase on power and influence, for they were close to the heart of Whig interests at a national level and able, after 1715, to share in the rewards of Whig hegemony. These were formidable and useful relatives.

Unfortunately, Robert Ellison (1665-1726) was far from being the best businessman among Cuthbert's sons and his advantageous marriage seems to have been about his only astute move. His inclination seems to have been for the life of a rather old fashioned country gentleman and his, "simplicity of manners" was remarked on. Unfortunately, an estate like Hebburn required efficient management and, during Robert's time, arrears of rents mounted. The Ellisons were comparatively new landowners, and Whigs at that, but Robert was more like the older squires, so many of whom found it difficult to run their estates profitably in this period. His younger brother, William, was a successful merchant and was Sheriff of Newcastle in 1705, while another brother, Cuthbert, became a fellow of Corpus Christi College,

Oxford. Merchant Adventurer and Hostman though he was, Robert Ellison was not successful in his business ventures and was heavily in debt when he died in 1728. He had for long been assisted by his brother-in-law, Colonel George Liddell, MP for Berwick upon Tweed, to whom he owed a considerable sum of money.

Robert fulfilled his duties as a Justice of the Peace punctiliously and, in that his actions in that office sometimes occasioned complaints from his relatives, probably dispassionately. Anne Clavering found his judgement wanting in 1709 and had, "...an inclination to shame him and putt myself into the Commission of Peace and come and sitt amongst you".[4] Henry Liddell, whom Anne married in 1711, was scathing about a decision made jointly by Ellison and James Clavering: "As to the 2 justices' behaviour I don't so much admire their conduct, especially his with whom I am so intimately acquainted".[5] The position of Justice of the Peace was, though honourable, arduous and time consuming. That he was referred to as "the Justice" in the coded letters written by Henry Liddell to William Cotesworth, suggests that this unpaid position was his consuming interest.[6]

His last years were not happy ones. When his wife was seriously ill in London during 1724, his letters to his son, Henry, reveal him to be both anguished with worry about her health and concerned about the expense of her treatment. George Liddell had to be applied to for money.[7]

Both trade and estate management on rapidly industrialising Tyneside were hazardous occupations in a hard tough world, where little quarter was given to the indebted. Much depended on the business acumen of the head of the family. Primogeniture and entailment have the great merit of keeping estates together over the generations but the disadvantage that everything can depend on the ability of the eldest son. The Ellisons would have fared ill had things been left to eldest sons. They were to be saved by advantageous marriages, linking them to the most able, and the most ruthless, families in the piranha pond of the North-East economy, and the good fortune and good sense of a younger son.

Robert Ellison's eldest son Cuthbert (1698-1785) had a successful career as a soldier but he spent more than his income from the estate and his army commission provided. He rarely visited his home at Hebburn so that the estate had an absentee landlord. The family's fortunes were, therefore, left in the capable hands of his younger brother, Henry (1699-1775). As Cuthbert never married, the Hebburn estate eventually came to Henry's son, along with the very considerable property and wealth left to him by his father.

Henry Ellison's successful life, in which he established himself as a country gentleman of substance in his own right, owed something to his considerable abilities but more to the Ellison facility for advantageous marriages. By the time of his marriage to Hannah Cotesworth in 1729, he was embarked on a career as the agent to the Ravensworth estate, a responsible and well paid position, which held out considerable opportunities by which a capable man could make profits for himself, as well as for his employers. But the marriage to one of William Cotesworth's two daughters transformed him into a rich man with a fine mansion (Gateshead Park), landed property and coal interests. To put Henry and his marriage into context, we need to consider the economic life of Tyneside in the early eighteenth century.

That Henry Ellison, despite coming from a line of Newcastle merchants, who were Merchant Adventurers and Hostmen, did not, as a youth, enter into the economic and corporate life of Newcastle, may seem surprising. His uncle, William Ellison, was a major figure in the town and the Newcastle companies were the traditional path to advancement for younger sons. The reasons are in part to be found in his family's gentry status, reinforced by his father's marriage to Elizabeth Liddell. They have also much to do with the beginnings of a decline of the monopolistic power of the Newcastle companies and the parallel increase in the importance of the economy south of the river and, especially, to the south-west of Gateshead, where the Liddells of Ravensworth owned so much land. Henry did become a Hostman in 1726 and a Merchant Adventurer in 1727 but it is significant that he was in his late twenties and already advanced in his career when he did so.

A further hundred years were to pass before the companies became largely honorific bodies and, in the early eighteenth century, there was still solid material advantage, as well as prestige, in membership but the monopolistic power of the corporate bodies of Newcastle and, indeed, of the town itself, was in retreat.

A freer economy gradually emerged, but not because of any widespread enthusiasm for free trade doctrines; protectionism was still the common sense of the day and mercantilism governed relations with foreign markets. A man like Sir Joshua Child, who expressed the view, "that all restrictions on trade are naught; and that no Company whatever, whether they trade in a joint stock, or under regulations called regulated companies can be for public good, except it be made easy for all or any of His Majesty's subjects to be admitted into them", was rare.[8] Many of those who opposed particular monopolies were men who wished to establish different monopolies. What aided the free market was that for legal and pragmatic reasons monopolies became more and more difficult to enforce as the economy expanded and became more complex.

It is important to distinguish between the gradual decline in the power of the corporate institutions of Newcastle and the position of the town as the region's economic and social centre and political capital. Despite incipient rivalry to Newcastle from Sunderland and the challenge to the Tyne from the Wear and even from Blyth, the increased wealth of the region continued to be channelled through Newcastle. Nevertheless, the business career of Henry Ellison was not to be located in Newcastle, itself, nor pursued, primarily, as a Merchant Adventurer or Hostman. It was a career devoted to the improvement of estates and the exploitation of their mineral deposits in the area to the south west of Gateshead, an area which exhibited dynamic economic growth in the period.

Historians have long argued about the suitability of terms like "industrial revolution" or "industrialisation" to describe the growth of the British economy in the eighteenth and early nineteenth centuries. The growth of the coal trade can be seen as so fundamentally altering the nature of the economy of the region as to have created, not only a new economy, but a new society. An alternative view is to fully accept the dynamic impact of the accelerating importance of coal throughout the seventeenth and eighteenth centuries but to see its effect as the energising of an essentially pre-industrial economy and society. J.U.Nef has argued that the expansion of the coal trade brought about a qualitative change in the nature of the economy and society[9], while a recent study of the parish of Whickham, so central to the development of the coal trade and to the lives and economic advancement of Cotesworth, the Ellisons and, as we shall see later, the Carrs, has seen it as "Britain's first industrial society".[10] Can even Whickham, much less the wider North-East economy, deserve such a description? Norman McCord has, in contrast, described Northumberland and Durham as late as 1800 as "...rural counties into which the coal industry intruded...".[11]

There can be no doubt that the economy of the area was transformed by the extraction of and the transportation of coal and by the attraction of other enterprises that could utilise the cheap supplies of coal. David Levine and Keith Wrightson's close study of the development of the area provides an invaluable picture of economic and social change. What is debatable is whether what emerged was an "industrial society", much less a "class society".

Coal mining provided in the long run a means of manufacturing but it is not itself a manufacturing process and the coal, which was produced in the area to the west and south of Gateshead, was overwhelmingly bound for domestic use. Abraham Crowley's iron works at Swalwell and Winlaton, a massive and paternally, if sternly, governed operation, constituted one of the biggest manufacturing operations in Europe, but was highly exceptional within the locality and region as without.

Levine and Wrightson argue that a "community" of copyholders had by 1700 been changed into an "industrial class society"[12] characterised by a large population of wage-earning industrial workers and superior orders of landowners, coalowners, substantial farmers and tradesmen, a society where older social bonds had been replaced by the economic relations of the coal trade. Yet, save in remote areas, which as we shall see included parts of Northumberland, the sort of socio-economic relationships found in sixteenth century Whickham had also been much modified by 1700 and certainly did not exist in rural areas close to substantial towns. Mining and the Crowley works had helped to destroy all but the formal legal framework of the manorial system in Whickham but so had the pull of prosperous Newcastle and the stimulus it gave to agriculture and market gardening in adjacent areas. The comment that social relations continued to be conducted in "an older idiom" and "adapted only slowly and partially to the realities of new structural contexts"[13] suggests a determinism based upon an idea of social change following an ordained pattern from economic developments, itself derived from a later period of history, while the "new structural contexts" are far from uncontentious.

Like all arguments about change and continuity, the question as to the nature of the North-East economy in the eighteenth century is in part a matter of emphasis and also involves definitions and periodisation. The debate impinges upon the wider controversy as to the nature of eighteenth century British society as a whole, an *"ancien regime"* society[14] or one hurrying on to "modernity". Comparisons of a society with what has been and what is to come utilise the inevitable yardsticks but can obscure its unique characteristics and what it was in its own right.

The concept of the North East as the crucible of British industrialisation ignores the leisurely pace, accompanied by setbacks, of the development of the region's manufacturing. As McCord has written:

> *...in some respects the impetus towards economic growth achieved in the North East by about 1700 seems to have faltered somewhat in ensuing years, in comparison with the increased pace of expansion in those other areas of Britain which were among the major centres of early industrialisation...If in 1700 the North East seems to have been as advanced as any region in Britain, the great days of the North East industrialisation were to be considerably delayed and this region was not one of the most obvious prodigies of early industrial Britain.*[15]

The idea of accelerated industrialisation as constituting a "revolution" in the late eighteenth and early nineteenth centuries has itself come under attack. J.C.D.Clark has commented that the developments in this period were "...neither very industrial, nor very revolutionary".[16] E.A.Wrigley's view of the transition from an "advanced organic economy" to a "mineral-based energy economy" is cogent, but it is important to emphasise that Wrigley sees this as a nineteenth century development.[17] Even that archetypal leading sector, cotton, did not embrace coal-propelled steam power to a great degree till the 1820s. The great period of the North East's application of steam power to manufacturing begins around 1850. That a number of manufacturing industries had previously emerged on Tyneside as epiphenomena of cheap coal (salt-making, glass and iron for instance), should not blind us to the fact that an industrialised North East was a late nineteenth century development.

The eighteenth century North East fits well Wrigley's concept of an "advanced organic economy" and the most "modern" aspects of it were to be found in commerce, law, landowning and even, sporadically, in its agriculture, rather than in the tightly-knit industrial and mining villages he describes as "industrial but not modern".[18] A *caveat* might well be, whether, in respect of mining villages, a process of hacking coal from holes in the ground with hand tools should necessarily be described as "industrial" though its organisation and distribution system were clearly "modern". Wrigley, like Levine and Wrightson, sees colliery workers as constituting "one class" with "few visible betters whose pattern of consumption could be aped". Miners were an identifiable section of society with manners and *mores* of their own but their designation as a class is suspect; miners into the twentieth century were to remain a section apart with their own solidarity and interests, distinct from other workers, while for much of that period their vertical ties to owners and landowners might be cut across by divisive interests but were enduring none the less.

The concept of a "long eighteenth century", encompassing the period 1688 to 1830, is a useful corrective to an overemphasis, in descriptions of the economy and society of eighteenth century Britain, on transition from "traditional" to "industrial" or to "modern". It allows a greater emphasis on unique characteristics evident over a time-scale, which is sufficient for them not to be seen as merely residual or as harbingers. The economic dynamism of Tyneside to the west and south of Gateshead and its social structure, for all their peculiarities, were readily explicable within the context of the wider economy and society. Landowning was dominant but closely involved with mineral extraction and trade. There was a freer market but one that worked within the framework of old laws, titles and restraints. Economic changes both fitted into and modified the existing social order, which adapted itself to the salience of the coal trade. Coal was extracted from land owned or leased by aristocrats, gentry or Newcastle merchants but a small number of large landowners dominated the coal mining of the area. Their lawyers and agents, relying often on old manorial law, safeguarded their rights and interests as to their mineral wealth as they did with their agricultural interests. Far from a "class society" this was one where vertical ties were as important as horizontal divisions.

Levine and Wrightson comment that:

> *Paradoxically, industrialised Whickham was a far more gentrified society*
> *than the Elizabethan parish had been. The restructuring of copyholder*
> *society that accompanied industrialisation saw the emergence of a large*
> *number of minor gentry families".* [19]

The "paradox" is, however, only there in the light of a specific historical scenario
for the ubiquity of such families, often merchant or ex-merchant families, all
around Newcastle, was central to the developing North-East economy and society. [20]

It was in this context that Henry Ellison as a younger son of a gentry family began
his career. He did the sensible thing and subordinated his prospects to the service of
wealthy and powerful relatives. His mother's family largely determined his early
career. Edward Hughes has commented on the rise of the Liddells:

> *....the period between the restoration and 1750 witnessed the liquidation*
> *of scores of ancient families, both great and small, and the rise out of the*
> *ashes of new men who gradually acquired vast agglomerations of estates*
> *and whose descendants have, for the most part, remained in possession*
> *until our own day. In some cases, the Liddells of Ravensworth, for*
> *example, it is possible to watch a slow-motion picture of this process.* [21]

By the early eighteenth century, the capable younger sons of Sir Henry, the third
baronet, Henry and George Liddell, were energetically expanding the family estates
and coal interests. [22] From 1701 until 1711, Henry Liddell supervised his family's
extensive interests in the Durham coalfield, after which he moved to London, from
where he was able, until his death in 1717, both to intimately influence the London
end of the coal traffic, and to retain overall responsibility for the family's fortunes.
His brother George took over the day-to-day management of the collieries, the
wagon-ways and the shipment of coal.

Henry Ellison appears to have been picked out by the Liddells as a useful recruit to
the family firm and to have been sent to London to study law. He was articled to
one of the leading attorneys of the day, Charles Sanderson, who, a north
countryman himself, acted for many of the gentry families of the North-East. He
was, Hughes comments, "cousin" to almost everybody. [23]

Henry's move to Sanderson's chambers at the Inner Temple did not part him from
kith and kin for the Liddells exhibited great fondness for London life and many of
them lived there. It was, perhaps, a mark of their new aristocratic social station that
the word "town" signified for them, London, rather than Newcastle. Henry's

mother, Elizabeth, having born her husband eight children, of which two died soon after birth, was settled in London by 1724 along with her daughters. Mrs Ellison's residence in London may have, initially, been occasioned by her poor health and the need for treatment by London physicians, but her parents and brother spent much time in London and she spent the rest of her life there, dying at Kensington in 1750. Her daughters, Jane, Elizabeth and Catherine were all buried at Kensington.

After his legal training at Charles Sanderson's chambers, Henry became the agent or steward of the Ravensworth estate at the generous salary of £400 a year. No doubt he had followed the advice given him by his uncle, George Liddell:

> *Now that you are about to come into the world on your own bottom, I earnestly recommend it to you not only to persevere but to redouble your diligence in this last year. I need not tell you how great an advantage it will be to you both in reputation and in your calling to see a sober and diligent young man in an age when virtue and industry are hardly known.*[24]

Edward Hughes has described the considerable duties of the agent or steward of an estate as follows:

> *The agent was responsible for setting farms, arranging leases, holding courts, collecting rents, keeping accounts, supervising the collieries, keeping an eye on poachers, and if the master and mistress happened to be away in town or recuperating at Scarborough or Bath, he took over control at the hall, reported regularly on "the infantry", engaged and paid the indoor and outdoor staff, and generally assumed responsibility.*[25]

A good agent was invaluable, while a poor one could prove disastrous for a family's fortune's. It is rarely sufficiently emphasised that, until the mid-nineteenth century, the most important and the most lucrative activities in the North East were the law and the administration and exploitation of landed estates. The two went hand in hand for so much litigation concerned inheritance and title to land. Manufacturing was small beer in comparison[26] and even the commerce of Newcastle merchants could hardly compete with the returns from land, while there could be no division between landowning and the coal trade because, for many, the coal trade and the exploitation of mineral resources in general were very much part of landowning.

The North East experienced rapid growth from the early years of the eighteenth century but manufacturing played only a small part in this. What were at the heart of growth were agricultural improvements, the development of the extraction of mineral resources, the improvement of roads and a web of legal innovation, banking development and more effective administration (this latter dependent on the increased ability of governments to raise taxes).

It is not therefore surprising that a major path to advancement was the time-honoured one of service to great estates, either as an all-round agent, a specialist in mining or as a lawyer and, either as a servant to a single landowner, or to several. Thus William Cotesworth, among his many business activities, acted as agent to a number of estates including those of the Milbank family and Lord Powlett, while John Carr of Dunston Hill was agent to Lord Thanet and others. The Allgoods were, for generations, lawyers to the Radcliffes, before acquiring their own considerable estates. More than a century later Thomas Taylor was able to establish himself at Chipchase Castle with a fortune accumulated while mining agent to the Duke of Northumberland.

Henry Ellison was, thus, embarked on a career with considerable opportunities and was, from the Liddells' point of view, that most desirable combination, a capable relative. What transformed his position, however, was not work but marriage, a marriage which made him an heir to much of the fortunes accumulated by three remarkable men, William Ramsay, his son, another William Ramsay, and William Cotesworth.

References

1. Of Robert's younger sons, Nathaniel and Joseph founded respectively, a Newcastle branch of the family and the Ellisons of Linz Green in County Durham, while Samuel married Barbara, daughter of Cuthbert Carr of St. Helen's Auckland. Samuel's son, Robert, was eventually to inherit the St. Auckland estate, changing his name from Ellison to Carr.

2. Halliday, "Social mobility".

3. The Newcastle Carrs and the Carrs of Cocken in County Durham shared a common ancestor in George Carr, who had been mayor ten times in the fifteenth century. By the 1660s, Francis Carr of Cocken was financially embarrassed and gradually mortgaged the estate to his relative, Sir Ralph Carr, who took it over in 1665.
    Sir Ralph, like Cuthbert Carr of St. Helen's Auckland, had been a staunch royalist during the Civil War. The inter-marriage between these families and the Ellisons shows how quickly political animosities could be forgotten.

4.   Anne Clavering to James Clavering, April 14, 1709. *The Correspondence of James Clavering*, H.T.Dickinson (ed.), Surtees Society, Vol. CLXXVIII, 1963.

5.   H. Liddell to W.Cotesworth, 18 July 1716, *Liddell-Cotesworth Letters,* J.M.Ellis (ed), Surtees Society, Vol. CXCVII, 1975.

6.   *Ibid*. In these letters from Liddell to Cotesworth, Liddell, fearful of their interception, attempted via nicknames and veiled references to disguise his meaning.

7.   Robert Ellison to Henry Ellison, 8 March 1724, 5 April 1724 and 24 April 1724. Ellison Documents, Gateshead Public Library, (A2). The Ellison of Hebburn Documents are divided into classes A,B,C,D. and subdivided into bundles, 1,2,3, etc. When an extract from a document is ascribed as (A9) or (A20) following references to the Ellison Mss. will be taken as belonging to that particular bundle of documents unless stated otherwise.

8.   Quoted in *Extracts from the Records of the Merchant Adventurers of Newcastle upon Tyne*, F.W. Denny (ed), Surtees Society, Vol. XCIII, p.XLIII.

9.   J. U. Nef, *The Rise of The British Coal Industry,* 2 vols. (1932).

10.   David Levine and Keith Wrightson, *The Making of an Industrial Society. Whickham 1560-1745* (1991).

11.   Norman McCord, "Some Aspects of change in the Nineteenth Century North East", *Northern History,* Vol. XXXI, 1995.

12.   Levine and Wrightson, *Making of an Industrial Society,* p.429.

13.   *Ibid.*

14.   J.C.D. Clark, *English Society 1688-1832* (1985).

15.   Norman McCord, *North East England. An Economic and Social History.* (1979) p.15.

16.   J. C. D.Clark, *Revolution and Rebellion*, (1986) p.39. See also Michael Fores, "The Myth of a British Industrial Revolution", *History*, Vol. 66, No. 217, June 1981.

17. E. A. Wrigley, *People, Cities and Wealth, The Transformation of Traditional Society,* (1987).

18. *Ibid,* p.74.

19. Levine and Wrightson, *Making of an Industrial Society,* p. 356.

20. Benton, which acquired a cluster of big houses during the eighteenth century, is a good example of this.

21. Hughes, p.5.

22. Thomas, the elder brother and heir was physically handicapped. He was known as "the deaf and dumb squire". John, the next oldest, had inherited an independent estate in Yorkshire from his maternal grandfather, Sir John Bright of Badsworth.

23. Hughes, p.77.

24. *Ibid*, p.379.

25. *Ibid* p.74.

26. Halliday, "Social mobility", identifies only one manufacturer, the ironmaster, Townley, of Stella and Stanley, among those who bought landed estates in Durham between 1610 and 1819.

Chapter 3

The Ramsays, "Black William" and the Making of Fortunes

"...a head and genius in business"

Henry Liddell on William Cotesworth

William Ramsay was a leading Newcastle goldsmith who, like many in that trade, was also a moneylender, providing credit and mortgages. He also dealt in bills of exchange on London. In 1687 he became the proprietor of lead-mines at Haydon Field and Settlingstones. Hughes provides us with one yardstick for the scale of this enterprise: the gross salary bill rose from £17.19s.0d., for the period November 1687 to the following January, to £213.18s.4d., for the period December 1689 to May 1690. He went on to take interests in lead-mines in Weardale and was in a position to take advantage of the high price of lead during Queen Anne's reign and the demand for the metal in Amsterdam and Hamburg. Ramsay was indeed, as Hughes suggests, something of an Alchemist, changing gold into lead, lead back to gold, and purchasing land with the gold when he bought the manors of Bellister and Hartleyburn, close to Haltwhistle, in the last year of his life.[1] Despite his wealth, his position as an Alderman and his marriage to Elizabeth Ellison, the daughter of the Robert Ellison who acquired Hebburn Hall, William Ramsay lived simply at his shop in the Side.

If the father made money, it was the son who made the social advance. A Merchant Adventurer, rather than a goldsmith, William Ramsay, junior, left the Side and went to live in Westgate House at the bottom of Westgate Road. He traded with the Baltic, Holland and Newfoundland, importing flax and madder and exporting lead, coal and grindstones. Like his father, he carried on a substantial business in loans and mortgages, while he retained the lead-mines and the Bellister and Hartleyburn estates. He made a prestigious marriage to the sister of Calverley Bewicke of Close

House and was Mayor of Newcastle in 1701. In 1712 he bought the manors of Gateshead and Whickham and moved from Westgate House to Park House at Gateshead, which he proceeded to improve at great expense. Ramsay died childless in 1715 and left Gateshead Park and the bulk of his estate to his brother-in-law and business associate, William Cotesworth.[2]

If the rise of the Ramsays over two generations had been rapid, the career of William Cotesworth represents one of the most spectacular advances in economic and social position, within a single lifetime, to be found in North East history. The younger son of a modest Teesdale farmer, Cotesworth was apprenticed to a Gateshead merchant and tallow chandler. The merchant, Robert Sutton, died before Cotesworth had completed his term but the widow carried on the business with the aid of her young son. Mrs Sutton appears to have been exceedingly fond of the apprentice and brought him into partnership; she provided most of his share of the capital and he paid only a nominal twenty pounds; she was later to be very generous to him in her will. In 1699, he married his late partner's sister-in law, Hannah Ramsay, sister to the wealthy William. The firm of Cotesworth and Sutton lasted for some fifteen years. It was engaged in a very varied trade as grocers, mercers, tallow chandlers and wine merchants.

Before its dissolution in 1706, the partnership had become a rather unequal one and Cotesworth was already acting outside it. He had become the local agent to the Hollow Sword Blade Company, arranging shipments of blades to London and paying the German craftsmen who ran the workshops at Shotley Bridge. In 1704, he made his first move into the coal industry, when he obtained an exclusive lease of wayleave rights belonging to the Dean and Chapter of Durham. Many of his activities were contrary to the terms of the partnership and the break-up was marked by some ill-will and allegations that Cotesworth had milked the joint capital for his personal ventures.

Cotesworth was probably not quite straight or, if he obeyed the letter of contracts, he strayed from their spirit. As Joyce Ellis has demonstrated, he manipulated the credit system, delaying payments while collecting promptly.[3] His nickname, "Black Will", was not affectionate. Whatever his methods, he had, by 1706, acquired sufficient capital to set up an independent business and branch out into the extremely risky and capital intensive salt and coal industries. He had already come a long way from humble beginnings and had also overcome the disadvantage of being apprenticed in Gateshead, rather than Newcastle.

Like many whose business interests lay outside Newcastle, Cotesworth was hot against the town's privileges and the control exercised by the charmed circle of its magistracy. The Crowleys, whose iron works were at Winlaton and Swalwell fought a running battle with the corporation over its insistence on levying tolls on goods passing through Newcastle. Robert Ellison complained of the tyranny of, "a few ill-bred, ill-natured and insolent inferiors", which seems odd when one considers he was a Merchant Adventurer and Hostman, with a brother prominent in the corporation. Even Thomas Liddell, who was Governor of the Hostmen, shared the irritation of landowners south of the river with the way Newcastle exercised its powers. Ellison's target may have been Richard Ridley, who was defending the corporation's powers and his own interest vigorously.

Newcastle was in a cleft stick, in that it sought the increasingly incompatible ends of maximising its tolls *and* enforcing the rights of the Merchant Adventurers over imports and exports, "foreign bought and foreign sold". The desire for tolls won and, as the town made £10,000 a year out of charges and tolls, Cotesworth and others were able, by convenient fictions, to trade unmolested, provided they paid the tolls.

Cotesworth was already, by 1706, a merchant of substance but it was in the next ten years that he was to transform himself from successful merchant to a landed gentleman, who was a force to be reckoned with in the coal trade.

The coal trade presents the historian of North-East England with many problems. From Elizabethan times it beat out the rhythms of prosperity and recession. As Sir Henry Liddell Bt. put it: "But what signifies all your Balls, Ridottos etc. unless Navigation and the Coal Trade flourish". Yet, historians have painted such a bleak picture of potential losses and the difficulties of the trade that one sometimes wonders why anyone ventured into it. Hughes, à *propos* William Ramsay, junior, and his commercial success, writes: "It is surely significant that prior to 1711, and thereafter only as a landlord, Ramsay was never a coal-owner or concerned in the salt industry at Shields, both notoriously precarious trades".[4] Joyce Ellis refers to the coal industry as "already notoriously expensive and risky" before the risks increased in the early eighteenth century.[5]

Newcastle had maintained its control of the coal trade, as over every type of trade into and out of the Tyne, until the late seventeenth century. It did so, in the first place, by its monopoly of the landing and the loading of goods along the entire navigable reaches of the river. This control was buttressed by the fact that many Newcastle merchants were also mine owners or worked mines, which they leased. Since the middle of Elizabeth's reign, certain Newcastle freemen had benefited from the Grand Lease of the manors of Gateshead and Whickham which contained the most profitable mines of the area.

A number of factors came together in the late seventeenth and early eighteenth century to change the nature of the coal trade and decrease Newcastle's dominance within it. The Grand Lease ran out, but at a time when the more easily worked shallow seams in Gateshead and Whickham were nearly exhausted, and pits near the rivers Wear and Blyth began loading significant amounts of coal at Sunderland and Blyth. The Tyneside coal industry had to choose between digging deeper or sinking new pits further from the riverside. Considering the state of mining technology, the latter was the more practical strategy but one bound, in the most litigious period of a consummately litigious nation, to lead to legal problems. Fanning out from the river involved the transport of coal over land belonging to many different individuals on its way to riverside staithes.

There were three major players in the coal trade, the mine owners, the fitters who were contracted to see to the loading of coal on to ships and the London dealers, to which can be added the ship-owners who had interests of their own. That the Hostmen's Company was not the power it had been, had much to do with the fact that many of the members were no longer coal owners, but simply fitters with different interests from owners. These factors and the state of the London market for coal, which was virtually static while output was rising, provide the background to William Cotesworth's career in the coal trade. In particular they explain two major steps, his becoming principal agent to a cartel formed in 1708 by several of the principal coal-owners of the Tyne Valley and his persuading his brother-in-law, William Ramsay, to purchase the manors of Gateshead and Whickham in 1712.

The two leading figures in the formation of the cartel in 1708 were Cotesworth and Henry Liddell. Their admiration for each other's business acumen turned into a lasting friendship. Liddell, as we have noted, was the principal manager of the extensive business interests of his family. His alliance and friendship with Cotesworth was, as Joyce Ellis, who has edited the Liddell-Cotesworth Letters, writes:

> ...at first sight an unlikely relationship: in contrast with Liddell's privileged background, Cotesworth was laboriously working his way up from humble beginnings as an apprentice tallow chandler, when they first came into contact, and was never fully accepted by many of the north-eastern gentry families.[6]

Liddell, referred to as "the Governor" in their circle because he was Governor of the Hostmen's Company, considered his friend, "Mr Mayor" [of Gateshead], to have, "...a head and genius in business".[7] Though a newcomer to the coal trade, Cotesworth was already involved in mining ventures with the Liddells when he was brought in by them to be principal agent to the newly formed coal cartel, the

Regulation. This was the first of many attempts to maintain prices on the London market by limiting production. Its failure was, probably, inevitable, because those outside the cartel could increase their production, while those within it were likely to squabble over their allocations. That it lasted until 1715 says much for the ability of Cotesworth and Liddell. The more broadly based Grand Alliance, which followed it and enjoyed some success for many decades, was, in essence, based upon it. But *agreement* with fellow coal owners was not the only way to regulate the amount of coal coming on to the market.

Another way was to control the access of coal from inland pits to the riverside. In 1712, Cotesworth, as we have seen, persuaded his brother-in-law, William Ramsay, to purchase leases on the manors of Gateshead and Whickham. In themselves, the manors were not a brilliant acquisition, as the more easily gained coal in the area had been worked and to go deeper was both expensive and risky. The real value of the estates lay in their strategic position. Cotesworth and Ramsay now controlled the passage of coal from many collieries south of the Tyne, which had to cross their land to get to the river. In 1716, after Ramsay's death and Cotesworth's inheritance of his estate, Bishop Crewe demised the manors to Cotesworth for 21 years, renewable as was customary every seven years.[8]

Cotesworth claimed that the majority of coal mined in the Tyne valley came to the market, "by my lycence or under my influence".[9] Thus it was, that, in a trade where success usually depended on the vast resources that the Liddells, Bowes or Montagu-Wortley families could draw upon, a relative minnow like Cotesworth, whose actual share of the industry was small, was able to have such influence and make a considerable fortune.

He, along with the Liddells and the Wortleys became active in the salt trade. He claimed by 1719 to be the biggest salt proprietor in the country. The salt from the salt pans at North and South Shields was of poor quality but was very cheap as the salt pans provided an outlet for the inferior coal, which was inevitably extracted, along with the high quality sea coal, from the Tyne valley pits.[10]

By 1715, after he had inherited Ramsay's estate, his income from land and industry was over £8,000 a year. He was now William Cotesworth Esquire of Gateshead Park, a Justice of the Peace and Lord of the manors of Gateshead and Whickham and of Bellister and Hartleyburn. The one time apprentice tallow chandler had come a long way.[11]

Cotesworth and the Liddells were allies in politics as well as business. The Liddells were strong Whigs as was Cotesworth. "I was in King Charles the Second's reign what was called a Whig and so have continued and am at this day", he wrote in

1720.[12] Henry Liddell's uncle, Sir Henry, was Whig MP for Newcastle upon Tyne for the first decade of the eighteenth century. The town was essentially Tory, however, and in 1710 Liddell and the other Whig MP, William Carr were defeated by Sir William Blackett and William Wrightson in an election dominated by the impeachment of the High Church divine, Dr Sachervell. There was a political split in the Ellison family at this time, with the Mayor of Newcastle, William Ellison, brother to Robert Ellison and cousin of both Sir Henry Liddell and William Carr, supporting the Tory candidates. "What", wrote Henry Liddell to Cotesworth, "could induce him to desert his relations".

In 1715 Cotesworth was active in despatching intelligence of Jacobite activity in the North East to Liddell in London.[13] Both the correspondents were zealous in calling for the firmest measures and strongest penalties to be invoked against Derwentwater and his supporters. Both were disappointed that, after the Rising, the government did not do more to reward loyal Whigs like themselves or to punish Jacobites. "Such coolness makes me sick", wrote Liddell regarding the Ministry's failure to take a stronger line on forfeitures. Cotesworth, was, however, the gainer from one forfeiture when he and Joseph Banks MP bought up the forfeited estates at Stella and Winlaton that had belonged to the Jacobite, Lord Widdrington.

It is not surprising that a man like Cotesworth excited considerable animosity. Sir Ralph Carr had him beaten up during a wayleave dispute, his friend Liddell warned him on several occasions to arm himself when he went out, and, in 1725, he was poisoned, when his gardener, on instructions from his butler, put arsenic in his coffee.[14] His housekeeper, Hannah Watson, found the remains of the poison and Cotesworth survived the attempt to murder him.[15] The accomplices were sentenced to a whipping and the pillory on the anniversary of the crime. This murder attempt seems to have been organised by a business enemy and, although Cotesworth had plenty, Richard Ridley, his major rival in the coal industry and also a political opponent, seems the prime suspect.

Cotesworth had several lawsuits against Ridley pending and the two were engaged in disputes at Whickham and to the east of Newcastle. At Whickham, Ridley was supporting Lady Clavering in a long lasting attempt to win the right to wagonways over Whickham common in Coteswoth's manor. On the north side of the Tyne, there was a bitter struggle over the refusal of Newcastle corporation, of which Ridley was an influential member, to allow Cotesworth wayleave rights, from his colliery at Heaton across Walker to the river. Ridley owned a neighbouring colliery at Byker and had, Cotesworth suspected, broken through the underground boundary and removed coal from the Heaton pit, while at the same time sabotaging attempts to drain it. Cotesworth was confident of victory in both disputes and Ridley and his allies were getting desperate. A fortnight after the murder attempt, Ridley's men caused an explosion at the Heaton colliery, blowing themselves up in the process.

Cotesworth's law suits cost a lot of money and he was not as rich when he died in 1726, as he had been at the height of his success in 1719. Nevertheless, he left his heirs a fine landed estate, a handsome country house in Gateshead Park and a respected position in society.

His hopes for a Cotesworth dynasty were, however, confounded. Of his five sons, three died in childhood. He had hoped to educate his eldest son, William, into a "more polite way of living" and had, accordingly, sent him to Sedbergh and Oxford for a gentleman's education and then had him articled to Charles Sanderson. William died in 1721 and it was his younger brother Robert, who inherited the substantial but complex, confused and encumbered estate. Robert sold off the salt pans and then sold the Whickham estate to the Liddells and was busy rationalising his inheritance and paying off debts at the time of his death in May 1729. The estate passed to his sisters Hannah and Elizabeth.[16]

The two girls had been sent to boarding school in London in 1717 and it is possible that Henry Ellison may have met Hannah Cotesworth while he was at Sanderson's chambers. He would definitely have known the Cotesworths while he was agent at Ravensworth. He and Hannah were married in September 1729 and a year later Elizabeth married Henry Thomas Carr of Cocken.

So, Henry Ellison, a younger son, was the co-inheritor of the rewards of the business careers of three remarkable men, William Ramsay senr., William Ramsay jnr., and William Cotesworth. Eventually, almost all of the Cotesworth estate was to belong to the Ellisons.

References

1. *Ibid* p.46.

2. Much to the disgust of his other brother-in-law, Calverley Bewicke, who had placed his daughter at Gateshead Park, in the hope that Ramsay might grow fond of her.

3. J. M. Ellis, "A Study of the Business Fortunes of William Cotesworth c.1688-1726". Oxford D.Phil. Thesis, 1975.

4. Hughes, pp.49-50.

5.   Joyce Ellis, "The Poisoning of William Cotesworth, 1725", *History Today* Vol. 28, Nov. 1978.

6.   *The Letters of Henry Liddell to William Cotesworth*, edited by J. M. Ellis (1987), Surtees Society, Vol. CXCVII, p.IX.

7.   Ellis, thesis, p.3.

8.   The demise of the manor of Gateshead did not include the third part of Tyne Bridge and the advowsons of the two rectories.

9.   Ellis, thesis, p.55.

10.   For a detailed analysis of the Tyneside salt industry see J. M. Ellis, "The Decline and fall of the Tyneside Salt Industry, 1660-1790: A Re-examination". *Economic History Review,* Second Series, Vol. XXXIII, Feb. 1980.

11.   In 1719 he was High Sheriff for Northumberland.

12.   Hughes, pp.268-269.

13.   Robert Neill's novel, *Black William* (1955), is largely based on Cotesworth's career and, in particular, his role in the '15 Rising.

14.   See Joyce Ellis, "The poisoning of William Cotesworth, 1725", *History Today* Vol. 28, 1978.

15.   William's wife had died in 1710 and Hannah Watson was, not only his housekeeper, but his companion and mistress.

16.   They had a half-sister, for William had fathered a child on Hannah Watson. On William's death, Hannah Watson was declared his wife, and she and her daughter, Henrietta, took his name. Henrietta became a governess to the children of George III.

Chapter 4

Brothers in Arms

General Cuthbert Ellison (1698-1785)

"I have been here near Six Weeks and I thank God I never yet saw so disagreeable a place, nor I hope ever shall."

Robert Ellison at Fort William

As his elder brother had no children, the family estate at Hebburn, as well as the Cotesworth inheritance, eventually came to Henry's son. Before following Henry and his family further, however, we must consider the careers of his two soldier brothers, his older brother, Cuthbert, and the younger, Robert.

General Cuthbert Ellison (1698-1745)

Had all depended upon Robert's eldest son, Cuthbert, it seems likely that the Ellison fortunes would have declined. It was not that Cuthbert was without ability and, indeed, he had a distinguished career as an army officer, rising to the rank of lieutenant-general, and he became MP for Shaftesbury in the Parliament of 1747-54. He had, however, little inclination for estate management and, as he hardly ever visited Hebburn, he was unable to deal with the many problems of the estate, which he inherited, encumbered by his father's debts.

By the early eighteenth century, it had already become the custom for the land-owning gentry to send their sons into the armed forces. Army pay assisted, though it did not cover, the expenses of a gentleman of independent means, though it might suffice for a younger son, who was not expected to keep up expensive appearances. A few did well out of military service: naval captains who were fortunate with prize money, those who rose to the highest rank or who were specially rewarded for service to a grateful nation, and those who profited from the control of supplies and victuals. At the other extreme was the fate of the half-pay officers, of whom it was said in Parliament, "tho' they hardly live, they never die".

Cuthbert Ellison joined the army in 1723, when he obtained a commission as captain in the 8th Dragoons, becoming major in the same regiment in 1731. It would have been conventional for him to leave the army on his father's death and look to the management of his estate, on which, not only his own welfare, but that of his mother and brothers and sisters depended, but he preferred the life of an army officer and the management of his estate fell upon the shoulders of, first of all, his cousin, Colonel Liddell, and then his younger brother, Henry Ellison.

Cuthbert has been described as follows: "Charming, mannered and easygoing, Cuthbert Ellison's inclinations led him to continue in the army, where he mixed with the best society and could gratify his considerable social instincts".[1] Something of a valetudinarian, he worried ceaselessly about his health. In 1728, he wrote from Bath, "I have been very much out of Order for this month past, my Old Disorders upon my Nerves & Chest having returned upon me with Violence".[2] From Dublin in 1730, he wrote that he was again off to Bath and that, "I still have frequent returns of my Disorder".[3] There are, indeed, few letters from Cuthbert that do not mention the Old Disorder. It was almost certainly dyspepsia and his two brothers suffered from the same complaint. He spent a great deal of time visiting spas, which enabled him to combine care for his health with social amusement. He was an early pioneer of sea bathing, visiting Brighthelmstone (Brighton) to see, "if it [sea bathing] should happen to agree with me".[4] He was also very fond of London, which eventually became his home.

The greater part of Cuthbert's career was spent in Ireland, a country that he rather disliked. During this time he was appointed to the position of aide-de-camp to the Lord Lieutenant, a post which he found enjoyable but expensive. He appears to have been quite an able soldier, proud of his regiment and well thought of by his senior officers.[5] During his eighteen years with his regiment of dragoons, there were several changes of colonels and, as James Hayes remarks, "they all thought well of him". His promotions, however, owed more to his connections than his ability. As he wrote himself at the time of his retirement:

> *I have long been ashamed of soliciting my Friends to make use of theirs, in my favour, having been entirely indebted to their Countenance and Protection for every Step I made in the army, and had I continued in It, must have been constantly easing them to lay themselves under Obligations on my Acct, to people perhaps they would not otherways choose to be obliged by. Sir H. Liddell was ever my constant protector, and I never wanted his Good Offices whenever they could be of service to me.[6]*

For most of his military career, Cuthbert was rather hard up. The estate brought in such a small income that, after providing for those relatives who depended upon him, he had to live upon his army pay, which his position and social life, with the added expense of being aide-de-camp to the Lord-Lieutenant, made insufficient. The possession of an estate was, he thought, almost a disadvantage:

> *I begin almost to think that the Name of It is a real Disservice to Me. For if I had not the Reputation of having a Fortune independent of my post I might have lived credibly upon the Income of the Latter, which I shall not find Great Difficulty of doing in this Ill-natured and Expensive Age.[7]*

Brother Henry had not only to look after the Hebburn estate as well as his own property but had to deal with the debts and loans Cuthbert contracted wherever he went. Thus, in March 1729, he wrote, "Three or four Days ago I drew a bill upon You for £80 payable to Ralph Carr, a debt that I have long'd owed him"[8] and, from Dublin in June 1830, "I took the liberty to draw upon Mr Fowler for Sixty Pounds not knowing how to draw upon you at this distance".[9] The account drawn up by Henry in November 1734, showing his brother's income and expenses, demonstrates that Cuthbert's expenditure was more than the estate could bear.[10] Having entrusted his affairs to Henry, he bombarded him with a ceaseless stream of letters giving advice, instructions, and complaints about his agent, Shute, and "the monstrous areas of rent". Ever the optimist, he urged, when the boring for coal on the estate had reached 36 fathoms without result, that they should continue to 50 fathoms.[11] Despite Cuthbert's generous language, "My house at Hebburn is entirely at your disposal as is everything else that I am master of"[12], it says much for Henry's brotherly loyalty that he doesn't seem to have complained about the onerous nature of his work for the absentee landlord.

In 1739, Cuthbert became lieutenant-colonel of the 23rd Dragoons. The expense of this promotion, together with debts incurred during his visits to spas, appears to have been too much for the encumbered estate to bear and Henry Ellison suggested that part of it be sold. Cuthbert readily agreed to this, though he was far from blaming himself for the decline of his inheritance:

> 'Tis a consolation to me however that this mortification did not proceed from any Excesses that I have been guilty of, but from an old gangrene that twas impossible for me to put a stop to, notwithstanding that I followed as close as possible the Advice of my friendly Physicians.[13]

In the event, the plan to give up the estates that the Ellisons had leased from the Dean and Chapter of Durham (Wardley with Heworth Mill and other small properties) since 1680 does not seem to have been acted upon, probably because George Liddell died in the same year, 1740, and his will may have helped to improve Cuthbert's financial position. Robert Ellison's debts to George were still a charge upon the Hebburn estate but Cuthbert had hopes that a legacy from his grandfather, Sir Henry Liddell, administered by George could now be used to cover those debts.[14] George, in his will as in his life, was ever a good friend to his sister's family. As Cuthbert wrote: "He has been very generous in his benefactions to all of us, and to me in particular".[15]

After the sale, Cuthbert's finances appear to have improved but his health did not. He served in Flanders during the War of the Austrian Succession and was present at the Battle of Dettingen. After Dettingen, he wrote:

> I am so happy to escape unhurt but had two men and ten horses killed out of my troop; Newchatel's brother who is my servant who attended me with a horse had the horse killed under him with a cannon ball.[16]

In October 1743, he was suddenly commanded to advance with his 300 dragoons and take Germersheim, a French strongpoint on the Rhine. His success in taking Germersheim points to his capabilities as a commander but his campaigning appears to have convinced him that his health was not up to an active army life and in 1745 he sold his commission. He desired, "a Little more ease and Tranquility than I can expect in the Profession I am in, and not a little Anxious to quit it". He, nevertheless, volunteered for service during the '45 rebellion and helped pursue the forces of Prince Charles through Derbyshire.

He remained on the Army List, acting as a Deputy-Adjutant-General for some time after the sale of his commission and obtaining the rank of colonel in this post. He was later made a lieutenant-general though his later service was purely nominal. The promotion probably pleased him, for he was never one to make light of rank or title, but he played it down: "I thank you for your Compliments on my promotion. the rank of Lieut. General is of Consequence to an Able and Healthful man, but tis of none to me who has for long been fitter for an Hospital than the Field".[17]

His retirement gave Cuthbert the opportunity to enjoy the social round of London and Bath and to spend time with his many friends. He was a regular visitor to Euston in Suffolk, the home of the Duke of Grafton. Lord Ravensworth, Cuthbert's cousin, was a close political associate of Grafton's and his daughter, Anne Liddell, married Lord Euston, later the third Duke. The Ellisons looked to the Liddells of Ravensworth for political leadership and preferment and through them to the Dukes of Grafton and, ultimately, until the 1760s, to the Duke of Newcastle, at the top of the tree of patronage and power.

In 1747 Cuthbert was elected MP for Shaftesbury, an extremely corrupt borough. The main competing interests there were those of the Earl of Ilchester and the Earl of Shaftesbury but, as it had a relatively large electorate of poor and bribable Scot and Lot payers, results could be uncertain and contests were always expensive. Cuthbert was invited to stand by Lord Ilchester and set about campaigning with military planning and a realistic appraisal of his chances. On 12 June he wrote that:

> *I have now been three days employed in walking from house to house solliciting Votes for my Self. If promises wou'd chose me, I should certainly be elected...At this time we are on by three Candidates, viz Mr Pitt [George] and Mr Walters, the present members, and Myself. These Gentlemen, are Young and Rich...They have the advantage also of having great part of their fortunes in this Neighbourhood, but as I am supported by Lord Ilchester's Interest and have the Returning Officer, Most of the Magistrates, and Better Sort of the People by that means in my favour, I may hope for success, but my election will be dubious, troublesome and very expensive.[18]*

That this eminently clubable man enjoyed being in the House of Commons cannot be doubted but he didn't stand again in 1754. Perhaps another contest was more than his purse could stand. Within a decade or so, the rising cost of elections in Shaftesbury had led to even the Ilchester and Shaftesbury interests withdrawing from them.

He never married[19] but he was very fond of his female relatives, especially Lord Ravensworth's daughter, Anne, to whom he was a good and loyal friend in the difficult circumstances of her sensational divorce from the Duke of Grafton. It must have been a great setback to her relatives when, after making a very advantageous marriage and becoming Duchess of Grafton, she first separated from her husband and then, in 1768, eloped with the Earl of Upper Ossory by whom she was pregnant. The scandalous impact of the subsequent divorce case, followed by her remarriage to Ossory, was all the greater because Grafton was Prime Minister at the time. General Cuthbert helped negotiate the terms of the Duchess's separation and, unlike Lord Ravensworth, who never communicated with her again, kept in close touch with her after her marriage to Ossory.

Despite his perennial worries about his health or, perhaps, because of his constant concern for it, Cuthbert lived to enjoy a comfortable and relatively prosperous old age. Well liked and respected, he continued to enjoy society. He died in 1785, as old as the century, and the second general officer on the establishment. Horace Walpole wrote to Lady Ossory, condoling with her on the loss, "of the good old general". Cuthbert's will provided for a legacy to Lady Ossory, which, as she was already very rich, may not have pleased his closer relatives, but, although the General had lived comfortably in his latter years on his annuities and the income from the Hebburn estate, he left little behind him. Walpole wrote that the legacy "…will scarce purchase half an acre of a modern hat".[20]

Cuthbert Ellison's life was not a dramatic one, but there can be worse epitaphs to a man than to say he was liked and trusted by almost all who knew him.

Colonel Robert Ellison (1710-1755)

The younger brother of Cuthbert and Henry, Robert was intended for the coal trade and went to study law in London. His mother wrote to Henry:

> *Your Bror Bob is yet undisposed of. I wish he might be thought capable of imbibing instructions in colliery affairs, as being most agreeable to his own inclinations and I may say constitution which is not of the strongest. He is sober, willing and desires to please But I'm afraide Engaging with a sharp master in the law would quite confound him.*[21]

Robert appears in fact to have been an intelligent and capable man and it was probably lack of inclination for the law, rather than intellectual shortcomings, which led him to abandon it for an ensigncy in the 3rd Buffs in 1732, when he was twenty-two. James Hayes sketches his subsequent military career as follows:

He became a captain of Marines in 1739, major of a short lived American regiment in1743 and lieutenant-colonel of yet another in 1745. In 1754, after a few years on half pay, he was given a colonelcy of the 44th. Only forty-four when he died, he would probably have gone far in the Army, for he seems to have been a keen and competent officer.[22]

For a man, who like all the three Ellison brothers, had a weak constitution, Robert was not lucky in his army postings. His first posting was to Fort William, where General Wade was busy building roads and bridges. He wrote to Henry:

I have been here near Six Weeks and I thank God I never yet saw so disagreeable a place, nor I hope never shall: the weather has been so bad for about a month of the time yet there was no stirring out of the baracks, but when we were obliged to mount Guard which comes to my turn every fourth day.[23]

On the outbreak of war with Spain in 1739, he was given command of a company in a new Marine regiment. This preferment was, as he acknowledged, due to Sir Henry Liddell's influence. His first job was to raise the company by recruiting in Yorkshire. He declined brother Henry's invitation to stay at Park House as he was too busy with his recruiting but asked that his brother's man, John Boyn:

...could pick me up 2 or 3 Men...they must not be under five foot five Inches without Shoes, Strong made; they shall have 6d a day from the Time of his Agreement with them & please to let him have money on that account if he is likely to succeed; and please to tell him, he may go as farr as a Guinea & a Crown advance, but as much under as he can.[24]

That the payment of soldiers was not a straightforward business but one in which paymasters had an almost private enterprise role is shown by the following:

I thank you for your kind advice in my Sister Jenny's letter about my accepting of the Paymaster's place in Partnership, but I think I cam Assure you that I run no Sort of Risque from it because the Major who shares with me in the Profits has nothing to do with the Money Affair, nor Nobody but Myself. Coll: Robinson gave it to the Major but Recommended me as a Proper Person to do the Business and what induced me to accept of it was, that it will be a Certain profit to me of near £50 a year without any expence...[25]

He was well satisfied with his recruits whom he considered, "...not in the least inferior to the best Parcell I have yet seen belonging to ye Regt."[26]

Alas, many of those fine recruits and many of the regiments officers were to die in the expedition sent against the Spanish colonies in the West Indies. Robert described the disastrous attack upon strongly fortified Cartagena in a letter to his brother Henry written in Jamaica:

> But as its [the fort of St Lazarus] Strength was not, I am afraid, sufficiently known before we were ordered to Storm it, we were obliged to Retreat with the loss of 640 men killed and wounded, among whom many more officers suffered in proportion than private men, for as the Spaniards had Trenches without the Walls of the Fort, which secured them from the Fire of our men, they had an Opportunity of Levelling at whom they pleased...[27]

Families were often without news of men serving in the West Indies for considerable periods and his sister, Jane Ellison, expressed her concern to their brother, Henry: "We have seen in the newespapers that there is 16000 letters come from Jamaica and as wee have had no Letters from the poor Captain we are a good Deal uneasy upon his account".[28]

As with many military expeditions, men were as much in danger from illness as from bullets and Robert refers to the great losses due to sickness and death and his own recovery from, "a very severe bloody flux". Nevertheless, war brings survivors promotion and in 1742 he was made major in a newly formed and American regiment. It was, however, soon disbanded and in 1743 he found himself back in England on half pay.

For the next two years he lived the unsatisfactory life of the half pay officer, staying with his relatives, visiting spas and attempting to use his own and his relations' influence to gain a new appointment. When one was secured with the help of his family and Lord Stair, on whose staff his brother Cuthbert was serving, it was to another American regiment, Shirley's Regiment, in which he was made a lieutenant-colonel. After the heat of the West Indies, he was to experience the cold and the winds of Cape Breton. Louisbourg had been captured from the French and Shirley's regiment was assigned to garrison duty there. Had he not changed ships at the last moment because of a disagreement over his baggage, he would not have reached America, as the first ship was lost on the westward voyage. On arrival he found that the regiment was not yet raised. It had to be recruited from the reluctant settlers of Massachusetts. The sums available with which to attract recruits were inadequate.

> The Price of Labour here is Extremely dear, besides the People of this Country are vastly averse to serve as Soldiers, especially under any other

*Officers than those of their own Country, all these are difficultys I
foresaw before we left England and Represented to Mr Pelham and Sir
William Yonge but was always told they apprehended the men were
raised at Louisbourg.*[29]

Louisbourg must have been far from the most desirable posting in the Army. Not
only was the climate unpleasant and the place so isolated that for almost eighteen
months Robert had no news from friends, but the garrison was potentially mutinous
because a parsimonious government made an arbitrary stoppage of 3d a day in pay.
The Governor and officers sympathised with the men for, as Robert pointed out,
everything at Louisbourg was twice the price it was in England.

Colonel Cuthbert considered his brother's situation an "extremely disagreeable, not
to say a melancholy one" and did his best to get him out of it:

*I have long endeavoured to find a Lt.Colonel that wou'd change with him
on consideration of a sum of money, but Louisbourg is now known to be
so terrible a place that none can be prevailed upon to go thither. I have
likewise applyed to the Secretary of Warr, to put him with any Regiment
in Europe, in case of a vacancy, but hitherto without success, but hope
with Lord Ravensworth's Assistance to get him removed before the next
year.*[30]

While at Louisbourg, Robert had hopes of being able to purchase a colonelcy. The
plan was that Colonel Shirley would get General Phillips's regiment and Ellison
gain Shirley's position. "Mr Shirley desired to know how much I would be willing
to give towards making a sum for General Phillips to resign in his favour and I to
succeed him." The scheme fell through and Robert had to wait several years for his
colonelcy but it provides an interesting example of the way a rank was a posession
and, just as one had to purchase a commission, so one expected proper
remuneration on giving it up.[31]

After the Peace of Aix-la-Chapelle, came respite from war and the pleasures of
peace, not altogether welcome to the professional soldier, likely to have to exist on
half pay (Robert's half pay for the year December 1750 to December 1751 was
£155. 2. 6d.). This was his fate for five years, but the youngest brother, with little
in the way of expectations from the family, was no slouch when it came to money.
He had managed to save on his army income, took a lease on Scaleby Castle in
Cumberland and was on his way to setting himself up as a country gentleman.

He had in fact acquired quite a substantial personal fortune. He was due, in 1749,
£887.16.7d from the Executors of George Liddell, back payments on an annuity of

£200 a year.[32] In January 1750 he wrote to Henry, asking him to put his money, about £200 he had to hand and another £850 by virtue of a bill on Mr Nicholas Walton, Lord Ravensworth's agent and executor of George Liddell's estate, out at interest.[33] A letter of Attorney of October 1754, giving Henry full powers over Robert's affairs while he was abroad, was followed by a list of his assets, which shows him to have been worth over £4,000.[34]

He still needed further advancement in the Army to make his ambitions come true. This came in 1754 when, assisted no doubt by the Liddell influence, but, one hopes, also by a recognition that he was a very capable officer, he was promoted to the colonelcy of the 14th regiment of foot.

This was a great opportunity for, as James Hayes has put it, "...colonelcies were lucrative posts and many colonels were known to have bought themselves modest estates on the proceeds of managing their regiments".[35] Robert did not, however, live to enjoy his new position for long. His fate seemed to lie in America for he had to follow the regiment there and, shortly after his arrival, he fell sick and died in Albany. His personal effects were auctioned according to custom and fetched £248.[36] His will provided that all his money and possessions be divided equally between his brothers and sisters.[37]

The lives of Cuthbert and Robert illustrate how very different careers in the eighteenth century army could be, some relatively comfortable and others very arduous, but both were competent officers and Robert a very good one, who might have achieved much had he lived longer. Of the three brothers it might well be said that either Henry or Robert would have made a better custodian of the family estate than Cuthbert. Yet as things turned out, Cuthbert went his charming, if not very dynamic, way, Henry brought increased wealth and influence to the family and Robert gave service to his country in inhospitable places.

References

1.   "Two soldier brothers of the Eighteenth Century" by James Hayes in *Army Historical Research*, No. 40 (1962) p.150.

2.   Cuthbert Ellison to Henry Ellison, 13, Nov. 1728.Ellison Mss. (A18)

3.   *Ibid*, 13 June. 1730.

4.   *Ibid*, 28, June 1759.

5. We learn little from his letters to Henry about the daily round of military life and of his attitude towards enlisted soldiers. That he had enlightened attitudes is suggested by his view of naval impressing: "that disagreeable and cruel service".

6. *Ibid*, 5, Feb.1745.

7. *Ibid*, 14 Nov. 1733.

8. *Ibid*, 20, March, 1730.

9. *Ibid*, 13, June, 1730.

10. Accounts of Cuthbert Ellison with Henry Ellison to Nov. 1734. Ellison Ms.

11. Cuthbert Ellison to Henry Ellison, 10, June, 1735 and October, 25, 1735.

12. *Ibid*, 9, Feb. 1730.

13. *Ibid*, 29, Sept. 1739.

14. *Ibid*, 9 Nov. 1740.A19.

15. *Ibid*, 23, Oct.1740.

16. *Ibid*, June 1743.

17. *Ibid*, 26, Feb.1759.

18. *Ibid*, 12,June 1747.

19. Cuthbert had little inclination for marriage."I'm sorry I Can't dance at your wedding", he wrote to Henry in 1729, "and that I had rather dance at It than at my own." But that he was attracted by women is shown by his comment in the same year on meeting a Miss Dove in the Carlisle area "...who is so pretty that I have quite forgot Miss Redesdale". (A18).

20. *Horace Walpole's Correspondence, The Countess of Upper Ossory,* 3 Vols.32-34. ed. W. S. Lewis (1965).

21. Hayes, "Two Soldier Brothers" *op. cit.* p.158.

22. *Ibid*, p.151.

23. Robert Ellison to Henry Ellison, 2 October 1733. This and another nineteen letters from Robert Ellison are in the Columbia University Library, New York. They were edited by Edward Hughes and published in *Archaeologia Aeliana,* 4th series, Vol. XXXI.

24. R. Ellison to Henry Ellison, 7 Jan. 1740. Hughes *Ibid* p.4.

25. *Ibid*, 27 Jan. 1740.

26. *Ibid*, 23 Feb. 1740.

27. *Ibid*, 30 May 1741.

28. Jane Ellison to Henry Ellison, September 1740. Ellison Mss. (A6).

29. Robert Ellison (Boston) to Henry Ellison, 31 Jan.1746. Hughes *op. cit.*, *A. A.*

30. C. Ellison to H. Ellison, 8, Sept., 1747 (A20).

31. R. Ellison to H. Ellison, 22 Nov. 1747. Edward Hughes, *op. cit.*, A. A., p.19, comments that this casts light upon the view that the purchase of a commission was a provision for retirement.

32. Colonel Robert Ellison to the Executors of George Liddell, 10 Oct. 1749. Carr-Ellison Papers, Northumberland Record Office 855, Box 6.

33. R. Ellison to H. Ellison, 21 Jan. 1750. Ellison Ms. (A5)

34. These assets included £500 invested at 5% in the Breamish turnpike road and £759 owed to him by Lord Ravensworth. Letter of Attorney, 11 Oct. 1754. List of principal sums due to R. Ellison, 15 Oct, 1754. Account of R. Ellison with Lord Ravensworth, Oct 1754. Ellison Ms. (A5).

35. Hayes, p.160.

36. *Ibid.*

37. A copy of his will of 2 Nov. 1754 is in the Ellison Mss. (A5). He was always a generous and family minded man and had helped to pay for his nephew Robert's apprenticeship.

Chapter 5

Henry Ellison. The Business Life of a Landed Gentleman

Henry Ellison (1699-1775) (by Pompeo Batoni)

What most impresses one about these people is their fine sense of service, mostly unpaid to the local community in which they lived.

Edward Hughes (1952)

With his elder brother away from the region, Henry Ellison had not only to look after his own estates and interests, but had also to manage the Hebburn estate. He was the custodian of the family's interests, though Cuthbert still considered himself to be the head of the family and bombarded Henry with letters containing advice about the running of the Hebburn estate. As it became clear that it was unlikely that Cuthbert would marry, it became accepted that Henry's eldest son would inherit both Cuthbert's and Henry's estates.

With such responsibilities Henry Ellison's life was not a leisured one. On the successful management of the estates depended the prosperity of his immediate family (the inheritance of his eldest son, provision for his younger and dowries for his daughters) and also the income of Cuthbert, together with the maintenance in comfortable and respectable circumstances of his mother and unmarried sisters. He had to maintain his position and influence in society. This involved unpaid and often expensive work as a justice, while he served a term as Sheriff of Northumberland in 1735 and was prominent in the support of worthy local causes and charities. He had to assist in the advancement of people who looked to him as their protector and patron; such persons ranged from servants, tenants and distant relatives to friends and minor gentry. The maintenance of influence also required an active participation in politics and elections, an activity that could be arduous but brought very tangible rewards. The life of a conscientious landowner who sought to increase his position and status in the world was no round of leisure.

The Cotesworth inheritance was a mixed and complex assortment of properties and interests, which required skilful management. Unusually, Cotesworth's properties were not separated but were run, jointly and prosperously, for many years by the husbands of the co-heiresses. H.T.Carr took a keen interest in farming matters, but it was Henry Ellison who provided the expert management.

A skilful manager was exactly what Henry Ellison was. His training in Charles Sanderson's chambers and his time as agent at Ravensworth had given him the right background for such a role. He was no Cotesworth, no daring entrepreneur, but one who cautiously consolidated his position. Cotesworth's buccaneering had almost overreached his resources and good management was what the mixed bag of the inheritance required: the manor of Gateshead and the adjoining estate of Shipcote, the manors of Bellister and Hartleyburn, together with adjacent Broomhouses, and West Park at Brancepeth in Durham. Henry Ellison's time as agent to the Ravensworth estate must have stood him in good stead when it came to managing these very varied estates.

The Hartleyburn and Bellister estates in west Northumberland had been acquired by Ramsay, probably in the hope that lead would be discovered beneath them, and during the eighteenth century periodic efforts were made to find lead seams. The land was not of high quality for agricultural purposes.

These estates were something of a lawyer's feast and a steward's nightmare, as they rested on ancient manorial law and, rather than the main income deriving from rents, there was a complex system of fines and heriots. At the death of every lord of the manor, a copyholder was required to pay a fine, while upon the death of a tenant his heir had to pay a fine and also hand over a heriot (the best beast he or she possessed) to the lord. Tenants at Bellister were also supposed to perform a number of services, which included one-day's mowing and two-days' shearing, carrying coal and spinning one hank of yarn. At Hartleyburn, such services had been commuted to money payments.

The system was not only anachronistic in the circumstances of eighteenth century Northumberland, but almost impossible for an absentee landlord to maintain. It was undesirable from the viewpoint of both landlord and tenant. Rents were low, a matter of shillings, so that the landlord was denied a decent annual income, but fines could be as high as £11. The estates had been sold by a Mr Blenkinsop to the elder Ramsay, inherited by the younger Ramsay, then bequeathed to William Cotesworth, gone to Robert Cotesworth on his father's death and, eventually, passed to Henry Ellison and H.T.Carr on their marriages to the Cotesworth heiresses. If the tenantry had paid the fines due on each death of a landlord, they would have been in a bad way. As it was, Robert Cotesworth and Carr and Ellison do not appear to have collected on the deaths of their predecessors.[1]

Such complex estates could not be efficiently managed from the distance of Gateshead Park and much depended on agents. Robert Sisson, who had been Cotesworth's agent, remained in charge until his death in 1736 but, for several years afterwards, manorial customs were allowed to fall into disuse with no manorial courts being held. Robert Lowes, a Hexham attorney, was appointed steward in 1752 and set about putting things right, holding courts and attempting to collect arreas of fines and rents.

Most of the Bellister tenants were poor and well behind with their rents and fines, though the prosperous leaseholder tenant of Broomhouses farm, which was also owned by Ellison and Carr, acquired the copyhold to land at Bellister. Hartleyburn had a distinguished copyholder in Sir Lancelot Allgood, who had acquired land at nearby Lambley with his marriage to his cousin and found it convenient to extend his interests in the area by becoming a Hartleyburn tenant.

If Allgood was an unusual tenant at Hartleyburn, he would not have been out of place at the manor of Whickham, sold by Robert Cotesworth to the Liddells, for here most of the copyholders were gentry and even aristocrats, who had acquired their holdings in the interests of wayleave rights from their coalmines: "In short, copyhold here had nothing to do with farming: it had come to signify no more than the proverbial egg-cup holding up the crust in the pie of colliery way-leaves and staith rooms"[2]

If Ellison's and Carr's Gateshead estate was, like Bellister and Hartleyburn, a manor with its copyholders and its court, it was very different to the west Northumberland estates with their not very fertile land. It had prosperous farms with high rentals, due to the ready market for milk and vegetables to be found in Newcastle and Gateshead and the extra money to be made by transporting coal along the wagonways. Thomas Thompson and his partners agreed to a rent of £140 for 113 acres in 1734.[3]

At Broomhouses and at Brancepeth in Durham, Carr and Ellison had land subject to more modern tenancy arrangements, based on leasehold. At Broomhouses the one farm was leased by the Tinlins, Thomas Tinlin and his son, for most of the century, while, at Brancepeth, there were half a dozen tenants on nine year leases.

Henry Ellison's skills in estate management were complemented by H.T.Carr's knowledge of modern agricultural methods. Together they attempted to ensure that their tenants did not exhaust the land and built into tenancy agreements such rules, as those at Brancepeth, where tenants were required to leave a third of the tillage fallow every year and to take only two crops, one of which was to be oats between fallowings.[4]

This was a period in which gentlemen prided themselves on a knowledge of progressive farming methods; even General Cuthbert Ellison sent his brother "Dr Wintringham's receipt" for treating diseased cattle. He wrote that, by far the best way to stop cattle distemper spreading was to, "kill infected cattle and burn or bury their carcasses as soon as possible But it is impossible to persuade or even force the Country People to do so".[5]

The unusual practice adopted by Henry Ellison and H.T.Carr of running the Cotesworth inheritance together worked well enough for many years. Much probably depended on the close friendship between the two men. They had mutual interests in gardening and fishing and they and their families formed a cousinhood or dynastic alliance in which business and political interests were mingled with friendship and mutual solidarity. This was not to carry on into the next generation.

H.T. Carr had always been a restless as well as an able man. Shortly after his marriage he had lived in Northamptonshire for some time, then, much involved with the affairs of the Durham Bishopric, he had left his house at Cocken and moved to Whitworth to "keep up an interest" with the Bishop and he then moved to Mobberley in Cheshire to be close to Sir Edward Stanley. In the mid 1750s he suffered a serious illness and was declared a lunatic. After this relations between the Ellisons and the Carrs deteriorated.

The problem was the debts the Carrs ran up. H.T.Carr may well have overspent and left his family with money problems. Henry's sister Katherine Airey wrote to her brother in 1758 that Henrietta Cotesworth was very worried about money, having lent Mrs Carr about £550.[6] The Ellisons took a great interest in the progress of the Carrs' two sons, Ralph and Robert. Cuthbert Ellison became concerned about debts owed by Ralph, who was intended for the church, to his tutor at Clare College. He also was generous with his advice and help to Robert who had embarked upon an army career.[7] He wrote in the following year that, "I can't think I could have done more for Capt Carr than speak to Ld Cornwallis in his favor and that I have frequently done."[8]

By the mid 1770s Henry Ellison was negotiating with Ralph and Robert Carr to buy out various Carr interests in the Cotesworth inheritance, including the manor of Gateshead which required an Act of Parliament. He needed financial assistance from his brother who sold stock to help him.[9] By this time the Carr brothers were to the General, "capricious and unpleasant gentry" and "unsettled, capricious people"[10] and in 1775 he wrote of his great pleasure:

> *...in hearing you had signed with Messrs Carr and that you would probably soon be in full possession of the manor. The Act of Parliament necessary to make a title to the Freehold will I hope be obtained this session and that the whole of the transactions with that family will be over in a few months.*[11]

Thus was the "Carr Treaty" concluded and with it a partnership that had lasted forty-four years. Henry was to die later that year in the sole possession of his estate.

Henry Ellison had, as we have seen, the added burden of managing his brother's estate, as well as his own. The Hebburn estate appears to have declined in Robert Ellison's time, if not before; the "old gangrene", as the medically minded Cuthbert put it, while absolving himself from blame. Certainly, on the agricultural side, there were "monstrous arreas of rent" and Cuthbert was always complaining that his agent John Shute was incompetent, when it came to collecting rents.[12] In July 1736, he wrote to Henry that he wanted a new agent to replace Shute[13] but in 1748 Shute was still there and Cuthbert had drawn a bill upon him "at 21 days sight. He will probably be surprised at my draught upon him as he has not heard from me in those terms for the three years past."[14] In 1749, however, he was requesting Henry to inspect John Shute's accounts:

The income I have had out of it [the estate] for many years past has not exceeded the Steward's Allowances, what I have most at heart is that he should not permit the Tenants to run for long in Arreas or suffer them to breach the Covenants of their Leases, which must bring ruin upon them, the Estate and everyone dependent upon it.[15]

It may be doubted whether this state of affairs was altogether Shute's fault. As an experienced agent himself, Henry Ellison, who had been given full authority to run the estate, would undoubtedly have got rid of Shute, if he had doubted his competence or probity. At any rate, Shute's widow was still in possession of a farm in 1758 and was behind with the rent. Cuthbert, when in straights, was inclined to demand that tenants be squeezed but he was, at heart, far too kindly a man to have dealt more harshly with the Shutes despite his strictures.

The Widow Shute's arreas, is very Great tho the times have lately been remarkably good for the Farmers, I am willing to try what she can do for herself another year…in my opinion no tenants except some very special cases should be suffered to remain in a farm, that is above one Year Rent in arreas.[16]

But he was prone to finding exceptions:

You mention in your Remarks that Jane Wright had two cows, one of which you ordered to be disposed off. If tis not sold I desire she may keep them both as I apprehend She and her Children are objects of Charity.[17]

But the management of both his own estate and the Hebburn estate required more than a knowledge of agriculture and an ability to receive farmers' rents. Henry Ellison had to look after coal mines, be knowledgeable about wayleaves and keep his eye on a number of disparate businesses: salt pans, grindstone quarries and the Hebburn ballast shore. He owned collieries, Gateshead Fell, Gateshead Park and the Saltmeadow, and possessed the valuable way-leave rights that the foresight of Cotesworth had bequeathed to him. The salt pans at Shields were in slow decline from the 1720s but still managed to produce profits until late in the century.

Relations with the Bishopric could be difficult. As the lords of the manor of Gateshead, Ellison and Carr were, in relation to the bishop, feudal inferiors, while their superiors increasingly approached the renewal of leases and fines in a businesslike manner.

In the late seventeenth century and early eighteenth century the affairs of the bishopric were both corrupt and inefficient as senior clerics, their relatives and stewards systematically plundered the church lands. It was in these circumstances that Ramsay and Cotesworth had managed to obtain the manors of Gateshead and Whickham on such easy terms. By the 1720s, though the motives were far from lofty, and were essentially the desire to increase the bishop's income, the management of the diocese's resources was being more efficiently pursued. The manors had not been "bought" in an absolute sense, for the Bishopric retained a reserved rent and the right both to adjust this and exact a fine at the renewal of the leases. Leases were for twenty-one years or three lives and were renewed on a seven year cycle, with rents generally low but with fines for renewal.[18] The reserved rent hardly changed but it was the new tough attitude of the Bishopric to fines that forced Robert Cotesworth to sell Whickham to Sir Henry Liddell. After 1728 fines seemed to have been paid annually, a system that suited Ellison and Carr as it was convenient to make a modest annual payment instead of a large sum every seven years.

Good personal relations with the bishop of the day were very important and here Carr, with his forte for cultivating the senior clergy came in useful. "On Tuesday last Mr Carr and I waited on the Bishop about our renewals" wrote Ellison in 1730.[19] This bishop, Bishop Chandler, proved relatively easy going about the terms of the lease, but Bishop Butler, who became Bishop of Durham in 1750, drove a hard bargain when he renewed the lease in 1751. Bishop Trevor was content to accept the same fine of £128 in 1754 as his predecessor had taken the previous year. But then came a period of steep increases for, during the times of Bishop Egerton (1771-86) and his successor Bishop Shute Barrington, the fines went up consistently and considerably from £159 in 1771 to £470-14s.0d in 1788, the last year of Egerton's rule, to £509.2s.2d in 1793.[20]

Henry Ellison had also to deal with the Bishopric in his capacity of custodian of his brother's interests but in this instance his dealings were with the Dean and Chapter, rather than with the Bishop. Things followed substantially the same pattern, however, with the Dean and Chapter leaving rents stationary but demanding increases in the fines. When, in 1738, seven years of Cuthbert's lease had expired, John Airey, the Ellison's attorney, found himself engaged in hard bargaining:

> *I attended the Chapter yesterday. Dr Johnson, Dr Sharp and Mr Bland present. They asked £500 for the fine. I bid then the old fine and gave reasons. After a good deal of debate, I withdrew....Again called in: the fine set at £440. I did all I could to have the old fine [£400] but they would go no lower.*[21]

Despite efforts to get the fine reduced, it was set at £440 in 1745 and again in 1752 and 1759. As Robert Swinburne, the steward at Hebburn put it, "Fines never go back even if rents fall". No wonder the incomes of the prebends of Durham went up so rapidly in the eighteenth century.[22] It was too much for Cuthbert Ellison who, in 1765, took the step he had contemplated in 1740 and gave up the estates he had leased from the Dean and Chapter.

In his cousin, Robert Ellison, Henry had a good friend and valuable adviser in his business activities. Robert, the son of William Ellison, was, like Henry, a Merchant Adventurer and a Hostman but was much more active in these bodies. He was prominent in the economic and commercial life of Newcastle where he held the valuable post of Collector of the Customs.[23] He was Sheriff of Newcastle in 1734. This useful cousin was Henry's eyes and ears in the commercial world of Tyneside.

The management of the Hebburn estate called for all Henry's skills. Its affairs were complex and involved Hebburn Quay, the ballast shore, Hebburn Mills, Hebburn Vale colliery, wayleave leases and other mining interests. Then there was the matter of the properties leased from the Dean and Chapter of Durham: the manor of Wardley with Heworth Mill and other smaller properties.

As we have seen, Cuthbert was very optimistic when it came to boring for coal on the estate, though his optimism was not rewarded. He was badly affected by the bankruptcy of Alderman Rudston in 1733:

> *Tho I was always apprehensive that I should be a sufferer by these Gentlemen [Rudston and his partner Reed], yet I never imagined that my loss could have been so very Great as I find now tis likely to be.[24]*

Two years later, he wrote:

> *I am very much obliged to you for the trouble you have taken with my Way Leave Treaty. If you can get me the same rent I was to have received from Mr Rudston, I shall think myself happy...[25]*

One does not envy Henry Ellison the job of looking after this difficult estate, with the absent squire looking over his shoulder. There was the complex matter of the enclosure of Hebburn Common to be seen to: "Is there no question of bringing Sir B. Rawling [26] into a division of the Common as it seems to be in his interests as much as mine. I am surprised he is not as desirous of it as myself".[27] The common was eventually enclosed in 1779 when General Cuthbert and the Cathedral church of Durham divided it between them.[28] Then there was the matter of letting Hebburn Hall; it was let first of all to Uncle Robert Ellison of Newcastle but, after his death, suitable tenants proved difficult to find. Nevertheless, the brothers were fond of each other and Cuthbert was zealous in looking after Henry's interests and furthering the careers of his nephews while, as Cuthbert got older and showed no inclination to marry, it became accepted that the estate would come to Henry's son.

Their association with the Liddells was very important to the Ellisons. Letters from one Ellison to another are larded with accounts of the latest news of members of the Liddell family or enquiries about them: "My uncle [George] had like to have had a nasty accident yesterday by an overturn but thank God neither he nor Sir Harry received any harm"; "Is Lord Ravensworth's gout better?"; or "Lady Ravensworth's cold is much improved".

That the Ellisons and the Liddells were a close and affectionate cousinhood is certain but there was a lot of mutual self interest in the relationship. People have always needed and relied on the help of friends and relatives to assist in their advancement in their business, professional and public life, though the twentieth century is discreet and even sanctimonious about this. The eighteenth century made no bones about it. This was a very personal world in which vertical ties stretched from the top to the bottom of society. Such ties stretched from the Duke of Newcastle down to, though he scarcely knew it, the under-gardener at Gateshead Park. You looked after your own and they, in turn, deferred to and supported you. This was, at once, the strength and the weakness of eighteenth century England. Those who suffered, who, for instance, felt the full rigour of the harsh laws, which could hang a man for stealing a sheep or have him transported for poaching, tended to be nobody's men. As for the majority, they openly recognised those to whom they owed loyalty and those to whom they owed assistance.

The Ellisons expected assistance in their careers from the Liddells and the Liddells expected support from the Ellisons, whether in a business or a political venture. The Liddells were a family of national importance and influence. Lord Ravensworth has been described as, "a strong Whig but not a very sensible one"[29] but his uncles Henry Liddell and George Liddell were both astute businessmen. The Liddells were close to the Duke of Grafton, standing in a similar position to him as the Ellisons did to them, and were within the outer ring of what many have seen as the Whig oligarchy. In comparison, the Ellisons were of regional importance but were, in the generation of Henry and Cuthbert, expecting to share in the rewards that, what has been called, the "fiscal-military" state could give.[30]

As we have already seen, Cuthbert and his younger brother Robert both followed military careers in the much larger armies that became the norm in the eighteenth century and their careers were considerably assisted by the influence of their mother's family. But Henry Ellison also had hopes for the advancement of his son, Henry.

After completing his education at Clare Hall, the young Henry spent several years at Joshua Geekie's chambers at Inner Temple studying law and preparing to be called to the bar. It is clear, however, that this legal training was intended to be of general utility to him, rather than preparing him for a legal career. It was hoped that by remaining in the south and by mixing in society close to government and court he might gain some "place".

He wrote to his father in 1758: "My Lord Ravensworth has recommended me to the Duke of Grafton, who has not only promised to advance me when he can himself do it, but also has undertaken to speak to the Duke of Devonshire...". A few months later he was able to inform him:

> *Before the Duke of Grafton left town he spoke to the Duke of Newcastle on my account who said there were so many applications that he could not promise anything of that kind but that he would speak to the king for a pension; but upon my Lord Ravensworth's declaring he would have nothing to do with that (for which I am obliged to him as for his first application, A pension being what I would by no means care to accept & what I apprehended you would be as adverse to as I am). He has promised he will endeavour to find some place for me.*[31]

Early in 1759, there was, thanks to Lord Ravensworth's endeavours, the chance of employment with the Duke of Bedford, who was then Viceroy of Ireland. Henry determined to take it: "because my position would at least be made better by it for that time & in the interim my friends might probably have it in their power to do something for me in England".

This possibility does not seem to have come off. Perhaps Ravensworth exaggerated the patronage at the disposal of a Viceroy. When the Earl of Northumberland was rumoured to be going to be made Viceroy in 1761, General Ellison reviewing his nephew's prospects of getting a place, concluded that the appointments at the disposal of Lord Lieutenants was sadly depleted since his day:

> *In the Civil branch very few indeed are in their gift... [They still nominated to some military positions but]...The only good things in their gift are Church preferments....the rest of their attendants... are usually disappointed in their expectations ... the place perhaps most to be coveted in the Lord Lieutenant's gift is that of Usher of the Black Rod. 'Tis almost a sinecure & worth £1000 each session.*[32]

Ravensworth was obviously persistent in his efforts for Henry," my near relation, one I value and love". The Duke of Newcastle replying in 1761 to Ravensworth's request for a place said:

> *Both these offices [at Newcastle] are sinecures of £400 or £500 per ann.*
> *The one Sir Robert Walpole gave to his nephew, Mr Horace Townshend,*
> *the other Lord Wilmington gave to Mr Sharpe, First Clerk of the Council*
> *and one who had served long and been of particular use to my Lord*
> *Wilmington while he was President of the Council. I have not given one*
> *sinecure to any one Relation I have ever since I was at the Treasury and*
> *indeed there is but one of any value that has fallen in my Time. Your*
> *Lordship will judge whether I must not have Friends and Relations of my*
> *own who may expect such sinecures when they fall. But tho'it may not be*
> *in my power to do this, I will find some way of providing for Mr E. as*
> *soon as I possibly can.[33]*

Henry Ellison senr. had himself a post with the Newcastle Office of Tax Farmer Inwards. As we have seen, his cousin Robert Ellison was Collector of Customs at Newcastle. The young Henry Ellison was able from London to keep an eye on his father's interests:

> *I yesterday met Mr Heron, who informed me of the death of Mr Stow,*
> *and told me, that tho' you had hitherto received and were certainly*
> *entitled to a moiety of the profits annexed at the Office of Tax Farmer*
> *Inwards in the Port of Newcastle, yet the present patent being made to*
> *Mr Gordon and his son and to you, might seem to vest an equal share in*
> *each of the patentees, wherefore he apprehended some declaration by Mr*
> *Gordon importing that you were still to enjoy the same proportion you*
> *have always had in that Place should be given to you to secure you in the*
> *possession of your moiety.[34]*

It was never intended, of course, that the persons to whom the patent was made should do the work. Some junior lawyer or lawyer's clerk, who would have to be a Whig, would do the work for fifty pounds a year and be very grateful for the opportunity.

This matter of Henry Ellison's share of the patent dragged on for some time. It was put in the hands of Geekie and Gordon's attorney Heron. By February 1761 it was planned that young Robert Ellison should receive the salary instead of his father and it was hoped that the patent might be made for life.[35] Gordon was particularly keen that this be done as he apprehended the possibility of a change of government:

As under the present Patent you enjoy the Place only during Pleasure,
Mr G thinking it probible that his friends may not always be in favor, and
that some person may hereafter be put into the Patent to the prejudice of
his son would be glad if the new Patent might be made for life...[36]

The warrant for making out the patent was in Geekie's office but awaited the attention of the Duke of Newcastle. Gordon was reluctant to approach Newcastle, feeling that as the warrant was in Ellison's interest, he should get Grafton to bring the matter to Newcastle's attention.[37] Grafton was indeed, at Henry (jnr)'s request, using his influence on Newcastle but when Geekie died suddenly later that month the patent was no further forward.

Gordon's worries about a change of government were, of course, justified. The classic Whig ascendancy was in its last days, though most of the leading Whigs would be back in office within a few years. The Duke of Newcastle clung to office with the tenacity of a barnacle, while George III's favourite, the Earl of Bute, acquired more and more power. As Henry Ellison jnr wrote in March 1761,"On Friday Lord Bute was appointed Secretary of State instead of Lord Holdernesse since which each day has produced so many changes..." It was not until 26 May 1762 that the Duke finally resigned after forty years in government. All patronage and the dispensing of all grants and pensions from the civil list were for the time being in Bute's hands. The Ellisons managed to hold on their Customs post, however, but it continued to be vested in the father rather than the son.

For all but the richest families, the careers of younger sons were a problem. The Ellisons decided that Henry Ellison's younger son, Robert, should be apprenticed to a London merchant, Godhard Hagen, a not inexpensive step as such apprenticeships had to be paid for. After Robert had served his apprenticeship, his father and elder brother decided to support him by negotiating a partnership for him with Hagen.[38] A partnership was finally agreed in 1763 at a cost to the Ellisons of £5000 but Robert grew worried at Hagen's risky business practices, which involved the extension of credit on trade with Amsterdam and withdrew from the partnership in 1766. When a subsequent partnership with a banker failed, Robert found himself in an embarrassing position and lived out the rest of his life abroad.

The political influence of the aristocracy and gentry and their purchase on patronage lay in the connections between their local bases and their contacts at Court and Westminster. A culturally homogeneous elite based its power on land and wealth set in diverse localities and on the influence it could wield in the administration and political life of provincial communities. An inward looking country squire with no metropolitan connections had a purely local significance, while a man about town who rarely visited his country estate had little to offer to political managers. The successful man had a grip on the relationship between central and local power.

It was essential to exercise political influence. At any election even the most apolitical of country gentlemen would be asked which way he was putting his influence and much could depend upon a wise answer. Not every election gave a clear choice to the most confirmed Whig or Tory and personalities, personal loyalties and obscure local prejudices and loyalties played their part.

The Ellisons were, like the Liddells, strong Whigs and were assiduous in their support for Whig and, particularly Liddell candidates at Election times. Sir Henry Liddell was MP for Newcastle for the first decade of the eighteenth century but in 1710 Newcastle demonstrated its Toryism when Sir William Blackett and William Wrightson defeated the Whig members, Liddell and William Carr.[39] Despite having the patronage of government behind them, the Whigs were unable to dislodge the Tory hold on Newcstle, though they won one of the seats in the double member constituency in 1722, when another William Carr came top of the poll.[40] In 1727 the Tories, Blackett and Nicholas Fenwick, topped the poll, though Carr petitioned parliament and was allowed to take his seat when Blackett died in 1728. This was only accomplished after the Whigs had packed the committee of enquiry. As George Liddell remarked: "I think there was scarce anyone believed the witnesses. However, Sir William was voted not duly elected and Mr Carr voted duly elected".[41] The Tory ascendancy in Newcastle continued, however, with Walter Blackett[42] and Nicholas Fenwick winning in 1734 and 1741. The '45 Rising brought about an end to the fierce rivalry between Tories and Whigs in Newcastle as in the region as a whole. Many of the most prominent local Tories, among them Walter Blackett, were conspicuously loyal to the Hanoverian throne in 1745. The result was, " a consensus which was to prevail in Newcastle in 1747 and for thirty years thereafter".[43] Although there were attempts at a second Tory candidacy from Nicholas Fenwick and William Ord, there were in the end two unopposed candidates, Walter Blackett and Matthew Ridley. As W. A. Speck has put it:

> *Blackett, though a Tory was no Jacobite. Ridley, though a Whig, as mayor of Newcastle during the 'Forty-Five , engaged in no witch hunt of Tories but brought the town united through the crisis.*

Ridley had, nevertheless, to work hard enough to consolidate his position before it was clear he would have no opposition. Even the absent Cuthbert Ellison's support was called for:

> *I yesterday received a letter from Mr Ridley desiring my interest at Newcastle, which is at his Service, but am afraid will not be of much Use*

*to him in this Occasion; however if there are any people that I can
influence, I desire they may be applied to, for their votes in Mr Ridley's
favour.*[44]

In the Northumberland county division Henry Ellison and H.T.Carr had an obvious
influence as some of their tenants at Hartleyburn and Bellister also had freehold
land and were therefore voters. The Ellison and Carr influence was, like that of the
Ramsays and Cotesworth before them, naturally put behind Whig candidates. One
of the two Northumberland seats was firmly controlled by the Whigs but in the
early years of the century there were usually fierce contests for the other. An
exception to this was when the Tory MP Thomas Forster was expelled from the
house for his part in the '15; the subsequent by-election saw a contest between rival
Whigs, Sir Francis Delaval, backed by the Court Whigs, and Oley Douglas.
Ramsay gave his freehoders leave to vote as they pleased. In 1722, however,
Cotesworth ordered his tenants to vote for the Whig, Ralph Jennison, in the by-
election won by his Tory opponent, William Wrightson.

After a series of closely fought and ruinously expensive elections, there was an
electoral truce in 1741 and 1747. Sir William Middleton, who was MP from 1722
to 1757, was the only Whig candidate while the Tories put forward a single
candidate, John Fenwick. The two were accordingly returned at both elections
though, in 1747, few expected the hard-drinking Fenwick to survive for long. As
Walter Blackett wrote to Lancelot Allgood in June: "That noble candidate Jack
Fenwick was to have been with me last night or the morning but I find he was so
ill (drunk I suppose, damnably drunk) that his excellency could not come". On
Fenwick's death, shortly after the election, the peace of the county was disturbed by
the Earl of Tankerville who, rather than give the Tories a free run, determined to
get his son, Lord Ossulston[45] returned at the by-election. The idea of running
Ossulston as a second Whig candidate had been mooted in 1747, when Lord
Ravensworth had suggested to the Duke of Newcastle that there had been
insufficient preparation for it.[46]

There can be little doubt that many Whigs had great doubts about Ossultston's
candidacy. The Tories adopted Lancelot Allgood, who had been scrupulously,
almost ostentatiously, loyal during the '45, while the Earl of Tankerville, the Lord
Lieutenant, had absented himself from the county during the time of danger. His
son had never been in Northumberland before.

For loyal Whigs like the Ellisons, Ossulston's candidacy presented a difficult
decision. Tankerville was in the ministry and a close associate of the Duke of
Newcastle from whom the stream of patronage and hopes of advancement flowed to
Grafton and from him to the Liddells and themselves. At the same time they

respected Allgood and knew he was no Jacobite and was popular in the county. From the time of the Ramsays, the freeholders of Harltleyburn and Bellister had, as we have seen, been instructed to vote in the Whig interest and so it had continued under Cotesworth and under Carr and Ellison. This time things were not so simple as a letter from H.T.Carr to his brother-in-law and joint proprietor demonstrates:

> *Our tenants have been asked not to engage themselves. Mr Algood has declared his intention of standing but was pretty well assured that you would be for Lord Ossulton...you will be home in time to direct our Freeholders yourself for Lord Ossulton. I should certainly vote for Lord O. if he had been opposed by any Person reasonably suspected of Jacobitism, but considering Mr Algood's good character and his zealous behaviour in the late Rebellion, I cannot bring myself to vote against him in favour of the son of a man who, though Lord Lieutenant of the County, deserted it so shamefully in the time of danger and who himself seems to have nothing said in his favour but that he is a Whig set up by the Whig Party, who I wish had made a choice of a man of more merit, as I think we shall look a little too sour and shew ourselves too irreconcileable to the bare name of Tory if we can't be so far softten'd and reconciled by Mr Algood's good behaviour as to look upon him almost as one of ourselves, but must to a man oppose him. And, if that should be the case I fear the consequences of it would be a reuniting of the Jacobites and Tories whom the latter at the time of the rebellion separated themselves from...*[47]

Nevertheless, the Hartleyburn and Bellister tenants were instructed, via the agent Sill and sub-agent William Tinlin of the family which farmed Broomhouses, to vote for Ossulston. They don't appear to have done so. Robert Ellison of Newcastle, reporting to Henry Ellison in January 1748, wrote that Tom Tinlin [William Tinlin's father and the tenant of Broomhouses] has either neglected that interest [Ossulston's] or his wishes are another way".[48] Allgood was clearly the most popular candidate in the Tynedale area in which he gained a large majority of the votes cast. Robert Ellison was pretty pessimistic about Ossulston's chances in general. After the Whig candidate had waited upon the Newcastle freeholders, he commented: "The general bent of the people's inclinations is to Mr Algood in preference to Lord O. and no less other circumstances give all the reason imaginable to fear all endeavours for his Lordship's success". Cuthbert Ellison, writing from London, was more confident that Lord Ossulston would be returned: "Mr Algood's friends here, say he will carry it, by a great majority; but I should think they will be mistaken, except Lord Tankerville is very much so in his calculations.[49]

Lord Ossulston came second in the poll, eleven votes behind Allgood, but the Sheriff of Northumberland , Nicholas Brown, who acted as returning officer, was a close friend of Lord Tankerville's. He promptly rejected a number of votes for Algood, making Ossulston the winner by sixteen votes. The Whigs had in fact used every corrupt and dubious practice in the book. Allgood's supporters petitioned parliament and Ossulston conceded the seat, largely to protect his friend, Nicholas Brown, whose conduct had been so scandalously partial and corrupt that had the matter dragged on he might have been charged. Cuthbert Ellison, commenting on Ossulstone's decision not to defend his seat reported that no prosecution would be commenced and added: "I am of Opinion that his Cause in General, was not the Best and the Conduct of some of his friends such as could not be supported".[50]

As Jacobitism waned, the essential unity of elite and polite opinion became apparent. As Henry Ellison wrote to his father after the Hexham riot against the militia ballot in 1761:

> The severe but necessary Measures taken to quell the riots at Hexham, have I hope secured the tranquility of the County for the future. In affairs of this kind it is a great satisfaction that all people approve the conduct both of the deputy Lieutenants and of the Militia.[51]

The constituency that mattered most to the Liddells and Ellisons was Berwick. Colonel George Liddell was MP for Berwick (1727-40) and the garrison town was a "Government borough" where considerable patronage was dispersed. Much of the patronage was military and George Liddell had a difficult task deciding between the many whom had some claim upon him and wished for an appointment for relatives and dependants. Liddell was on close terms with Sir Robert Walpole who called him "the wise man of the North" and he had the support of the Government interest at Berwick elections.

Normally there was no opposition but in 1734 there were rival Whig candidates when Lords Barrington and Polwarth opposed Liddell. "It is no very agreable thing to have fresh candidates leading up the dance two years before the probable time of Election",[52] wrote Liddell, bemoaning that it would be expensive while expressing confidence in victory.

A well organised campaign was co-ordinated by Henry Ellison assisted by his cousin Robert. They had the assistance of all those in Berwick whose interests were bound up with those of the Liddells or who gained from the Court patronage of garrison positions. Such supporters included the governor, the mayor, the collector of Customs and the Commissary. Even with such support, victory could not be taken for granted. Liddell treated the considerable number of Berwick voters who lived in London to dinners at the Bedford Arms and sent a thousand guineas to Henry Ellison in Berwick to spend on hospitality for voters there. No doubt the eventual total of money spent by Liddell on the election was considerable, though certainly less than the £5000 to £10000 spent by George Bowes in his unsuccessful attempt to win Berwick in 1722. Liddell's campaign was successful. He topped the poll, the second seat going to Lord Polwarth, and remained MP until his death in 1740.

Compared to the search for place, sinecures and positions, the dispersal of patronage may appear both simple and rewarding. One gained honour, prestige and influence from it but, even to the most machiavellian, it posed problems. There were always more applicants than posts. To the conscientious man, who sought to steer a course between a proper recognition of what was due to friends and supporters and at the same time make good appointments, agonising decisions had to be made.

When it came to the appointment of a Vicar to Whittingham, the correspondence between Sir Henry Liddell and Henry Ellison[53] makes it clear that a suitable candidate had to have several qualifications: he had to be a Whig but he also had to be a scholar, a man who would be content with rural life and enough of a gentleman so that he would not let down his patrons; he had also to be a native of Northumberland or Durham. Hughes describes the deliberations of Henry Ellison and Sir Henry Liddell over this appointment as "patronage at its best" and it is significant that an Ellison relative, Nathaniel Ellison, Vicar of Kirkwhelpington, who was a candidate, was not chosen: "I fear he would scarcely justify me naming him, even to the Parish and the character he would carry in the neighbourhood".[54] The system would no doubt shock devotees of equal opportunity legislation but it probably made no less and no more mistakes than subsequent systems of appointment.

That England remained tolerably well governed during the eighteenth century depended greatly, at county level, on men like Henry Ellison, who combined the search for place, power and money with a sense of what was fitting and was in the wider public interest.

References

1. As Hughes points out, it was a moot point whether, after the sale of a manor, the fines and heriots had to be paid on the death of the purchaser or of the vendor.

2. Hughes, p. 129.

3. *Ibid*, p.140.

4. *Ibid*, p.135.

5. Cuthbert Ellison to Henry Ellison, 15, April 1749 (A20).

6. Katherine Airey to H. Ellison, 11 Sept. 1758 (A8).

7. Cuthbert Ellison to H. Ellison, 25 March 1758 (A20).

8. *Ibid*, 9 July 1759.

9. *Ibid*, 12 July 1774 (A23).

10. *Ibid*, 25 Sept. 1774 and 26 Nov. 1774.

11. *Ibid*, 30 March 1775.

12. *Ibid*, 3 April 1736 and 23 May 1736 (A18).

13. *Ibid*, 25 July 1736.

14. *Ibid*, 24 Dec. 1748 (A20).

15. *Ibid*, 27 June 1749.

16. *Ibid*, 22 March 1759.

17. *Ibid*, 25 Feb. 1758.

18. This was very much the standard system and can be compared with what happened at Hartleyburn and Bellister and, as we shall see in section 2, with the conditions of Ralph Carr's lease of the tithes of Ponteland and Embleton.

19. Hughes, p. 317.

20. *Ibid,* pp.317-329.

21. J. Airey to Henry Ellison, 1738. Ellison Mss. (A40)

22. Hughes, p. 325.

23. Henry Ellison, himself, held a post in the office of Taxfarmer Inwards and thus controlled the positions of Customs House Officers for Newcastle and Sunderland.

24. Cuthbert Ellison to H. Ellison, 14 Nov. 1733 (A18).

25. *Ibid*, 10 Dec. 1735.

26. Sir Benjamin Rawling was a relation of the Ellisons. On his death, Elizabeth Ellison, daughter of Nathaniel Ellison of Newcastle inherited about £140,000 of personal property.

27. C. Ellison to H. Ellison, 3 Jan 1740.

28. Alfred J. Ellison, *Ellison Portraits 1510-1936 (*Unpublished 1936) p. 38. South Tyneside Central Library.

29. John Brooke, *King George III (1974)*, p.81.

30. See J. Brewer, *the Sinews of Power* (1989).

31. Henry Ellison jnr. To his father Henry Ellison, 21 Feb. 1758 (A1).

32. Cuthbert Ellison to Henry Ellison, 31 Jan. 1761 (A21).

33. Quoted in Hughes, p. 283.

34. Henry Ellison jnr. to Henry Ellison, 6 March 1760 (A14).

35. This does not seem to have happened as, after Henry Ellison's death, his son wrote to Mr Wells at the Custom House, Sunderland, thanking him for his condolences, promising to recommend him to his father's successor and instructing that all profits from the office up to the time of Henry's death be paid to him.

36. Henry Ellison jnr. to Henry Ellison, 24 Jan. 1761.

37. *Ibid*, 17 Feb. 1761.

38. *Ibid*, 15 June 1759.

39. William Carr was the son of William Carr of Newcastle.

40. This William Carr was, "..of St Helens Auckland by marriage with a co-heir through Ellison of a family of the same name....Carr of Auckland was also of Coxlodge." *Memoirs of Ambrose Barnes*, p.56. He was the son of Joseph Carr of Coxlodge and a cousin of H. T. Carr.

41. Hughes, *p. 260*.

42. Born Walter Calverley, he married an illegitimate daughter of Sir William Blackett and inherited the Blackett estate on fulfilling the condition of changing his name.

4.   W. A. Speck, "Northumberland Elections in the Eighteenth Century", *Northern History,* Vol. XXVII, 1992.

44. Cuthbert Ellison to Henry Ellison, 12 June 1747 (A20).

45. Ossulston's name is spelt in a variety of ways. W.A. Speck favours Ossultstone. Edward Hughes uses Ossulton which the contemporary H. T. Carr used. Modern reference books give the junior title of the Tankerville Earldom as Ossultston.

46. Edward Hughes, p.266.

47. H. T. Carr to Henry Ellison, 1748. W. A. Speck in his "Northumberland Elections" wrongly attributes this quotation to a Henry Cust.

48. Robert Ellison to Henry Ellison, 15 Jan. 1748 (A17).

49. Cuthbert Ellison to Henry Ellison, 23 Feb. 1748 (A20).

50. *Ibid*, 24 Dec. 1748.

51. Henry Ellison jnr. to Henry Ellison, 17 March 1761 (A14).

52. Hughes, p.275.

53. See Hughes, pp.337-340.

54. The Newcastle Ellisons produced a distinguished line of clergymen but it would appear that not all of them were above reproach from those of the strictest morality. The Rev. John Ellison (1694-1773) was the subject of "an indecent rhyme" entitled, "The Will of a Northern Vicar", while the Rev. Cuthbert Ellison, who was Vicar of Stannington, "published some sermons and a coarse rhyme". *The Family of Verge* by Colonel Ralph Edward Carr and Cuthbert Ellison Carr (1891) p.31 and 38.

Chapter 6

Family Life

I hope my dearest jewel will remember the charge I gave him to take care of himself.

Hannah Ellison to her husband Henry.

The marriage of Henry Ellison to Hannah Cotesworth was clearly advantageous to both parties. Henry gained her share of the considerable Cotesworth inheritance, while the daughter of the erstwhile tallow chandler married into an established gentry family. Cuthbert wrote to Henry congratulating him upon his engagement, "the young lady has a gt many good qualities and I suppose a very good fortune".[1] But, if there was sense in the marriage, there was also sensibility. Five years after their marriage, Hannah began a letter to her husband, "I had the favour of my Dearest's most obliging letter" and concluded, I hope my dearest jewel will remember the charge I gave him to take care of himself".[2]

It was a happy marriage, which lasted for forty-six years, until Henry's death in 1775. The notion that affectionate marriages were something of an innovation in this period is one of the wilder fancies of historians of the family. It is true, however, that, as life spans increased amongst the upper classes, a mere alliance of property interests was increasingly seen as, by itself, an insufficient basis for wedded life. The couple produced five children over a fifteen-year period, not a large family by contemporary standards, all of whom lived into adult life.

The family home was Gateshead Park, not Hebburn Hall, the seat of the absent Cuthbert, and Henry had the wealth and the taste to make it a fine and a comfortable house.

The country house, designed for ease and comfort and to impress, but with no thought for defence, came late to North East England (the Jacobean mansion, Denton Hall, is an early example) but, by the first decades of the eighteenth century, the prosperous aristocracy and gentry were, as at the Liddells' Eslington Park or the Delavals' Seaton Delaval Hall, building houses fit to rank with anything in the south of England.

Gateshead Park House (by W. H. Knowles) (Gateshead Public Library)

Gateshead Park was a more modest house but there were three successive rebuildings in fifteen years. Ramsay had it rebuilt in 1714-15 and Cotesworth embarked upon extensive alterations when he went to live there in 1716, as did Henry Ellison, after his marriage to Hannah Cotesworth. Ellison employed James Gibb, a London architect, and the result, a house built in brick with a pantiled roof and sash windows, must have been the acme of modernity.[3]

Gardens, both for food and ornamentation, were laid out carefully under the watchful eyes of Henry himself, Allan Brown, the head gardener, and Colonel Liddell, a very knowledgeable horticulturist. They did not always agree. It says much for contemporary gardening skills that non-native fruits, like apricots and peaches, were able to be grown on south walls, while the Ellison pippin apple testifies to the expertise with native fruits at Park House.

"What we have in the north at this time", wrote Edward Hughes, "is rather like a Caucasian spring, a sudden blossoming of civilisation with the melting away of political and social disorder under the warming influence of economic prosperity."[4] Park House reflects a mixed picture: beds could have bugs, dogs were still used to turn spits (though, Cotesworth insisted, "The dog must shit in the pot...") but the house, managed by housekeeper Peggy Gates, had a high reputation for comfort and good food.

Yet a country house, like Gateshead Park, remained something of an outpost, reliant, for many of the goods its inhabitants consumed and wore, on parcels from town, and town was London, not Newcastle. Furniture came from London as did tea, ordered from Twinings, hats and dress material for the ladies and wigs and fishing rods for the men. There was a continuous two-way traffic of parcels between those members of the Ellison family at Gateshead Park and those in London. To London went potted woodcock, pickled salmon and other delicacies, while from London came orders, such as that sent to Henry Ellison by his son in 1745, of "wigs, stockings and razor straps", as well as goods that had to go by ship, a coach shaft and breeding fowls. The expansion of provincial polite society and a consumer industry catering for its needs would, by the end of the century, make a town like Newcastle a much better shopping centre but, for the wealthier gentry, London would remain the place where one shopped for fashionable or luxury goods.

What surprises the modern reader of the Ellison Papers is that, though the time it took to travel between London and the North East and the difficulties of the journey were so much greater than today, the psychological distance was not commensurately greater. The Ellisons and their friends and relatives took the three or four day journey on bumpy roads as a matter of course. They rarely went by sea.

The upbringing and education of the children reflected these links with the south of England. The two boys, Henry (1734-95) and Robert (1738-83), were sent first to a local grammar school at Houghton-le-Spring and then to Eton, while the eldest girl, Hannah (1731-99), was at school in Chelsea by the age of ten. This was part of the general trend amongst the gentry to become less provincial and aspire to a national upper-class education, culture, acquaintances and, most importantly, accent. It was made more convenient for the Ellisons because so many of the family lived in London.[5]

Elizabeth Ellison, Henry's mother, had lived in London since her serious illness in 1724. This was in part to be close to eminent doctors but also because she preferred London to the North East and her Liddell relatives spent much time there. Her daughters, Jane and Elizabeth, who never married, lived with her in Rathbone Place and the third daughter Katherine, who married Newcastle attorney, John Airey, spent most of her life there. Henry's children, though far from Gateshead Park, were, thus, never far from close relatives.

Relationships between the parents and their children, though formal by twentieth century standards, were affectionate and considerable thought and care was given to the children's' upbringing. In his early twenties, Henry Ellison jnr. expressed his gratitude to his father thus: "...I shall be always much obliged to you for the care with which you attended to my education, the Affection which you have always born towards me and the constant anxiety you have expressed for my welfare".[6] The young Hannah Ellison wrote to her father from her school in Chelsea: "I will take care to make very great improvements in every part of my education as I know it will oblige so good a Papa as yourself".[7] It was not an age in which the facts of birth were supposed to be a closed book to a well brought up girl and the following year the eleven year old hoped that, "...mother will soon be safely delivered of a new baby".[8]

Amongst the responsibilities of Cuthbert and Henry Ellison was the maintenance in appropriate style of their mother and sisters. Mrs Elizabeth Ellison had been seriously ill in 1724 with some sort of mental illness, probably what would be referred to today as a nervous breakdown.

The treatment prescribed seems harsh and dangerous to a twentieth century way of thinking and, as the case of George III was later to demonstrate, position and status did not save you from the worst humiliations, once you were considered not to have full possession of your mental faculties. Robert Ellison had begged Henry, who being in London at the time was in charge, not to suffer "any harsh methods to be used which as I sayd before will instead of doing good will make her worse".[9] Harsh methods do seem to have been what the doctor ordered. Mrs Ellison was removed from the care of her daughter, Katherine, who was considered too indulgent to the invalid, and the treatment recommended by the doctor was begun. For some time Mrs Ellison seems to have refused to take the medicaments required. Cold bathing seems to have been part of the cure, suggesting that the diagnosis was hysteria. Perhaps surprisingly, the doctor's administrations seem to have been successful or at least did no harm and Mrs Ellison recovered to live for many years and to develop her own views on medicine, which included a great faith in the efficacy of bleeding. Her daughter, Jane, seems to have suffered a similar illness in 1761 and her nephew advised: "as she is easily governed, she should still continue in her own home but constantly attended by her nurse and servant".[10]

As Robert Ellison left the estate in debt, his widow and daughters were ill- provided for at first, but the sons were able with the assistance of George Liddell to improve their circumstances. As Cuthbert wrote to Henry, George agreed to allow his sister (Cuthbert's and Henry's mother) "...£100 pa in case you and I will allow her £50 each to enable her to keep a house and coach and live in a more reputable Manner than she does at present. He recommends some certain restrictions which she must submit to and am afraid are but too necessary to be insisted on."[11] The widow and daughters settled at a rented house in Rathbone Place in genteel, if not luxurious, circumstances.

That only one of the three sisters, Katherine, married is perhaps explained by the fact that they came from a gentry family but had little money. Henry, of course, became wealthy but he had his own family to think of and the incomes of his mother and sisters came from the Hebburn estate, which scarcely supported Cuthbert, and gifts and legacies from the Liddells. Only marriage with social equals was desirable but such equals would expect a sufficient dowry.

Katherine Ellison had an unhappy love affair in the 1720s. Robert Doubleday wished to marry her and she was clearly very attracted to him but both her brother,

Henry, and her uncle, George Liddell opposed the match. Doubleday had apparently a reputation for sharp practice in business matters. George Liddell called him a "loose chapman". In 1738, when she was 36, she married the family's north-country attorney, John Airey of Crow Hall in Felling. She was his third wife and it is clear that her relatives felt she had married beneath her. Mrs Elizabeth Ellison wrote that she had heard that "...your sister is to be married to a country attorney".[12]

Many historians have painted dismal pictures of the position of women prior to the Married Women's Property Acts of the late nineteenth century but such pictures largely concentrate upon the middle orders and leave out the aristocracy and gentry. Most of the latter were only too well aware of the need to protect the position of women and effectively did so by settlements.

From Airey's first formal offer in January 1733 to the marriage in March 1738, negotiations were detailed and protracted. "The exceeding great regard" he professed for Miss Ellison, "whose virtues and goodness I am sure must make her the most agreeable consort",[13] were not enough. He had to lay bare his financial position and was asked to accede to demands that he found unacceptable. In March 1735, asked to make further settlements of his furniture and £500 on his proposed bride, he declared, "I can consider ye demand only as intentional to break the affair off; or some alteration of the lady's mind".[14] John Airey must have wished he'd never asked.

This long engagement or business negotiation ended with a marriage settlement which placed many of Airey's assets under the supervision of a group of trustees who would see them transferred to his bride in the event of his death.[15] It may not have been a brilliant match but Airey had a fair amount of property and investments and Kitty ended up in more prosperous and independent circumstances than her unmarried sisters.

The world of Rathbone Place in Kensington seems to have been polite and comfortable with much in the way of tea and card parties. It was enlivened by the occasional excursion into that grander world, close to court and government, inhabited by their Liddell relatives. There were also visits from Cuthbert Ellison who lived in St James's Square and from other male Ellisons.

Illness and its treatment were constant preoccupations at Rathbone Place as at Gateshead Park. Much ill-health and considerable suffering were the lot of most people and neither the Ellisons nor the Liddells had strong constitutions. Mrs Elizabeth Ellison had great faith in a doctor called Small. When her daughter Jenny was ill with an inflamed throat in 1735, she described her as "having undergone a weeks severe discipline by the assistance of Mr Small who you know spares nobody". Whether because of Small's treatment, which included "opening ye jugaler of each side her neck and taking away a good quantity of blood...together with ye help of a blister and other evacuations" or in spite of it, Jenny was soon able to eat the breast of a chicken. Mrs Ellison's daughter Elizabeth was less impressed by the formidable Mr Small and when, a few years later, Jenny was again being treated by this doctor commented, "I think he has troubled himself just to put his fees in his pockett". For young and old, strong and weak, bleeding seems to have been an inevitable treatment. Young Robert Ellison was bled when ill at Eton as was Mrs Elizabeth Ellison in her last illness, her doctor believing that "people in years require more bleeding in their disorders than young people"[16]. Dr Hayes, the Eton school doctor, prescribed doses of Dr James's Powder for Robert's serious illness. This powder, concocted by a man who, according to Dr Johnson, "for twenty years was not sober"[17], was considered efficacious for both men and animals. Robert recovered. Modern medical opinion would, at any rate, have approved the alacrity with which the Ellisons accepted the practice of inoculating children against smallpox. Such inoculations were almost literally passed round between relatives and friends. "Miss Bright has been inoculated", wrote Robert Ellison to his brother, Henry, "and has had the Smallpox very favourably...I believe that 2 of the Duke of Richmond's daughters will be inoculated from Miss Bright".[18]

Gossip and scandal were, as ever, great sources of pleasure. When the Carr's daughter, Betty, went to live in sin with Sir James Lowther, Katherine Airey's horror was overshadowed by her delight in having a good tale to tell:

> ....*as every step B-C has taken, for some time past, has seemed to point at the way of life, she is now said to be in; this shocking story, I had mentioned to me, privately, ten days ago; but did not care to mention, so bad and disagreeable piece of intelligence to you....there is no room to doubt; of the truth of B.Carr's being now supported, (I will not give it the usual epithet) by a Person well able to do it even to the indulging her in her extravagances, as his fortune will allow it ; When I have said this much , I need not mention that it is Sr J----s L-----r...She sat at the head of that Person's table, when he had company din'd with him, so that I guess she glories in her shame . My heart bleeds for poor Mrs Carr who only wanted this to make her completely miserable.*[19]

Even the Carr scandal paled beside the Grafton divorce case. This was the major scandal of the day and, even twenty years later, when Lady Elizabeth Foster was preparing to give birth in secret to the Duke of Devonshire's child, she was reminded of the Duchess of Grafton's desperate attempt to conceal her pregnancy.[20]

The Ellisons had taken pride in their relative, Anne Liddell, who had made such an advantageous marriage and become a famous society beauty. Katherine Airey wrote to her brother in 1758:

> *The Duchess of Grafton was at Lord Ravensworth's on Sunday evening when we got there: Her Grace has got a little flesh since I had the honour of seeing her...She looks better than I ever saw her and is indeed a most charming fine figure; I do not imagine Lady Coventry can exceed her, either in face or in person.*[21]

The events of March 1768 were succinctly summarised by the *London Chronicle*: "It is remarkable that a lady who was a Duchess on Thursday last, descended to plain Miss on Friday, and rose into a Countess on Sunday". As we have seen, that man of the world, Cuthbert Ellison, was a pillar of strength to his niece during her troubles but there are no further references to the Countess of Ossory in the letters of the female Ellisons.

As we have seen in the case of Kitty Ellison, within the aristocracy and gentry specific legal agreements usually protected the property rights of married women. Even the most spectacular instance of fortune hunting, that of Stoney Bowes's marriage to the Dowager Countess of Strathmore, demonstrates just how hard it was for Bowes to get his hands on the fortune of which she had a life tenancy.[22] When Anne Liddell first separated from Grafton, Cuthbert Ellison and his fellow general, Henry Conway drew up an agreement protecting her interests and the fortune she had brought to the marriage, more than £80,000, was returned to her at the time of the divorce. Similarly, Katherine Ellison's brothers ensured that her dowry was kept separate from John Airey's estate at the time of her marriage. These upper-class women were well protected by their male relatives.

They were often pretty good at looking after their own interests as well, keeping a close watch upon the details of wills and upon their investments and property. On the death of her brother, George Liddell, Elizabeth Ellison was quick to ask her son Henry how she stood in the will, while she went over the accounts John Shute sent her as to her income from the Hebburn estate with an eagle eye.[23] Henry's sister Elizabeth was quite prepared to give her opinion as to the desirability of selling the lead mines left by George Liddell[24] and was quick to point out that she was not only entitled to her share of three lottery tickets, but to the interest due upon them.[25] Katherine Airey was equally sharp when it came to looking after the property she inherited from her husband and soon detected that her agent was in arrears to her.[26]

For all the Ellisons a rich and varied world of leisure was available. The eighteenth century saw an explosion of new leisure pastimes and habits founded on greater wealth, the rise in numbers of the genteel, greater mobility and better education. Previously, many of the gentry had been content with a country life of blood sports and early dinners, leaving balls and masques to the select few who spent time at court and London or who were invited to the great houses of grandees, while the gentleman with a large library or a wife and daughters with musical ability, was rare if not an oddity. Now, richer gentry went to London for the season, visited spas and travelled abroad. Libraries became normal in country houses, periodicals like the *Spectator* and *Tatler* became essential reading, the novel became established as a literary genre and music lessons were *de rigeur* for young ladies. While, in the country, an outdoor life with riding, shooting and fishing continued to be the essential routine, the aristocracy and gentry increasingly eschewed the cruder and more brutal blood sports and returned from the field to houses of refinement and comfort. Gentry of more modest means, in conjunction with merchants, bankers and provincial polite society made towns, like Newcastle, York, Exeter or Norwich, cultural centres, providing assembly rooms, circulating libraries, baths, concerts, theatres and literary and philosophical societies.

The leisure life of the Ellisons reflects these developments. Plenty of time was devoted to the traditional pursuits of the country gentleman, which included hard drinking as well as strenuous exercise. "My Saterdays wine reproved me eno'(without your wife)", wrote George Liddell,"for I was not well till yesterday morning's coursing with canny Frank set me to rights". Good dogs were highly prized and George Liddell's uncle, Sir John Bright of Badsworth near Pontefract, was a well known breeder of beagles, spaniels and foxhounds. Robert Ellison wrote to his brother in 1731: "The Master has an old Dog for you to breed of but would not have you put your bitches you got from him to Snowball because they will be too mettled". Foxhunting had yet to become the organised sport and the dominant pastime of the gentry it would be a century later but beagling was very popular.

Horse racing combined two English obsessions, love of horses and a delight in gambling. Like most eighteenth century sports, its organisation was rudimentary by modern standards. The layout of even the top courses left much to be desired. At Newmarket only the end of the course was enclosed with ropes and the judges sat in a wooden hut on wheels, which was moved, as the course was lengthened or shortened, opposite to the winning post. Both Henry and Cuthbert Ellison were fond of racing. In 1736 Cuthbert wrote to Henry from Ireland, wanting to know "the character of Lambton's Grey Mare which had run by the name of Miss Doe and sometimes by that of Shylooks. Last summer she won at Penrith by the name of Smiling Betty and at Morpeth and Carlisle by the name of Miss Doe". Horses could cost a great deal of money but the sport retained a wonderfully unprofessional character and Henry Ellison allowed his groom, Robin, to enter one of their coach horses at Chester races. Close to home there were races at Newcastle, with a gold cup on the town moor, and on Gateshead Fell. The Ellisons were basically cautious men but must have mixed with a wilder set. General Cuthbert was able to astonish Henry with the news "...from Newmarket that our countryman, Shafto [Jennison Shafto], has gained a complete victory, having rode 50 miles yesterday morning in less than one hour and fifty minutes. One may say he grows rich at a Great Pace".[27] Shafto was supposed to have won £80,000 by this feat.

So one could go through the list of country sports. Shooting was something everyone did and there was no great fetish about it. You went out by yourself or with a friend or two and a couple of dogs and shot what materialised. There were no game books, no drawn game and no hundreds of birds; a gentleman might be quite pleased that he had shot a brace of partridge, a snipe and a hare. Fishing was taken very seriously and Henry Ellison and H.T.Carr would travel to Grindon, near Haydon Bridge, or Wooler in search of good sport with their single unit rods purchased in London; Carr was an experienced fisherman while Ellison was a novice who enjoyed his sport. His brother, Robert, was also an enthusiast and wrote from Berwick while serving in the garrison there: "As the Time of Year for Fishing is now Coming on shou'd be glad to meet you at Woolerhaugh head at any time...".[28]

The leisure life of the Ellisons and their friends demonstrates that wonderful entwining of the physical and the cultured that makes the world of the eighteenth century English upper classes, at its best the apotheosis of civilised existence. Robust pursuits were punctuated by time in the library, music in the drawing room, the cultivation of gardens, visits to theatre or opera and excursions abroad in search of the classical inheritance.

Hannah Cotesworth had had music lessons as a girl while her brother Robert played the flute. Henry Ellison went to the opera whenever he was in London. There was a spinet at Gateshead Park and Hannah's and Henry's children were all musical; the young Hannah sang and played the guitar, while her brother Robert sent her scores from the latest London musical productions. The Ellisons, the Liddells and their circle of friends were equally involved with the theatre. Henry Ellison jnr recounted in 1781 how the aged Lady Ravensworth was attracted back to the theatre by the fame of Mrs Siddons and was herself given applause as a tribute to her lifetime's patronage of the stage.

The burgeoning world of leisure was essentially a commercial one and was increasingly accessible to the prosperous as well as the rich.[29] Better roads made travel easier, not just to London but to spas, to the seaside, to *beauty spots* and to the continent. Entrepreneurs of the new leisure industry, from the famous Beau Nash at Bath to obscure men, who sought to provide facilities at Boston Spa or even

Shotley Gate, attempted, not only to advertise waters that might cure dyspepsia or gout, but to provide a fashionable milieu and entertainment. General Cuthbert, as we have seen, spent much of his life at spas or watering places but the Ellison females and the Henry Ellisons, father and son, visited them as well. Henry Ellison senr. was at Bath in 1741 under a strict regime set by his doctors. The Liddells, the Carrs and the Ellisons rarely let a year go by without visits to Bath, Buxton, Scarborough or Harrogate, combining the benefits of physical recuperation with social stimulation. Luckily for children, contemporary medical opinion's obsession with the beneficial effects of water made sea bathing and therefore the beach fashionable and Henry's daughter, Anne, Mrs Ralph Bates, took her family to Tynemouth every August.

The search for health was one of the reasons for foreign travel. Having tried Bath in 1741, Henry Ellison senr. was at Spa in the Austrian Netherlands in 1743 and was pleased with the company he found there:

> *As far as I can yet judge the society seems to be on an agreeable and easy footing arising from the concourse of people from all nations. The English are by much the most numerous, and among them we have...Lord Northington and Lord Clive.*[30]

Cuthbert urged him to return the following year, seeing he had received benefit from his visit, but Henry found it more convenient to get consignments of Spa water at £20 a time, from the English physician at Spa, Dr Alexander Hay.

There were, however, other reasons to travel abroad. The Grand Tour was increasingly seen as putting the final touch to a gentleman's education and the northern gentry were soon exploring the continent. Henry Carr wrote to his brother-in-law from Rome on 1739: "for people who have any taste for antiquities, statuary, painting or music here is sufficient entertainment for almost every hour." Sir Henry Liddell, later Lord Ravensworth, was a great traveller who visited Paris in 1729, attending a great fireworks display and, afterwards dancing with the Duchess of Pequigny at a royal ball. He and Sir Hugh Smithson, later Duke of Northumberland, were allowed to visit the French army near Mantua during the War of the Polish Succession. Henry Ellison jnr was abroad in 1764 and 1765. He "passed the Alps without danger and almost without difficulty" but then became ill in Paris in 1765. To fall ill while travelling could be a serious problem. In a major city like Paris medical attention was available though, as a historian of the Grand Tour has commented, such attention, "was a mixed blessing in this period".[31]

Financial embarrassment was another reason for long sojournes abroad and Henry Ellison's second son, Robert, who as we have seen was involved in a banking failure, spent the last years of his life in Switzerland. This turned out to be no great hardship for he delighted in the Swiss landscape and his descriptions of the scenery reveal a feeling for nature that looks forward to the Romantic Movement. In 1782 he described to his brother his evening walks around Geneva:

> *[I] stayed till after the sun was set behind the Jura mountains-The shades on these hills and the lights in the Alps opposite them, and the calmness of the lake between them, very striking";[the following evening, he] "...sat down beside the lake before sunset...saw the sun go down behind those mountains-The shadow on the hills gradually changing from light to misty grey to darker, till they became of a deep and glossy blue in some parts verging to purple. Above them a clear and bright sky, without a cloud excepting a few that atended the sun at his setting and were beautifully illuminated by him, some of them fringing the blue tops of the hills.*[32]

Robert died in his beloved Switzerland the following year and was buried at Lausanne.

Two generations had brought the Ellisons a long way from the provincial life of Robert Ellison, "the Justice". The comforts of their domestic life, their familiarity with London society, their cultural interests and their experience of travel, make them representative of a prosperous, confident and highly cultured ruling class.

References

1.   Cuthbert Ellison to H. Ellison, 30 Aug. 1729 (A18).

2.   Hannah Ellison to Henry Ellison, 27 April 1734 (A3).

3.   Gateshead Park remained the Ellisons' main residence until 1790, when Hebburn Hall was extensively rebuilt, and it remained an Ellison residence until 1825. In 1891 it was burnt down and its remains became an industrial building. In 1995 the factory of NEI Clark Chapman was demolished and at the same time a fire again raged through the remains of the old mansion. For a few months its shell still stood, though only the discerning eye could perceive something of its past glory. Nothing now remains of it.

4.   Edward Hughes, p30.

5.   A very high proportion of the Ellison family died in London or other parts of the south of England.

6.   Henry Ellison jnr. to his father, Henry Ellison, 24 Jan. 1758 (A14).

7.   Hannah Ellison (his daughter) to H. Ellison, 2 Sept.1742 (A3).

8.   *Ibid*, 10 Dec. 1743.

9.   Robert Ellison to his son, Henry Ellison, 5 April 1724 (A2).

10. Henry Ellison jnr. to Henry Ellison, 12 March, 1761 (A14).

11. Cuthbert Ellison to Henry Ellison, 8 Jan. 1730 (A18). What aspects of the lifestyle of Mrs Ellison and her daughters were considered so unsuitable we do not know.

12. Mrs E. Ellison to Henry Ellison, 5 March 1733 (A2).

13. John Airey to Henry Ellison, 17 January, 1733 (A38).

14. John Airey to Henry Ellison, 9 March 1735.

15. Airey-Ellison Marriage Settlement, 2 May 1738. Cotesworth Mss.(CD.1.38). I am indebted to the late Dr. P. Hurley of Crow Hall, John Airey's house, for information about John Airey and his marriage.

16. Elizabeth Ellison (sister) to Henry Ellison, 6 March 1746 (A3).

17. Edward Hughes, p.101.

18. Robert Ellison to Henry Ellison, 28 April 1750 (A4).

19. Katherine Airey to Henry Ellison, 1758 (A8).

20. Dorothy Margaret Stuart, *Dearest Bess* (1955) p.27.

21. Katherine Airey to Henry Ellison, 24 Jan. 1758 (A8).

22. Bowes, a wild and desperate character, ill-treated his wife and, when she left him, had her kidnapped in Oxford Street. See, Ralph Arnold, *The Unhappy Countess* (1957).

23. Elizabeth Ellison to Henry Ellison, 18 Nov. 1740 and 1748 (no day or month given) (A3).

24. In 1737 George Liddell purchased from the Greenwich Commissioners leases on the Alston Moor and Derwent Valley lead mines, which the Commissioners had gained from the sequestration of the Earl of Derwentwater's estates. He divided the share capital of his company into 96 shares keeping 74 for himself. Although he accepted all risks for these 74 shares, he apportioned 26 of them to his relatives: 4 to Cuthbert Ellison, 2 to Robert, 2 to Katherine, 2 to Jane, 2 to Elizabeth, 2 each to Lieutenant Bright and Miss Kitty Bright and 2 each to three Stockdales, Thomas, William and Mrs Letitia. Amongst the ordinary shareholders were John Airey and John Carr of Dunston Hill. This lead-mining venture was not a great success and was wound up by the Executors of George Liddell. See R. A. Fairbairn, *The Mines of Alston Moor*, 1993, p.22.

25. Elizabeth Ellison (sister) to Henry Ellison, 13 Oct. 1744 and 7 Sept. 1744 (A3).

26. Katherine Airey to Henry Ellison, 11 Feb. 1762 and 3 April 1762 (A8).

27. Cuthbert Ellison to Henry Ellison, June 28, 1759 (A20).

28. Robert Ellison to Henry Ellison, 15 March 1738 (A4).

29. See J. M. Golby and A. W. Purdue, *The Civilsation of the Crowd* (1984) Chapter 1.

30. Jeremy Black, *The British Abroad. The Grand Tour in the Eighteenth Century* (1992), p.183.

31. *Ibid*, p.185.

32. Robert Ellison to Henry Ellison,23 and 24 August 1782 (E1). Quoted in Jeremy Black, *Ibid*, p.302.

Chapter 7

The Zenith of the Ellisons

Cuthbert Ellison (1773-1860) by John Hopper

"Mr Ellison need not have walked in, we would have carried him in."

On Cuthbert Ellison's withdrawal from the 1830 Election

On the death of Henry Ellison in 1775, Gateshead Park and the bulk of the Cotesworth inheritance passed to his eldest son, Henry Ellison jnr. After another decade, on the death of the long-lived General Cuthbert Ellison, he also inherited the Hebburn estate. This joint inheritance made him one of the principal landowners and richest men in the North East.

As we have seen, Henry Ellison had, after Eton, gone to Cambridge and then on to the Middle Temple to study law. He had thus had a gentleman's education and one which would give him the legal knowledge invaluable in managing his inheritance. He had travelled on the continent and had his picture painted by Pompeio Batoni while in Rome. He was forty when his father died and he became responsible for the Gateshead Park estate. Polished by foreign touring, at home in London society and a devotee of music and opera, he was a confident member of a national elite. It is noteworthy, however, that he still felt it necessary to burnish his mercantile and Tyneside connections, becoming a Merchant Adventurer in 1765 and a Hostman in 1777.

What he lacked was a wife. The Ellisons appear to have been exceedingly cautious about embarking upon marriage. As we have seen, of the generation of Henry Ellison senr., only he and his sister Katherine married, while of the younger generation, two brothers and three sisters, only Henry jnr. and his sister Anne married.[1] It was not until he was forty-five that, more than three years after his father's death, Henry married Henrietta Isaacson in May 1779.[2] The nineteen year old bride was the daughter of John Isaacson of Newcastle and was a considerable heiress. They proceeded to produce eight children in the next ten years: Hannah, Henry, Cuthbert, Henrietta, Elizabeth, John and the twins, Robert and Anne.

Gateshead Park had been the principal Ellison residence since the 1720s, although, after General Cuthbert's death, Henry became Henry Ellison of Hebburn Hall. The hall was no doubt somewhat old-fashioned in Henry's eyes and he decided to rebuild it. He turned it into an imposing and spacious house in classical style with eighty-five rooms, one of the most splendid mansions on Tyneside. Considerable landscaping and planting of trees, together with the rerouting of the Newcastle road to the north of the house completed the transformation. The work was completed in 1790 and Henry and his large family moved in.

This fine house epitomised the fact that during the last decades of the eighteenth century the Ellisons became extremely rich. Henry Ellison had inherited, not only his father's extensive Gateshead estate, but General Cuthbert's property at Hebburn and Jarrow. Yet, as we have seen, although Henry Ellison senior had had a good head for business, he and his brother had had to extend themselves to buy out the Carr interest. Henry's marriage to Henrietta Isaacson brought him further property in Newcastle and his son Cuthbert's marriage to Isabella Grace Ibbotson was in the next generation to bring further property at St Anthony's, Byker, Durham City and Jarrow as well as in the south of England.

The develoment of mining also provided a considerable boost to the family's income in the shape of rents and mineral royalties. As we have seen, there had been coalmines at Hebburn since the early seventeenth century and General Cuthbert Ellison had been an enthusiast for new sinkings. Improvements in mining technology meant that in the late eighteenth century new mining operations were able to begin with mines more than 600 feet deep. At Hebburn intensive mining operations began in 1790 with the sinking of "A" pit, followed by "B" pit in 1794 and "C" pit shortly afterwards. It was in "B" pit that Sir Humphry Davy tested his safety lamp.[3]

Despite this mining activity and the bustle on the river bank as coals were loaded and ships discharged their ballast, Hebburn, like nearby Jarrow, still presented a largely rural appearance. This was not to last, for the Ellison lands at Hebburn and Jarrow were where, in a hundred years, would be much of industrial and urban Tyneside. As economic development and the need to house the growing urban population transformed the banks of the lower Tyne from farms and fields into coal mines, factories, warehouses, shipyards and rows of workers' houses, the Ellison fortune increased.

In the last decade of his life Henry Ellison transformed Hebburn Hall into an elegant mansion and made it his principal residence. Only forty years later, his son Cuthbert, "…finding that the increasing trade of the district rendered it unpleasant to live at or in the neighbourhood of his family estates, removed to the south of England…".[4] His country seat had been ruined but he had become a great deal richer in the process.

Although in some upper class circles there was something of a cult of childhood in the late eighteenth century with children being treated with greater indulgence than previously, the childhood at home of the eldest sons of Henry Ellison was short indeed. At the beginning of 1789, when young Henry was six and his brother Cuthbert was five, they were sent to a preparatory school at Bradenham near High Wycombe. Poor Henry was to die at the age of sixteen and he spent much of his short life far from home. The long journeys north for the holidays were a problem for such young children and, despite the headmaster's wife packing salve for the coach journey, they arrived at Gateshead with chilblains at Christmas 1789. From their letters home, the boys seem, nevertheless, to have been happy enough. The headmaster, Rev.Thomas Lloyd, and his wife, seem to have been kind and conscientious and the dowager Lady Ravensworth lived in London and was able to take them out for excursions.

The tendency of northern families to send children to new fashionable prep schools far from home (the Ellisons were not the only northern boys at Bradenham) grew during the late eighteenth century. Schools such as Bradenham were expert at providing the grounding in Latin, which prepared their pupils for the classical curriculum of the public schools and universities; while they also eradicated northern accents and standardised manners and mores. Better communications were assisting the creation of a national elite which a common educational background also helped to form; the wealthy squire with his provincial accent and rustic manners, so long the butt of playwrites, was becoming a rarity. Ambitious families like the Ellisons were no longer content with a northern public school like Sedbergh, where Cotesworth had sent his sons early in the century, still less with a private school like Mr. Croft's at Beverley, where, as we shall see, the merchant, Ralph Carr, sent his sons. The Ellisons', Tyneside accents were ironed out but not one suspects without embarrassment and difficulty. The Reverend Lloyd reported to their father after four terms: "It was impossible their manner of reading should have escaped you; it has long been a subject of conversation here, sometimes of mirth, at other times we have treated it very seriously particularly to Master Ellison".[5]

Master Ellison was not, as we have seen, to live to benefit as an adult from the pains taken over his education. He became head of the family at the age of thirteen upon the death of his father who died at Bath in 1795, where he had gone to try to save his failing health, but died himself while still a schoolboy at the age of sixteen.[6]

The fifteen-year old Cuthbert (1783-1860) thus inherited the family estates while he was at Harrow. He went on to Exeter College, Cambridge and graduated. Like many who inherit early in life, Cuthbert married young and, not unusually for an Ellison, he married an heiress, Isabella Grace Ibbetson, daughter and co-heir of Henry Ibbetson of St. Anthony's Newcastle.[7] They were married at Dorking in 1804 when Cuthbert was twenty-one and she was nineteen. She was born at Kingsbury and land in Surrey came with the marriage. More important was the fact that Isabella was the heiress to the Leven-Ibbetson, formerly the Bonner, estates at St Anthony's. During the Interregnum those two successful puritans, Robert Ellison and William Bonner, had respectively acquired estates and the ballast shores at Hebburn and St Anthony's, on opposite banks of the Tyne; they had also divided much property at Jarrow between them. In 1734 Thomas Lewen had married Anne Bonner and inherited St. Anthony's, much of Byker, part of Jarrow and further property in Durham City. He bequeathed these considerable estates to Mrs Ibbetson, daughter of Mrs Sarah Morton, herself a Bonner, in 1784. By the marriage of Henry Ellison to Mrs Ibbetson's daughter, Isabella, these estates were now combined in the possessions of the Ellisons. Sixty-four years later the entailed estates of the Ellisons were to be inherited by Ralph Carr, the descendent of Bonner's apprentice, although St Anthony's was left to Cuthbert Ellison's daughter, Lady Northbourne.[8]

As one historian has written: "from merchant adventurers in sixteenth century Newcastle, they had risen to be one of the richest commoner families in the north, owning thousands of acres of coal and land on both banks of the Tyne as well as estates in Surrey and a town house in London".[9]

The marriage was preceded by a complex ante-nuptial settlement [10] which illustrates once more the way in which female interests were provided for in marriage settlements. When Henrietta Isaacson had married Henry Ellison arrangements had been made for her security in the likely event that she survived him. With the deaths of Henry and then his son, Henry, (under the age of twenty-one and unmarried) and the forthcoming marriage of Cuthbert to Grace Ibbetson, these arrangements needed reviewing. Property at West Park and Oakenshaw, Stockley, Whimmey Houses, Evistones, Nettlehouses, Syles and Syleburn (in the Parish of Elsdon), West Harle, the manor of Bellister, Broomhouses and several closes in Gateshead were reserved for the widowed Henrietta[11], whose residence became Gateshead Park.

Two years before Cuthbert's wedding, his elder sister, Hannah, had married John Carr, the heir to Ralph Carr of Dunston Hill. This match, which joined together the two families of our study, was to lead to the inheritance of much of the Ellison estates by Ralph, the couple's eldest son, who was to take the name Carr-Ellison. It must be emphasised, however, that, in 1802, there seemed little reason to believe the Ellisons would lack a male heir.

Two other sisters, Henrietta and Elizabeth, were to marry respectively George William Aylmer of London and Frederick Edward Morrice of Betteshanger in Kent. His younger brother, Robert, was, as we shall see, to have a distinguished career in the Grenadier Guards and married Mary, daughter of Matthew Montague, later fourth Lord Rokeby.

As the head of one of the wealthiest and most influential families on Tyneside, Cuthbert had a natural position both in county society and in Newcastle and Gateshead. He looked after his inheritance well, exercised the patronage, which came with it, responsibly and gave generously to local charities. When, in 1808, the living of Jarrow-with-Heworth became vacant, Cuthbert, who was patron, gave it to the curate of St. Mary's, Gateshead, the Rev. John Hodgson. He thus gave the parishioners a fine Parson and enabled the great historian of Northumberland to write the first volumes of his history of the county in comfortable circumstances. He also, in 1836, gave the chapel of St. Edmund's monastery, which was in a ruinous condition to the Rector of Gateshead; the remains of the chapel were incorporated into the new Holy Trinity Church, which was built on the site.

The normal public and charitable offices were to almost inevitably come his way: High Sheriff of Northumberland 1808, High Sheriff of Durham 1826, Justice of the Peace and Deputy -Lieutenant of Durham, Mayor of Hartlepool in 1809, President of Gateshead Infirmary and Vice-president of Newcastle Infirmary. He maintained the family tradition of becoming a member of the Merchant Adventurers' Company, which though now an honorary rather than a practical body still had influence. Cuthbert was much involved, like his brother-in-law John Carr and other county gentry, with the volunteer forces raised in the locality to meet the threat from France as this local report shows:

> *1803. November 16-the Gateshead volunteers, commanded by Cuthbert Ellison, of Hebburn Esq., received their colours. About half- past twelve o'clock they arrived on the ground, which was previously kept by the Newcastle volunteers, and formed into line opposite to a stand which had been erected for the accommodation of the ladies. As soon as Mrs Ellison, who presented the colours, had taken her station, supported on the right by the Right Honourable the Earl of Strathmore, and on the left by John Carr esq., she was received with a general salute; the ceremony then commenced by the regiment going through the manual exercise, after which three sides of a square were formed by the corps, the stand in front making the fourth. Mrs Ellison then stepped forward , and after making some appropriate remarks , delivered the colours into the hands of Colonel Ellison, who replied in a strain of manly eloquence....After going through various manoeuvres , the whole was concluded with a general salute, the colours were then taken to Mr. Bertram's, the Goat Inn, Gateshead , where they were deposited.[12]*

Such non-political offices and honours came his way as a natural leader of North-East society but Cuthbert was a serious minded man and decided to pursue a political career. The Ellisons had as we have seen been strong Whigs for much of the eighteenth century but along with the Liddells they had become Tories towards its end. Cuthbert was, however, at best a very moderate Tory and, indeed, a late nineteenth century authority describes him as a Whig.[13] He was described by Sir Charles Monck in 1812 as follows: "He has been born and bred a Tory but is considerably Whiggized by living with the Ridleys and Bigges and others of this country and also by his own opinions upon the conduct of the Tories in power during the last few years...".[14] He can perhaps best be described as a liberal Tory of independent inclinations though he was to become a Whig in the 1830s.

His first venture into politics came in 1807 when he was twenty-four and contested Durham County. At the previous election in 1806 there had been no contest, Sir Ralph Milbanke Bt. (Whig) and Sir Thomas Henry Liddell (Tory) being returned unopposed. At the general election of 1807 there were initially five candidates, Milbanke, Sir Henry Vane Tempest, Bt. (Tory), Sir Thomas Liddell, Bt. (Tory)[15], Rowland Burdon (Tory) and Cuthbert Ellison. On the nomination of the candidates upon the hustings, however, Burdon and Liddell withdrew and, despite their supporters persevering, they agreed to transfer their influence to Ellison. He was not, however, elected, withdrawing after three days of contest when it was clear Milbanke and Tempest were well ahead.

In 1812 he was unopposed when he stood at Newcastle as the running mate of Sir Matthew White Ridley. "That", R.T.Welford argued, "was thought to be a thoroughly safe position, and so, for eighteen years, it proved to be."[16] It is easy to see why Welford considered being MP for Newcastle along with a Ridley a safe position, for there had not been a contested election since 1777 and since 1747 one of the MPs for Newcastle had been a Ridley.

This long hold on the representation of Newcastle by the Ridleys was a remarkable achievement and probably took more effort on their part than appeared.[17] Historians are increasingly realising that contested elections were but the tip of an iceberg so far as the political struggle in constituencies was concerned. In a town like Newcastle with its large number of freemen voters, elections were always expensive, sometimes riotous, and they put a stop to business for several days. They were in short greatly to be welcomed by many voters but were a horror to be avoided from the viewpoint of the town's elite. To avoid such a horror a negotiated compromise resulting in shared representation between different political interests would often be achieved. A challenge from a new candidate or interest would only result in a poll if, after a long period of soundings and extensive canvassing, a serious prospect of success justified the expense of proceeding further. Much careful management was required to nurse a constituency and a great deal of electioneering preceded even uncontested elections.

The Ridleys were Whigs but Newcastle as we have seen was far from a Whig stronghold in the eighteenth century and part of the reason for the Ridleys' long tenure lay in an accomodation among the elite of Newcastle by which the representation was shared between a moderate Tory and a Ridley. For a large open constituency the stability of Newcastle politics and the lack of elections is surprising. One authority has claimed that this can be explained by the absence of any large landowners interfering in the constituency: "The business community, left to its own devices, consistently managed to produce two equally strong interests to share the constituency".[18] But this needs modifying, for the Blacketts, the Brandlings and the Ridleys *were* large landowners, as indeed was Ellison. The point is perhaps that they were not landowners whose influence came from outside the town but were what might be termed merchant-gentry, men who retained substantial interests within the town and its immediate environs as urban landowners, merchants and/or coal owners. Unlike those great aristocrats whose land encircled cities, their landowning had radiated out from the town. Within a generation or so their gentry status would be unqualified and their influence within Newcastle the less for it, but that time was not yet. The balance of power may have been helped it is suggested "...by the fact that the freemen-thanks to the corporation's monopoly of the Tyne coal trade-were relatively better off than their counterparts in other cities".[19] Thus between 1747 and 1774 Matthew Ridley and Walter Blackett, heads of the two families most prominent in the city's trade and commerce, were unopposed and though there was a contest in 1774, Sir Walter Blackett and Sir Matthew White Ridley easily topped the poll. The Tories found some difficulty in finding a satisfactory replacement for Blackett and the election of Trevelyan at a by-election in 1777 and the adventurer, Stoney Bowes, along with Ridley in 1780, were both subject to unsuccessful petitions to parliament. From 1784 until 1812 the Brandlings, first father and then son, provided the Tory balance to the Ridleys. It was this role that Cuthbert Ellison then took on.

It is often said, and with truth, that elections and parliamentary representation in this period have more to do with local issues, personalities and concerns than with national politics. This does not mean that in the Newcastle context the terms Whig and Tory did not have meaning but rather that they had a local meaning. They represented different interests within the corporation and the town and though these interests had each an ethos, which loosely paralleled a national notion of Toryism or Whiggism, these were far from the fundamental basis of political affiliation.

The seemingly effortless way in which the dominant factions controlled Newcastle politics is misleading. Influence was expensive and the Blacketts and the Ridleys had spent a great deal of money in the eighteenth century maintaining it. Even when an election never resulted in a poll, the successful candidates had usually had to spend time and money warding off potential candidates and cosseting voters.

As elsewhere, the sitting candidates or their nominated successors did not want contested elections, while much of the electorate did. The reasons were, of course, financial: expense for the candidates and rewards for voters. Cuthbert Ellison's great uncle General Ellison had found out how expensive a campaign could be when he won Shaftesbury in 1747.

In Newcastle, although many of the lower burgesses wanted elections, they found it hard to get third candidates. Potential third candidates knew that those most eager for them to stand were precisely those who were committed by ties of influence to one candidate; they wished for an election to raise the price of votes but the best a third candidate could hope for was their second votes.

Cuthbert Ellison may have not been opposed in 1812 in the sense that there was no poll but he, nevertheless, had to work hard and spend money to secure the seat. As the Tory candidate, he had obviously inherited an election machine. Nathaniel Clayton, the Town Clerk of Newcastle, and partner in Clayton and Brown, Solicitors, was in charge of it. It could not have been in more capable hands.

As that leading historian of North-East England, Norman McCord, has written, "the town council and local offices of importance were dominated by members of a number of leading families, Claytons, Bells, Andersons, Cooksons and Brandlings passed municipal office among themselves".[20]

Such offices were lucrative as the corporation's income was high. The Mayoralty was worth £2000 plus expenses and the position of Town Clerk was worth 500 guineas, although the special knowledge and influence that attended it were more valuable than the salary.

> *Thus in 1817 Nathaniel Clayton was Town Clerk; he had held that office since 1785, and was to be succeeded in 1822 by his son, John; his brother Robert was mayor and Robert's son William was sheriff: in the following year, although Robert and William were out of office, Henry, another son of Robert's was sheriff.*[21]

With Clayton's guidance, Ellison prepared for his election as if there was every possiblity of opposition. All the guilds or mysteries of the ancient town had to be visited in turn and their support solicited: the Merchant Adventurers, the Hostmen, the Upholsterers, the Coopers, the Slaters and the Mariners etc.(some 28 calls in all). Freemen were able to vote whether or not they resided in Newcastle and the solicitation of their votes required sub-agents; thus John Cockerill of North Shields accepted a retainer to take care of the out-voters there and John Reed respectfully declined Clayton's request to do the same job for voters on the Hexham area (he reminded Nathaniel Clayton that Mr Smith of Haughton Castle and Mr Watson of Humshaugh were freemen of Newcastle).[22] The London based freemen had to be "refreshed" and the candidate had to see personally to the refreshing of Newcastle voters. Thus Cuthbert was cordially invited to a meeting of the "Free and Easy John's Society: "The officers and Brothers of the above named Honorable Society which is composed of upwards of Two Thousand, the greater part of whom are desirous with being honoured with your company at the Lodge Rooms at the Cock Inn, Head of the Side".[23] Sir Matthew White Ridley and Charles Brandling had apparently been initiated into this body at the last election and it was obviously an invitation Ellison could not refuse. One imagines it proved to be an expensive evening as no candidate could be backward at picking up the bill at such an event. Advertisements were placed in the Tyne Mercury and handbills distributed in

Shields, Sunderland, Blyth, Morpeth, Alnwick and Hexham. Ellison was even offered support from within Newgate Gaol by a debtor, W. G. Waddell, who wrote to Clayton: "I beg you will accept my grateful thanks for your polite enquiry of Mr. Gee concerning my certificate which has been obtained from the Commissioners a few days since. At the same time I take leave to observe that should my liberation be obtained previous to the election, you may rely that my humble efforts shall be exerted for your friend".[24]

In an address he gave at the opening of his canvass, Ellison cleverly both wrapped himself in the mantle of his Tory predecessor, Brandling, and affirmed his desire to go into Parliament as an independent man unshackled by any party. Had Brandling not expressed his intention to retire he would not have put himself forward as his successor. Listing his qualifications, he was forthright about his wealth and interests:

> *...if the records of the town be examined the names of my family will, for centuries past, be found among them. My interests Gentlemen are identified with yours. I do not say because I happen to be the proprietor of a portion of the land of the Empire but as a considerable share of wealth accrues to me from the great staple and source of prosperity to this neighbourhood, I mean the coal trade, a trade which employs as it does an immense quantity of Shipping is the Nurse, in fact the chief support of our Naval power and supremacy.*[25]

In the event, an election was avoided and in 1818 there was again no formal contest, though opposition was threatened by a number of local Tories, friends of the Tyneside born high Tory, the Lord Chancellor, Lord Eldon. Dissatisfied with Ellison's liberal Conservatism, they floated the idea of William Scott, Eldon's son, as a third candidate. They found some support and were led by the influential Sir Thomas Burdon but the handbill from "A Free Burgess" suggested solid reasons why the voters of Newcastle should not support Scott:

> *And yet for this attention to your wishes, you are called upon to visit him [Ellison] with your censure, and embroil the Town in all the trouble and vexation of a Contested Election. And I would ask you, who is to be called on as a Candidate- a Young Man of whom we know nothing, and nearly unconnected with the Town- whose only Claim can be that he is the Son of Lord Eldon? What would the Freemen derive from such a connexion? If we are to judge from the past, Nothing, Look at your Infirmary, your Hospitals, your different Charities. Have that Family contributed to the Support of any one of them? Is the name of Scott to be found supporting any one public Institution in the Town, or is their Name*

to be found in any list of Subscriptions for the Benefit of the Poor, or the Improvement of the Town? If Mr Scott was elected your Member would he reside among you?

The message was clear, the Scotts were a mean lot compared to the Ellisons. In the event, Scott did not show up in Newcastle in time to further his promised candidature and once more the 5,000 or so resident and non-resident voters were denied the pleasure of a contest.

At the election following on the succession of George IV in 1820 Newcastle enjoyed its first proper election contest for forty years. Some Tories continued to be dissatisfied with Cuthbert Ellison's independence. He had not voted consistently with the government and, it was suggested, thereby lacked the connections with which to protect local interests. There was a move afoot to move the customs office at Newcastle to Shields and it was felt that Ellison lacked the influence to prevent this. In addition he had been abroad because of ill health for some time and was still abroad as the imminent death of George III made an election in the near future likely. Ellison was in Italy and according to Lord Elgin who had seen him there, "very feeble".[26] Nathaniel Clayton wrote to Cuthbert who was at Naples telling him he was putting out an election address on his behalf and referring to "wicked attempts to excite discontent in the lower orders".[27]

As Welford comments, "the opportunity seemed to be favourable for an effort to replace him".[28] A number of local Tories supported by the lower burgesses, many of whom simply wanted the joy of a contest, brought forward once more Lord Eldon's son, William Scott. In his brother's absence it fell to Major Robert Ellison to organise Cuthbert's campaign, which he seems to have done very efficiently.

Although a candidate's chances are scarcely enhanced by his absence from his election campaign, Ellison had the advantage that the Scott candidature was an odd coalition of ultra-Tories, radicals and thirsty electors. As the handbill entitled *The Bubble will soon Burst* put it, the burgesses were "called upon to support an *ultra ministerial* Candidate, nominated by a *radical* Baker and an *ultra radical catholic* Cobbler, and these worthies are parading the Town with a Band of Music, in humble imitation of Mr Polito, the wild beast man".[29]

At the nomination on 9 March, there was a singular lack of candidates. Only Ridley was there, for Ellison had not returned from Italy and Scott, as in 1818, had not turned up. Scott was nevertheless proposed and the show of hands went to Ridley and Scott. Major Ellison then demanded a poll. Polling commenced two days later but was called off on 12 March when Alderman Forster declined the contest on behalf of Scott, who had not arrived in Newcastle as he had promised. As Scott, to the great embarrassment of his supporters, never actually appeared and the sheriff declared the election not to be fully contested, the voting figures do not really provide a fair test of the candidates' popularity. Ellison and Ridley were returned by a large majority (Ridley 614, Ellison 477, Scott 217) but Scott's intervention must have made their re-election much more expensive.

In 1826 Ridley and Ellison were again unopposed but in 1830, as George IV's death grew near and an election loomed, a third candidate, John Hodgson, came forward and Cuthbert Ellison announced his retirement. John Hodgson, a wealthy coal owner from Elswick, was a Tory who differed little from Ellison in his political views. Both favoured a modest measure of parliamentary reform. The explanation put forward by Richard Welford has long been accepted: "Hodgson was brought out with the avowed intention of breaking down the influence of the Ridleys. That, however, was too firmly rooted in Newcastle to be disturbed, but the movement so seriously endangered the seat of Mr Ellison who was a Liberal-Conservative that he declined to go to a poll".[30] This interpretation has recently been challenged by P. D. Brett, who considers that it was not Ellison who was threatened by the twenty-three year old Hodgson but Ridley and that Ellison could easily have been re-elected if he had not withdrawn.

Sir Matthew White Ridley was not popular in Newcastle in 1830. He had progressively withdrawn himself from the society and commercial life of the town and based himself at his country seat, Blagdon Hall, leaving his town house unused. He had a reputation for aristocratic pride and didn't mix easily with the burgesses. As John Clayton wrote to Cuthbert Ellison, "The hostile feeling towards Sir M. seems to be founded on the supposed "hauteur" of his manner towards the Burgesses"[31] Just as important was his failure to treat and reward those on whose support he depended. Armorer Donkin, Ridley's agent, told him directly that his popularity suffered from not giving the burgesses the occasional "blow-out". He had not provided them with drink to mark the coming of age of his son and had failed to comply with a request to supply game for a dinner for the corporation auditors, while Ellison had sent a large quantity of game. There were also charges that he had neglected the interests of the town. He had, it was supposed, not spoken out against the shilling tax on each chaldron of coal shipped from the Tyne known as the "Richmond Shilling".[32]

The essence of Ridley's unpopularity was that he was increasingly perceived as remote from the town and its civic and economic life but whether this was enough to make him vulnerable even to a free-spending candidate like Hodgson, who was to spend a reputed £10,000 on his campaign,[33] is doubtful. The structural reasons for the Ridley's long domination of the town's representation were still in place. "In addition to a large interest among the freemen, and one of the biggest stakes in the coal trade, they owned 17 acres of prime land in the city, 100 acres acres in the expanding suburb of Elswick, 600 acres in nearby Heaton and a splendid 30,000 acres in south-east Northumberland."[34] As Brett demonstrates, once the threat from Hodgson was properly appreciated, Armorer Donkin put the Whig/Ridley electoral machine in motion and support for Ridley rallied. Sir Matthew would have taken a lot of beating and Hodgson's support could well have melted away leaving the old regime intact, Hodgson the poorer, and the lower burgesses the happier for having been well wined and dined amidst the delight of a contest. As it was, however, Cuthbert Ellison withdrew.

There seems little doubt that Ellison's reasons for withdrawing were those that he stated, his health and the desire to withdraw from public life. Clayton was quite confident that his candidate would win. He thought there was some threat to Ridley but none to Ellison and that the likely outcome was a defeat for Hodgson whose support was flimsy and venal: "...If the king lives a few months longer, the ale barrels at Elswick will be emptied".[35] Hodgson, he thought, would "soon discover the frail nature of the support of the rabble".[36] "The Freemen", he wrote a few days later,"are quite unanimous in their support for you but they may vary in their support for Sir Matt. W. Ridley or Mr. Hodgson.[37] On 2 June Ellison wrote to Clayton, letting him know that he intended to retire,[38] and, despite Clayton's attempts to dissuade him, persisted in his resolution. His withdrawal was announced on the hustings on June 10 and was much regretted by his agent: "The bitter hour is past- and I have gone through the Duty of communicating to your friends and the burgesses at large...your determination- I hope it may not be my fate to keep such another day in what remains to me of life".[39] A politician's ostensible reasons for retiring are rarely believed, and posterity suspected that Ellison feared defeat, but his contemporaries for the most part appear to have accepted them. Most probably he would have soldiered on if he had been unopposed, but he was in no mood to face a gruelling and expensive election even if he was almost certain to win.

He received a fulsome vote of thanks:

> *That the thanks of the Free Burgesses of Newcastle-upon-Tyne now assembled be offered to Cuthbert Ellison, Esq., their late able and faithful Representative in Parliament, for the services he has rendered to them and to the Town at large during the last eighteen years, and that he be assured that his late Constituents will ever retail a grateful Remembrance of those services, and of his uniformly friendly and courteous Conduct towards them, which would have secured for him their Unanimous Support had he sought again the Station he has so long and honourably filled, and which excite their deep and sincere Regret at his Retirement from it.*[40]

That such sentiments were sincere is attested by the widespread regret throughout the town. As Clayton informed the retiring candidate:

> *-one of the stewards of the companies, a hard iron-faced fellow, came to me on other business during the morning-I gave him your address to read (he is one of Hodgson's committee) he had it and burst into tears, and as soon as he could speak at all, he said, "Mr Ellison need not have walked in, we would have carried him".[41]*

Forty-six is an early age at which to retire from public and indeed from active life but this is precisely what Cuthbert did. He resisted the offer to become MP for Gateshead when that town achieved parliamentary representation in 1832. He had by this time drifted away from the Tories and can be best described as a moderate Whig, but it is significant that he was asked to stand by W.H.Brockett and his associates, who were advanced Liberals.[42] One of Brockett's helpers wrote: "...I think he is legitimately, as it were, the proper person, & and he certainly has many of the esential requisites- & I think he would be elected almost unanimously..."[43] This was both a tribute to the Ellison influence in Gateshead and the personal popularity of Cuthbert. His decline of the pressing offer makes it even more certain that the health and family reasons given for standing down in Newcastle were genuine. The Ellison influence in Gateshead was so strong as to secure the seat for his grandson, Walter James, in 1874.[44]

Cuthbert Ellison seems to have inherited the weak constitution of many of his forebears. Like his great uncle General Cuthbert Ellison this forced him to give up his chosen profession at an early age. His retreat from public life may also have had something to do with the fact that, although he had seven daughters, five of which lived into adulthood and married well, he had no son and heir. It may well have seemed a pleasanter prospect to live the life of a gentleman of leisure in the south of England and with much time spent abroad than to have nursed a North-East inheritance, the entailed part of which, would eventually go, so he assumed, to his brother's heirs. He had his town house in Whitehall Gardens and his estate at Box Hill, Surrey. Neither Hebburn Hall nor Gateshead Park[45] held great attractions now that industrial development increasingly hemmed them in.

The five daughters, Isabella, Henrietta, Louisa, Laura and Sarah married respectively: Lord Vernon; Hon. W. H. Lambton (brother of the first Earl of Durham); William David Murray, Lord Murray and Viscount Stormont (later Earl of Mansfield); William Edwards (later Baron Kensington); and Sir Walter James Bt. (later Baron Northbourne).

The heir to Hebburn Hall was Cuthbert's younger brother, Robert. He married Mary Montague, daughter of Matthew Montague, later Lord Rokeby, and had a distinguished career in the Grenadier Guards. He joined the regiment in 1807 and participated in the ill-fated expedition to Walcheren in 1809, took part in the Peninsular campaigns of 1811 and 1812 and was at the investment of Bayonne and the storming and capture of Peronne in 1815. He then fought at both Quatre Bras and Waterloo.

At Waterloo he commanded a company defending the chateau of Hougoument. This chateau was on Wellington's right flank and at the beginning of the battle of Waterloo came under attack from French regiments under the command of Prince Jerome Bonaparte. Its stout defence, combined with Jerome's mistake in continuing to pour men into the attack when he could have by-passed it or destroyed it with artillery, played a crucial part in determining the course of the battle.

Robert Ellison was in the Guards for thirty-six years. After his dangerous years of wartime soldiering, he served on in peacetime, achieved the rank of colonel and was sent to Canada at the time Lord Durham was appointed Governor in the aftermath of the rebellions of 1837. He was a friend of the Duke of Wellington. He died suddenly on parade at Hyde Park in 1843 at the age of 53. His son, Lietenant-Colonel Cuthbert Ellison, also had a distinguished career in the Grenadiers and was Brigade-Major to the Guards in the Crimea, participating in the battles of Balaclava and Inkerman.

Like his father, Colonel Cuthbert Ellison died young and his death in 1867 came only six years after the death of his uncle Cuthbert. He was unmarried and his inheritance of the entailed portion of the family estates went to his sister Mary and, with her death in 1870, to Ralph Carr.

The connection of the main line of the Ellisons with the North East had really been broken in the early 'thirties when Cuthbert Ellison retired from politics and decided to live in the south of England and abroad. Hebburn Hall had for long been little used when Ralph Carr inherited it. The Ellisons withdrew from Tyneside just as its industrial heyday was beginning but their role in the development of Newcastle and of the vibrant North East economy, which preceded and nurtured industrialisation, had been considerable.

References

1.   Anne Ellison married Ralph Bates of Halliwell and Milbourne Hall.

2.   The Isaacsons were a wealthy family. An Ellison had married an Isaacson in a previous generation when Nathaniel Ellison, son of Robert Ellison (1634-1678) married Elizabeth Isaacson in 1691.

3.   Paul Perry, *A Portrait of old Jarrow and Hebburn,* Vol.2 (1992) p.82.

4.   *Family of Carr*, p.114.

5.   Hughes, pp.364-367.

6.   Of the eight chidren of Henry and Henrietta Ellison, three were to die before they were twenty, Henry, John and Anne.

7.   This was not the first marriage between an Ellison and an Isaacson for the Rev. Nathaniel Ellison, son of Robert Ellison, MP, had married Elizabeth Isaacson, daughter of Anthony Isaacson in 1621.

8.   The records of the Leven–Ibbotson estates 1756-1830 are to be found in the Cotesworth Mss. CN/13.

9.   T.J. Nossiter, *Influence, Opinion and Political Idioms in Reformed England 1832-74* (1975) p.109.

10.   Ellison Mss. (C3).

11.   Ante-nuptial Settlement 13 July 1804. Ellison Papers (C3).

12.   *The Family of Carr,* Vol 1, p.122

13.   William Wardell Bean, *The Parliamentary Representation of the Six Northern Counties of England* (1890).

14.   Quoted in P. D. Brett, "The Newcastle Election of 1830", *Northern History,* Vol. XXIV 1988.

15.   He was the sixth baronet and was created Baron Ravensworth in 1821. This was a new creation, the first creation of 1747 having died out when the first Lord Ravensworth left no male heir.

16. R. T. Welford (ed.), *Men of Mark 'twixt Tyne and Tweed* (1865) p.150.

17. See Brett, "Newcastle election 1830".

18. David Stoker, "Elections and Voting Behavoiur, a study of elections in Northumberland, Durham, Cumberland and Westmorland 1760-1832". Unpublished Ph.D. thesis, Manchester, 1980, p.4.

19. *Ibid*.

20. N.McCord, *North East England, The Region's Development 1760-1960*, (1979) p.75.

21. W. L. Burn, "Newcastle upon Tyne in the Early Nineteenth Century", *Archaeologia* Aeliana,1956. Quoted in McCord, p.75.

22. John Cockerill to Nathaniel Clayton, 2 Oct. 1812 and John Reed to Nathaniel Clayton, 2 Oct 1802. Cotesworth Papers, CH2, Gateshead Public Library.

23. J. W. Lowes to Cuthbert Ellison, 6 Oct. 1812. Cotesworth Papers.

24. W. G. Waddell to N. Clayton, 2 Oct. 1802. Cotesworth Papers.

25. Cotesworth Papers.

26. Lord Elgin to Charles Brandling,30 Jan 1820. Cotesworth Papers CH 3.

27. N. Clayton to C.Ellison, 5 Feb. 1820,Ellison Ms.(A66).

28. Welford, p.151.

29. Handbill in Cotesworth Papers.

30. Welford, p.151.

31. John Clayton to Cuthbert Ellison, 1 June 1830, Ellison Ms. (A66).

32. Brett, pp.110-113. As Brett points out, Ridley had in fact done his best to get the Richmond Shilling repealed but the fact that coal from his own coal mines was shipped from Blyth and escaped the tax aroused suspicion.

33. *Ibid,* 109.

34. T. J. Nossiter, *Influence, Opinion and Political Idioms* p.108

35. John Clayton to Cuthbert Ellison, 1 June 1830. Ellison Papers (A66).

36. *Ibid*, 3 June 1830.

37. *Ibid*, 6 June 1830.

38. Cuthbert Ellison to John Clayton, 2 June 1830.

39. J. Clayton to Cuthbert Ellison, 10 June 1830.

40. Welford, p.151.

41. John Clayton to Cuthbert Ellison, 10 June 1830. Quoted in Brett, "Newcastle Election 1830".

42. Ellison's political progress was in the opposite direction to that of Sir Matthew White Ridley who by his death in 1835 had all but joined the Conservative Party.

43. N. McCord, "Gateshead Politics in the Age of Reform", *Northern History* Vol. IV (1969).

44. Walter James was elected Liberal MP for Gateshead in 1874. It was well-known that he owed his seat to his mother's connections with the town. His father's recommendation of him to Gladstone was frank: "He is very young, and without any great intellectual power but singularly noble-hearted and full of good sense". W. C. James to Gladstone, 3 Nov.1868. Quoted in T. J. Nossiter, *Influence, Opinion and Poliical Idioms* (1975) p.110.

45. After the death of Mrs Henrietta Ellison in 1805, there was little need of Gateshead Park House and in 1825 it was let to Isaac Cookson. A succession of industrialists rented the property, Charles Bulmer, Alexander Grey and Henry and Alfred Allhusen. In 1857 the manor of Gateshead passed back into the hands of the Church and the Ecclesiastical Commissioners sold much of the parkland for building purposes. Park House was bought by the firm of Clarke Chapman in 1884 and converted into offices. It was burnt down in 1891 and the remains became an industrial building.

Part 2

The Carrs of Dunston Hill

Chapter 8
The Carrs of Hexham

Yeomen, merchants and lawyers who had made their fortunes, were perpetually recruiting the ranks of the landed gentry; while the younger sons of the manor-house were apprenticed into industry and trade. In these ways old families were kept in personal touch with the modern world, and the country was kept in touch with the town.

G. M. Trevelyan, English Social History

In 1655, a young man of yeoman stock, John Carr, set out from Hexham for the town of Newcastle to take up an apprenticeship as a Merchant Adventurer. His success in that bustling and prosperous town, if not Whittingtonian, was solid and he was to found a line, which, within four generations, would have moved from being wealthy merchants to gentry. The Carrs of Dunston Hill, the house and estate bought by John's son, would, by the early nineteenth century, rank among the substantial landowners of Durham and Northumberland.

The Carrs of Hexham were people of modest substance. They were yeomen and burghers and were of consequence in the small world of the market town and the surrounding Hexhamshire. They had grander relations in gentry families like the Carrs of Hetton, of Ford and of St Helen's Auckland, and their closer relatives, the Carrs of Eshott and of Ditchburn, for Carrs had established themselves throughout the North-East and had already played some part in its history.[1]

As Colonel Ralph Carr, author of *The Family of Carr*, put it:

...while the other branches maintained good positions as landed proprietors, and kept up their family traditions, that which remained in the neighbourhood of Hexham settled down as small landowners or in the quiet life of burghers and municipal office-bearers in that ancient town which was then of high relative importance in the county, and the centre of an active trade.[2]

We are thus confronted with that important distinction in social rank between the gentry and those immediately beneath it. It is a distinction that becomes more difficult over time as the meaning of the word "gentleman" becomes wider and vaguer and as a legal order gives way to a social stratum which can include "urban gentlemen".

The unsettled and turbulent nature of life in Northumberland meant that an earlier, feudal, basis of gentry status still existed: knights, esquires and gentlemen were expected to maintain households, retainers and stables for the defence of the border. But, if only in the sense that a gentleman has always had to maintain the lifestyle befitting his position, wealth had always been the essential underpinning of gentry status. The order of knighthood was intended to be assumed by all landowners with more than a certain annual income (£20 in the late fifteenth century but later raised to £40). The fact that there were only some five hundred knights in England in 1500 points not only to income levels but to the tendency for many, who would have qualified, to evade their obligations because of the cost and onerous duties involved. A coat of arms was essential but the College of Heralds was empowered to register any person, "not vile born", who had at least £10 a year in land or £300 in movable goods.[3] The duties that gentry were called upon to perform, acting as sheriffs or justices of the peace, gave honour and status but could be time consuming and expensive.

The gentry became the leaders of Northumbrian society during the sixteenth century because of the diminution of the power of the native aristocracy, a process that the Earl's Rebellion of 1569 accelerated. In 1586 there was only one resident aristocrat in Northumberland, while it has been estimated that in 1615 there were 89 gentry families in the county, "one gentle family for approximately 900 inhabitants"[4]

This then was the class to which men like William Carr of Woodhall and Thomas Carr of Ford, ancestors of John Carr, belonged and from which the Hexham Carrs had sprung[5] and to which their descendants in the Dunston Hill line would rise again. In what lay the difference between gentry and the burghers and small Hexham landowners that were the Hexham Carrs? In terms of wealth, not a great deal, for as we shall see the leading members of that cousinhood, the Bailiffs of Hexham, were prosperous men, while thirty-six of the eighty-nine gentry of 1615 had incomes of under £100 a year.[6] Nor, despite the fact that a superior education was widely given as a characteristic of the gentry, was there necessarily in Northumberland a great discrepancy between the education of the gentry and that of smaller landowners. Only seven of the heads of gentry families extant in 1615 had themselves attended a university or the Inns of Court, though it has been estimated that twenty-two of the next generation did[7]. Schools were scarce in Northumberland, though from 1525 there was the grammar school in Newcastle, from 1552 one in Morpeth, and from 1600 a school at Hexham. It was probably from the grammar school at Hexham that Ralph Carr, son of Richard, Bailiff of Hexham, who was one of the school's founding governors, went on to St.John's College, Cambridge, a college which has long maintained a particular North- East connection; in 1637 Ralph presented the school with seven acres of land lying in the west field of Hexham[8].

It was unlikely that the gentry were superior in manners to yeomen or burghers for this was a rough age in the border county. Macaulay almost certainly exaggerated when he pictured the squire of the seventeenth century as "...with the deportment, the vocabulary, and the accent of a carter, yet punctilious on matters of genealogy and precedence, and ready to risk his life rather than see a stain cast on the honour of his house."[9] Yet Sir Thomas Carr of Ford, gallant commander that he was, has been described by one historian as permanently drunk.[10] Addicted to blood feuds (the North Northumberland Carrs had a long quarrel with the Forster family and a famous dispute with the Herons of Chipchase over the inheritance of the estate of Sir William Heron of Ford), the gentry led violent lives. As late as the seventeenth century, Ferdinando Foster was killed in a street in Newcastle, while Thomas Carr of Ford Castle and John Swinburn of Capheaton met their deaths by murder. Certainly the Hexham Carrs as small landowners, burghers and municipal office holders, may have led more orderly, if less grand, lives.

In the histories of most families there are switch-backs in wealth and social position, even in the main lines. Younger sons must necessarily step down a rank, albeit they may rise again with an advantageous marriage or a successful career. Below gentry status, primogeniture is less common and the chances of all offspring experiencing some diminution as estates are subdivided increases. James Carr of Hexham, styled yeoman, left his property at Hexham in equal shares to all his four sons. No doubt some of the brothers left no more than they inherited and that in some instances this was further subdivided in their wills, but his eldest son Richard added to his inheritance the property of Le Lee in Hexhamshire which he got from his relative, Lancelot Errington. His son, another Richard, advanced his fortunes further. Inheriting the Le Lee property, fields to the west of Hexham and two burgages with two shops in Hexham market place, he became Deputy Steward of the Manor Court of Hexham and was referred to as Bailiff.

Hexham had been, until the dissolution of the monasteries, dominated by the Prior and Priory. From then on the manor of Hexham, comprising the Liberty of Hexham and Allendale, previously in the possession of the Archbishops of York, belonged to secular Lords. Although Hexham remained part of the archdiocese until the nineteenth century, it became in civil matters part of Northumberland in 1571.

Sir John Fenwick was Lord of the Manor when Richard Carr became Bailiff. Manorial Courts were held in the Moot Hall and the Bailiff was the chief governor of the town and was appointed for life. He governed along with the four companies or corporate trades (Weavers, Tanners and Cordswainers, Skinners and Glovers, and Hatters) in this unincorporated town, the market town to the surrounding rural area and a centre for the leather trades. Richard was the first of a family dynasty of Bailiffs as the office was held by his son, another Richard, and his grandson, Benoni Carr.[11] He was clearly one of Hexham's leading citizens and a man of substance. He owned a town house adjacent to the Priory and lying between it and the market place but was by 1617 also in possession of the manor house of the Spital, which stood on the site of the old St Giles's Hospital. In Volume iii of the county history, Allen B.Hinds wrote that the Carrs along with the Allgoods occupied, "...an important, if not the foremost, position" in Hexham.[12]

But if Richard, Bailiff of Hexham, and his successors in a family line of bailiffs were wealthy and important, then his brother Ralph, styled as "of Slaley and Le Lee, Yeoman", who obtained the moiety of Le Lee from his brother in 1614, enjoyed a more modest prosperity. He lived into his eighties and had, by the time of his death in 1627, given his property and the bulk of his possessions to his family, yet his will gives some indication of the personal effects of a yeoman farmer of the period:

> *To be buried in the church yard of Slaley; and to Isabel Humble, my daughter, 40 shillings, or else a whye and one swarm of bees. To William Carr of Hexham, my son, 10 shillings. To Mathew Carr, my son, 20 shillings. To Richard, Thomas, Jane and Lucy, children of the said Mathew Carr, 10 groats a piece. To Ralph, son of the said Mathew Carr, 5 groats. To George Humble one dublet, one jerkin, one hat, one pair of hose, one pair of shoes. To Agnes Carr 5 shillings, or else half a stone of wool. To William, son of Richard Carr of Hexham, one gimmer lamb or else 3 shillings. To Agnes, daughter of John Oliver, one gimmer lamb. To Ralph Carr of Eastwood 2 shillings. To Mathew, son of John Carr 2 shillings. To Ralph, son of Thomas Carr, one gimmer lamb. Residue to my wife Alice, my executrix.[13]*

Ralph had been given a half part of the Le Lee lands which he left to his son William Carr, who is described as "William Carr, Glover", though, as anyone who was anyone in Hexham had to be enrolled in one of the companies, this doesn't necessarily mean he was a glover by trade.[14] William had three sons of whom one, James, inherited the Le Lee lands and Richard inherited a house in Priestpopple to the south-west of the town centre and land on the outskirts of the town. Richard appears in the lists of landowners in the Manor Rolls for 1647 and 1654, while in

1663 he was Bailiff of Hexham, which office he may well have only held briefly until his cousin Benoni was senior enough to take it on. At a Manor Court held in 1665 he and his brother James are described as "gentlemen" and it as such that Richard is described in the record of the enrolment of his son John as an apprentice to the Merchant Adventurers' Company.[15]

The "quiet life of burghers and office holders" described by Colonel R. E. Carr may not be the most apt description of the experience of several generations of Carrs at Hexham. The Henrician Reformation lay heavily on Hexham and Henry's Commissioners were strongly resisted there. The Archbishop of York made a special plea for Hexham's exclusion from the Dissolution, dwelling upon the house's position as a centre of safety and a force for stability in the border area: "and men feare if the monasterie goo downe, that in processe all shal be wast moche within the land".[16] This failing, there was armed resistance. When Sir Reynold Carnaby, the new Lord of the Manor, went to take possession he was told by an armour-clad canon: "We be twenty brethren in this house, and we shall die all, ere that ye shall have the house".[17] John Heron of Chipchase played a double and deceitful game, intriguing with the monks on the one hand and the King's Commissioners on the other, and had no small part in the events leading to the Pilgrimage of Grace of 1536-7.[18]

Henry's instructions to the Duke of Norfolk were forthright: " ... that you shall without pitie or circumstance, nowe that our baner is displayed, cause all the monks and chanons, that be in anywise faultie, to be tyed uppe, without further delay or ceremony,to be the terrible example of others...".[19] But no such fate awaited the canons of Hexham. Colonel Ralph Carr properly refutes the legend, repeated even in twentieth century publications, that the last Prior, Edward Jay, was hanged outside his Priory and in fact the canons submitted after the failure of the Pilgrimage of Grace and those over twenty four were given pensions.

The town and its hinterland were to be centres of recusancy for some time. The "Rising of the Northern Earls" or 1569 Rebellion had its subdued end at Hexham to which the Earls of Northumberland and Westmorland and their followers fell back before fleeing to Scotland. Among those indicted for their part in the rebellion were John Carnaby of Langley, a member of one of Hexham's principal families, Thomas Errington of Walwick Grange, a relative by marriage of the Hexham Carrs, and two of their cousins, Robert Carr of Ford and Robert Carr of Wylton.[20]

The Hexham Carrs, like so many of the burgesses of Hexham and the local gentry remained recusant in sympathy and, to the extent that it was compatible with public office and well-being, in practice. Thus Richard Carr of Hexham and Le Lee was prosecuted in December 1585 for not attending church. The York Ecclesiastical

Records report that he and his wife "did not repair to the Parish Church and receive the Holy Communion as by law they were bound-(ruled) To bring a certificate, and Mr Carr was bound over to attend, as it was alleged he was doubtful to the Church".[21] His brother John had to surrender a bond in August 1563 for the same offence of not attending church. Richard's son, Richard Junior, who became Bailiff, could not have held that office without outward conformity and, indeed, he sent a son to be educated at Cambridge, but he seems to have fulfilled the important role of looking after the property of recusants to which their religious beliefs denied them formal title. It is most likely that Hexham's dynasty of Carr bailiffs continued the surreptitious Roman Catholicism which was typical of the town itself. Benoni Carr's name appears in a list of recusants of Northumberland of 1677 and he was associated with a leading local recusant, Edward Radcliffe, in undertaking business transactions for Catholic families. The burial of his son, Richard, occasioned the following entry in the Hexham parish register: "March 28th 1691.Richard, son of Mr Benoni Carr Attorney, Papist (in) Choir". Nor was it only the senior line of the Hexham Carrs who had Catholic inclinations, for Ralph Carr of Slaley, who was a churchwarden of Slaley, was found wanting by a Visitation of the Deanery of Corbridge, which found that he and another churchwarden had failed in their duties: "They lacked a table of the ten, a covering for the communion table, a communion cup and a book of canons".[22]

This was the background of John Carr, Richard's second son, who left Hexham to be apprenticed as a Merchant Adventurer in Newcastle in 1655. He came from a line of yeomen and burgesses in Hexham with Roman Catholic sympathies that were common in the town and Hexhamshire and which were probably no more than an occasional inconvenience, rather than a disadvantage, in business life. His father, Richard, was, as we have seen, described as a "gentleman" both in the records of Hexham Manor Court and the Merchant Adventurers' Company's entry of his son's apprenticeship; although of modest wealth in comparison to his cousin, Benoni, he was nevertheless, briefly, Bailiff of the town.

It was not easy to become indentured to the powerful Newcastle Company and we may wonder about the nature of the Hexham family's influence and contacts in Newcastle. Two generations previously, two of the sons of Richard Carr, the first of the family to be Bailiff, had been enrolled as apprentices in the Merchant Adventurers' Company. William Carr was enrolled as an apprentice in the Boothmens' (Corn-merchants) Company with Bertram Anderson as his master in 1600 and Arthur Carr was enrolled as an apprentice Mercer under John Milbanke in 1607. The Boothmen, the Mercers and the Drapers together made up the Merchant Adventurers. Neither William nor Arthur appears to have been subsequently admitted to the guild as full members. Colonel R.E.Carr comments that, "the fact that Richard Carr, while residing at Hexham, had sufficient influence in the neighbouring town of Newcastle to obtain the admission of two sons, as apprentices, in the leading Guild of the Freemen shews that he was a man of mark not only in his native town but in the district, since admission to this city company was restricted within limits which rendered it an object of request among families of wealth and position in Newcastle and its neighbourhood".[23]

It is true that admission to the Company was highly prized as an avenue for younger sons and that the sons of existing merchants had first right of entry but a scrutiny of enrolments shows that many apprentices came from quite far afield, from elsewhere in Northumberland, from Durham, Cumberland, Westmorland and Yorkshire. Newcastle was where wealth was created and a steady stream of younger sons of gentry and yeoman families made their way there via a web of kinship connections. There were Carrs who were prominent in the Merchant Adventurers Company and in the civic life of Newcastle though they were not close kinsmen of the Hexham family. The Carrs of Benwell Tower and then of St. Helen's Auckland were an important merchant family and one of them, Cuthbert Carr, was to play a heroic part in the defence of Newcastle against the Scots in 1643. It seems likely that it was a kinship connection that enabled William and Arthur to be indentured; the daughter of Bertram Anderson, a member of an influential family who served as sheriff, mayor and MP for Newcastle as well as being governor of the Merchant Adventurers, married a Ralph Carr.

Hexham was a respectable enough sort of place and John Carr as a son of one of its leading inhabitants would have been an acceptable apprentice. If he had come from a few miles away, from Tynedale or Redesdale, things would have been very different for an order of 1564 forbade admission of their inhabitants to the Merchant Adventurers Company: "the parties there brought up are known either by education or nature not to be of honest conversation. [They]...commit frequent theft and other felonies," and therefore no apprentices are to be taken "...proceeding from such lewde and wicked projenitors."

The only surprising thing about John Carr's indenture is the master he was placed under. Phineas Allen was an up and coming merchant but he was a member of the puritan faction, then in the ascendant in Newcastle in the circumstances of the Interregnum[24], and was as such a strange choice as master to a member of a family with Catholic sympathies. John Carr's move from the small world of Hexham to one of the most prosperous and populous towns in the kingdom was a decisive step, which not only took him into a bustling commercial world, full of opportunity, but into a town which had been rent by the political and religious divides of the Civil War and the Protectorate.

The young John Carr must have found his transition from the familiar and intimate world of Hexham, where almost every inhabitant would have been known to the rest, to the populous town of Newcastle, with over 10,000 inhabitants, somewhat unnerving. The town was busy and prosperous but it was, at the same time, politically and socially volatile. It had, as we have seen, recently undergone the dramatic events of the 1640s: the occupation by the Scots of 1640-41, the siege and capture of 1644, and the replacement of royalist by parliamentary supporters in the highest positions of authority. By the time of John Carr's arrival, the puritan faction led by the Dawsons was firmly in control.

It was thus a confused, turbulent and dynamic world into which the young John Carr stepped in 1655. He was not to find himself a quiet haven with some neutral family, which simply sought to survive and prosper amidst the vicissitudes of national and local conflict, but rather he worked and lived in the counting houses, the warehouses and the homes of the puritan and temporarily dominant faction of Newcastle merchants led by Henry Dawson.

He was apprenticed to Phineas Allen, Merchant Adventurer and boothman, by his indenture of 29 September but was "set over" or transferred to William Johnson the following September to serve out his time.[25] No doubt it had always been intended that he be apprenticed to Johnson, for merchants were only allowed to take one apprentice at a time and it was quite common for a temporary master to be found for one, while another served out his time.

Phineas Allen was a minor figure in the pro-parliamentary and puritan faction headed by Henry Dawson.[26] He was a signatory to the petition sent to Parliament in 1648 by the Mayor, Thomas Ledgard, the Mayor-elect, Thomas Bonner, some of the Council and the "well affected of the town", demanding justice on the King and "the formentors of, and actors in, the first and second wars and the bringing in of the Scots".[27] William Johnson was a more important figure in the puritan establishment and a protege of Henry Dawson's. He first appeared in the Common Council in 1652 as an Alderman and served as Mayor during the next two years, a meteoric rise.

How did John Carr, coming from what appears to have been the Catholic recusant background of the Hexham Carrs, come to be placed amongst the new men who had taken advantage of the events of 1640-44 and formed the now dominant puritan faction in Newcastle? To be apprenticed to a Merchant Adventuer was a good start in life and probably John's father Richard did not worry over much about the religious affiliations of his son's masters, if indeed he knew of them. The opportunity was probably made available via the Carrs of Eshott who were connected by marriage with that key figure in the Dawson clique, Thomas Bonner, who after Henry Dawson's death in 1653 was the leading politician in the town until the Restoration.

His prosperity was probably relative. On the fringe of the new elite, he would have had advantages but this was a hard time for most inhabitants of Newcastle. The town was luckier than many other places; the "meaner sort in Cumberland" were said to have left and gone to Newcastle only to find that that not much help was to be had there where "...corn is very dear...the poor almost ready to starve".[28] John, as a minor figure in the merchant elite and within the wider family of those whose fortunes waxed with the progress of the Parliamentary cause, would have enjoyed some immunity to hardship. Nevertheless, if his association with the dominant puritan families was a blessing, it was not an unmixed one, as a reckoning would come with the Restoration. In the meantime his expectations increased as he proved himself a worthy, industrious and puritanically devout apprentice. The political influence, the religious persuasion and the financial fortunes of his master William Johnson and his circle, the Dawsons, the Bonners, the Allens and the regicide MP, John Blakiston, were in the ascendant.

As we have seen, the leading puritans enriched themselves during the Interregnum. William Johnson, Mayor of Newcastle in 1653-54, to whom the young John Carr was apprenticed, bought an estate and substantial mansion at Kibblesworth, four miles south west of Newcastle, and the Bonners also acquired land there.[29] The purchase was witnessed by John Carr shortly after he had begun his temporary apprenticeship with Phineas Allen.[30] Johnson, who as Mayor had had dedicated to him and the corporation Cuthbert Sydenham's puritan tract, *The Greatness of the Mystery of Godliness; Opened in Several Sermons,* was leading a busy successful life, concerning himself not only with business, religion and politics but with the proposed establishment of a university at Durham.

As we have seen, the treatment of those that had supported parliament against king and then controlled civic affairs during the Interregnum was comparatively mild when a swift reversal of fortune saw the restoration of the monarchy and the royalists back in charge of Newcastle's government. There was no wholesale purge for, indeed, the majority of men in the town's government had always been moderates in politics, who had adjusted to changes in central government and concentrated on looking after the wealth and welfare of themselves and the town. Just as the only the strongest royalists had been ousted in the 1640s, so only those whose support for the Commonwealth had been energetic were ousted in 1660-62.

Roger Howell has argued that the changes made in 1660-62 had probably as much to do with the internal politics of Newcastle as with the restoration of the monarchy. Perhaps we should conclude that local and national politics shadowed each other but that the shadows only partly overlapped, national events providing the opportunity for changes in the town. The list of those removed from civic positions and of their replacements is short but significant:

> *Five aldermen were removed, all clearly associated with the Bonner-Dawson groups; five members of the old inner ring of pre-Civil War days replaced them. Those whose early careers and family connections had cut them out for inner ring politics survived, their activity in the Commonwealth and Protectorate corporations notwithstanding.[31]*

The removal of five aldermen may seem a small "purge" but one must remember that others depended upon the support and patronage of prominent men.

The young John Carr, still an apprentice in 1660, was a minor figure but he was both a puritan and dependent upon the fortunes of his masters and patrons in the puritan faction. William Johnson was among the removed aldermen[32] and his fall must have seemed to threaten his apprentice's prospects. Nor was Johnson or John Carr prepared to make that religious accommodation with the Anglican Church that would have made for a quiet life. To John Carr, the Restoration with its reverse to his friends, patrons and co-religionists must have come as a shock.

The young Carr had been making steady progress. He was clearly not like those dissolute and cavalier apprentices who had defied the regulations brought in by the Merchant Adventurers in 1649 as to, "their haire, manners ,and apparell" and who had their hair cut and their "superfluos ribbining" taken off in 1649.[33] Nor can he have approved of his fellow apprentice under Phineas Allen, Allen Gilpin, who had his hair cut in open court in 1649 and was in 1651 sent to the apprentice's prison for calling Judeth Hall, a Merchant Adventurer's wife, a "base slut" when she rebuked him while he was drunk.[34] Carr seems to have been, not only a dutiful apprentice, but one who embraced his masters' puritanism and quickly won their confidence.

His circle was a tight, inter-locked group of puritan merchant families. William Bonner, son of Thomas, had married Abigail, daughter of William Johnson, while William's brother, Joseph married Prescilla, Abigail's sister. John Blakiston, son of the regicide MP, married another sister, Phoebe Johnson. On the death of William Bonner in May 1665, John Carr, who had recently been admitted a Merchant Adventurer, was named as one of the trustees in Bonner's will. In the following year he married the widowed Abigail.

That this group of puritan merchant families continued their dissenting ways into the Restoration is shown by the information laid before Ralph Jennison, Mayor of

Newcastle, in July 1669 as to an illegal prayer meeting, "in the howse of Richard Gilpyn, minister in the White Freers". Among those found to be present after the doors were broken down were William Johnson, Robert Johnson, Thomas Dawson, Thomas Ledger and John Carr.[35]

John Carr appears to have set up in business for himself almost immediately on gaining his freedom as a Merchant and we find him taking the fourth part of a lease on a wagonway together with Henry Hudson in July 1665. He and Hudson continued to have interests in the development of mines and wagonways in the Whitley Bay area, for a further indenture of January 1667 refers to an agreement between Hudson of Newbiggin and Carr as to a joint interest in a colliery in the township of Whitley.

Advantageous marriages were as important to merchants as they were to aristocratic and gentry families and by marrying the daughter of the man he had been apprenticed to John Carr materially assisted his economic and social advance. A year after his wedding, on the occasion of the birth of his son, John, he is referred to as "of Kibblesworth, gentleman". His father-in-law left a substantial estate in 1678, which included interests in lead mines in Cumberland and Westmorland and a colliery at St. Anthony's. His mother-in-law, on her death in 1681, left £80 each to all her Carr grandchildren save one, Nathaniel.[36]

The Johnson family was to have a distinguished and interesting history. Abigail's brother, Sir Nathaniel Johnson, was Mayor of Newcastle in 1680 and went on to be Governor of Carolina. He must have quickly cast off his father's dissenting faith for as Governor he was responsible for carrying out the policies against dissenters in that episcopalian colony. His son Robert also became Governor of Carolina. The head of the family in 1724, another Nathaniel Johnson, had the sonorous and, no doubt, profitable post of "Chief Farmer of the Chimney-money of his Majesty for the four Northern Counties".

By the time of his death in 1682 (he was only some 42 years old) John Carr was obviously a comparatively wealthy man. His will reads as follows:

> *1682,Nov.12. Will of John Carr of Newcastle, Merchant. To my wife Abigail my household stuff, books and horses; to my son John Carr, £400; to my son Richard Carr, £400; to my son Nathaniel Carr, £500; to my daughter Mary Carr, £250; in confidence that my children will receive what is allowed them by their grandmother's will before my son John be fit to put out to trade, I therefore order the aforesaid sums of £400 be paid unto my sons John and Richard when they attain 24 years or so or on the expiration of their apprenticeship. Whereas my son*

Nathaniel is not considered in his grandmother's will I therefore desire my wife and friends hereafter named as trustees or supervisors that at such time as my son Nathaniel be of fit age to put to trade they do out of the aforesaid £500 give him such sum as may be agreed upon to pay for his binding money not exceeding £100 and the other £400 when he attains 24 or on the expiration of his apprenticeship entreating that care may be taken for their disposal into sober families that they may have the advantage of a pious example for their imitation." Testator requests that John Blakiston of Newcastle, Esq., Mr Thomas Shepherd of London, merchant, brothers in law, and Mr Henry Hudson of Newbegan, Northumberland, "be supervisors of this my will, that they will content themselves in putting money out at interest into good and safe hands and that my share and proportion of the profits arising by Whitley colliery, Shildon Lead Works [the new trial at Red Deane], and Byker Moor Colliery, that they be paid to my wife.[37]*

Only three days after he signed his will, John Carr, merchant, was buried at St.Nicholas's Church on 15 November 1682 "in woollen according to the Act". Despite his comparative youth, he had accomplished much in a business career of 17 years though his marriage to his ex-master's daughter must have helped him financially. If it had not been exactly a spectacular progress, it had been a solid advance .One has only to compare his will with that of Ralph Carr of Slaley, sums of £400 as against "one gimmer lamb or else three shillings", to see the extent of the advance.

This was the will of a prosperous merchant who left not only money but solid investments in coal and lead mining which would continue to yield profits after his death. His father, Richard, had given him a good start in life when he enrolled him as an apprentice Merchant Adventurer. Did John look back to his Hexham boyhood and keep in touch with his relatives there while he was making good in Newcastle? Probably not, for Colonel Carr's exhaustive researches failed to find evidence of this and he suggests that the Carrs of this line were later confused as to their antecedents and seemed to think they sprang from the Carrs of Cocken, rather than from the Hexham Carrs. If this was so, were religious differences at the bottom of it, a puritan dissenter not wishing to broadcast a relationship with recusant Catholics? We cannot of course know and perhaps it would be unwise to guess.

What John Carr's will reveals are the wishes of a decent man on his death-bed who is concerned for the future of all his children and especially for Nathaniel, cut out of old Mrs Johnson's will.

His wife, Abigail, survived him for the considerable period of 46 years. She also continued to enjoy the fruits of his investment in mining in the Whitley Bay area. In 1691 she was still a lessee of the colliery and pier at Cullercoats in partnership with John Blakiston, John Rogers and her husband's old partner, Henry Hudson. In 1709 she and the other partners negotiated a new lease of the coalmines at Whitley and the pier at Cullercoats with the Duke of Somerset and, as late as 1728, she and others conveyed to Henry Hudson certain premises at Whitley in return for £250. By then she was living in London where her will was proven in April 1729. She left most of her money to her Johnson relations and to the children of her first marriage to William Bonner; only trivial bequests went to the Carr children and Colonel Carr suggests, "some coolness between her and her Carr offspring".[38] The Johnsons were obviously an awkward lot when it came to wills, what with Abigail's mother cutting out the young Nathaniel and she, herself, doing much the same to all her Carr children.

John Carr, himself, had, however, provided for his children and had left a substantial estate. Future generations would build upon his achievement but the first step is not to be undervalued.

Newcastle during the tumultuous years of the Civil war and the Interregnum had seen a struggle for power amongst the merchant elite in which self-interest loosely allied itself with religious and political affiliations. The struggle was muted and qualified, however, by a common interest in the town's prosperity and by ties of kinship. The old inner circle was pushed aside and then returned to its own but many who had gained in the 'forties and 'fifties·retained the substance of their acquisitions. Robert Ellison, as we have seen, emerged much the richer and even the apprentice, John Carr, found that he and his puritan patrons were able to thrive after the immediate aftermath of the Restoration.

References

1.   See Appendix 2.

2.   R. E. Carr and C. E. Carr, *The History of the Family of Carr,* vol. I (1893) p.3.

3.   G. E. Mingay, *The Gentry* (1976) p.4.

4.   S. J. Watts, *From Border to Middle Shire 1586-1625*, (1975) p.60.

5.   See *Family of Carr* and Appendix 2.

6.   *Ibid,* p. 66.

7.   *Ibid,* p.91.

8.   Northumberland County History Committee (eds), *A History of Northumberland,* Vol. III by Allen B. Hinds (1896), pp. 218-9.

9.   T. B. Macaulay, *History of England, Vol. I* (1906 edition) p.205.

10.   Watts, *Border to Middle Shire*, p.67.

11.   Northumberland *County History,* Vol. III, p. 300.

12.   *Ibid.*

13.   *Family of Carr* p.24. If Ralph Carr's personal effects seem paltry, it is worth noting that William Blenkinsop of Blenkinsop, head of a well-known gentry family, left household goods and apparel worth only £13.3s.2d in 1581, though there may have been a residue beyond this. Watts *Border to Middle Shire,* p.43.

14   Glove-making was one of Hexham's main trades.

15.   J. R. Boyle and F. W. Dendy (eds.), *Extracts from the Records of the Merchant Adventurers of Newcastle upon Tyne, Surtees Society* Vol. XCIII, 1895. Vol. II, p.280.

16.   *Northumberland County History.* Vol. III, p. 157.

17.   *Ibid.*

18. *Ibid.*

19. *Ibid.*

20. Cuthbert Sharp (ed), *Memorials of the Rebellion of the Earls of Northumberland and Westmoreland* (1840 reprinted as *The Risings in the North* 1975).

21. *Family of Carr,* p.17.

22. *Ibid,* p.23.

23. *Ibid,* p. 18.

24. See Roger Howell, Jr, *Newcastle-upon-Tyne and the Puritan Revolution* (1967).

25. J. R. Boyle and F. W. Dendy eds. *Extracts from The Records of the Merchant Adventurers of Newcastle upon Tyne*, Vol. II Surtees Society, (1899) p.280.

26. We can, in respect of Newcastle, talk of Puritanism without having to distinguish too closely between Presbyterians and Independents because, for the most part, Presbyterian and Independent ministers worked in harmony. See Claire Cross, *the Church of England 1646-1660,* p.119.

27. Longstaffe, *Memoirs of Ambrose Barnes* (1867) Surtees Society, pp. 351-2.

28 Brian Manning, *The Crisis of The English Revolution* (1976) p.81.

29. Mackenzie and Ross, *Durham,* p.154.

30. *Family of Carr*, p.30.

31. Howell, "Newcastle and Nation: The Seventeenth Century Experience" in *Puritans and Radicals in North England* (1984), p.27.

32. They were: George Dawson, Christopher Nicholson, Henry Rawlings, William Johnson and Peter Sanderson. They were replaced by Sir James Clavering, Sir Francis Anderson, Sir Francis Liddell, Henry Maddison and Cuthbert Carr. Howell, ibid , p.41.

33. Boyle and Dendy, Merchant Adventurers Records, p.154.

34. *Ibid*, p.161.

35. Memoirs of Ambrose Barnes, pp.408-409.

36. Family of Carr, p.32.

37. *Ibid*, p.33.

38. *Ibid*, pp.34,35.

Chapter 9

Prospering in England's Peru

England's a perfect World! has Indies too! Correct your Maps:
Newcastle is Peru.

William Ellis, *News from Newcastle* (1651)

John Carr (1667-1739) was referred to by successive generations of Carrs as "the Patriarch". This view of him as the father and ruler of the tribe undoubtedly owes much to the fact that he had a dozen children and may have also been because of the authority he exerted over them. It seems probable, however, that the term was also used in the sense of the founder of a family for the Carrs were rather cut off from their roots.

John was only fifteen years old when his father died at the age of 42 and although his mother, Abigail, lived to a ripe old age, she does not, as we have seen, appear to have been fond of the children of her second marriage. Perhaps because of the first John Carr's early death, the family seems to have been ignorant of its Hexham origins. To the "Patriarch's" children, he must indeed have seemed the founding father.

That the family was in some doubt as to its ancestry is shown by their appropriation of the wrong coat of arms. Ralph, John's son, placed on his father's tomb a coat of arms that was a mixture of that of the Carrs of Hetton and Eshott and the Carrs of St Helen's Auckland. In later generations, however, the family adopted the arms of the Carrs of Cocken. It was not until the researches of Colonel R. E. Carr established the Hexham ancestry that it became clear that the correct coat of arms was that of the Carrs of Hetton, a chevron with three estoiles.[1]

John and his two brothers, Richard and Nathaniel, were all admitted to the Merchant Adventurers Company as boothmen by right of patrimony.[2] In the same year of 1690 as he became a Merchant Adventurer, John applied to be admitted to the Roll of Burgesses of Newcastle and, although he was turned down because of his age, his application was successful the following year.

He seemed therefore to be set on a career as a Newcastle merchant, but the records of the Merchant Adventurers show that his membership ceased only two years after his admission, almost certainly because he had not paid his dues. This was not unusual, for many merchants allowed their membership to lapse if they left the area or went into some other form of business; they were generally allowed to pay off their arrears if they wished, once again, to avail themselves of the privileges of the Company. It would appear that John Carr allowed his membership to cease because his main business had become not that of a merchant but of an agent or factor specialising in mineral rights and coal mining.

Here we find interesting comparisons with the career of Henry Ellison, though Ellison was both a third of a century younger and of superior social rank. Ellison did not become a member of the dominant Newcastle societies until he had already established himself, while Carr became a Merchant Adventurer and then let his membership lapse. Both, however, became involved with landowning and coalmining in the same part of County Durham. Their careers point to two significant developments: the decline in real importance of the old monopolistic guilds and of the corporation of Newcastle; and the increasing economic significance of the area to the west of Gateshead.

The term "England's Peru" was applied to the coal-field about Newcastle in the mid-seventeenth century and, as we saw in Section 1, a recent study of the parish of Whickham has seen it as "Britain's first industrial society".[3] The former is probably a more accurate description than the latter, for black gold was what made the area tick, even if there existed in the iron-works of Abraham Crowley at Winlaton and Swalwell one of the most substantial manufacturing businesses of the day.

However we classify its economy, it is certain that the area within and around the parish of Whickham was the scene of dynamic economic activity. It had by the late seventeenth century lost much of its agricultural character and its mines, wagonways and furnaces amazed visitors. A great deal of money was to be made and lost there and its pursuit did not always constitute innocent employment for the coal trade could be a rough and desperate business.

Whereas Henry Ellison entered at the top of this booming economy due to his membership of a leading family, his appointment to the post of agent to his Liddell relatives and, finally, to his marriage to a Cotesworth heiress, John Carr's entry was more difficult. He came from a comfortable background but was of modest means and prospects. His advantage seems to have been, besides ability and determination, an intimate knowledge of the landscape and economy of the area in which he had been brought up, together with a wealth of contacts.

John Carr was brought up at Kibblesworth in the chapelry of Lamesley, which was separated from Whickham by the Blackburn. His family had knowledge and experience of the mining industry: his father had had part shares in Whitley Colliery and Byker Moor Colliery; his mother continued, after her second husband's death, to have, in conjunction with her Johnson relatives, interests in mines at Whitley and the coal-shipping pier at Cullercoats. His uncle, John Johnson, was land agent and coal factor to Anne Clavering of Chopwell, a formidable woman with a strong interest in business, who later married Henry Liddell.[4]

Growing up in such a family in this centre of mining activity, the young John Carr must have acquired much of the knowledge and expertise that would lead to his success as an agent and man of business. He would have known the topography of the Whickham area well and have had a good grasp of its geology. He would have known about coal seams, mining methods, wayleaves and wagonways. He would have been aware of the profits that could be made and of the losses and bankruptcies that awaited the incompetent and the unfortunate. The ownership of each acre of land, the difference between copyhold and leasehold and the details of manorial law, of leases, rents and fines, would have all been known to him by the time he was in his teens.

It seems probable that it was by his uncle, John Johnson, that John Carr was introduced to Sir James Clavering Bt. of Axwell and became his agent. By the time of his marriage to Sarah Wynne, daughter of William Wynne of Gateshead, in August 1700, John was living at Whitehouse near Swalwell and was agent to Sir James. At this time the Claverings were living at Old Axwell on the Whickham side of the Derwent. Whitehouse was close to the site of the later Clavering mansion of Axwell Park (designed by Paine and built in 1758) and was probably demolished when that house was built.

Sir James, the first baronet, died in 1702 and he was followed by a rapid succession of Clavering baronets: his grandson, James, who died in 1707, another grandson John, who died in 1714, and the latter's son, James, who died in 1726. As John Carr purchased the estate of Dunston Hill in 1704, partly from the Shaftos and partly from the Claverings, and because he seems to have continued to have been involved in business activities that were concerned with Clavering mining interests, it is probable that he continued to be the Claverings' agent for many years. There could have been few tougher or more demanding jobs, for the Claverings were soon involved in a bitter and violent dispute over wayleave rights with the lord of the manor of Gateshead and Whickham. The lordships were bought by William Ramsay in 1712 but the man behind Ramsay was William Cotesworth who inherited them from Ramsay in 1715.[5]

Cotesworth used the purchase of the Whickham leases to control, in conjunction with his allies who formed "the Regulation", the amount of coal coming on to the market from collieries more distant from the Tyne and beyond the extent of Whickham manor. This brought him into conflict with Sir John Clavering and his fellow mine-owners, George Pitt and Thomas Brummel, who wanted passage to the Tyne for coal from the collieries of Byermoor, Fawdonfield, Ridingfield, Bucksnook and Tanfield. They set out to build a new waggonway, the Bucksnook, down to the Swalwell and Derwentshaugh Staithes against the fierce opposition of Cotesworth and Lady Bowes. The building of the Bucksnook was accompanied by extraordinary events, including the destruction of the line by Lady Bowes's men, and a welter of lawsuits.[6] In April 1716 Lady Clavering, who continued the dispute after her husband's death[7], was arrested in her own house and required to give a bond for good behaviour. But the new waggonway continued and Cotesworth, cutting his losses, acquired his own share in the Bucksnook line.

In 1720 the quarrel with Cotesworth started up again with different sets of allies. Lady Clavering, this time with the Bowes interest, in the shape of the young William Blakiston Bowes, and Richard Ridley of Newcastle on her side, decided to build another wagonway, the Western Way. William Cotesworth responded by allying himself with the Liddells and the Wortley Montagues in the building of yet another wagonway in 1724-5 to bring the coal from the Stella Grand Lease collieries and Blackburn in Lamesley down to Dunston Staithes and Redheugh Staithes. When this wagonway was extended via the Causey Arch to the Wortley Montague collieries at Tanfield and Causey, coal was being transported six miles to the Tyne. The resulting competition and consequent drop in the price of coal enabled Cotesworth to persuade his allies and rivals that the time was ripe for a further attempt at regulation and the Grand Allies were formed in the summer of 1726; this alliance was to attempt to control the Tyne valley coal trade for the next quarter century.

What was John Carr's part in all this? Clearly so long as he was agent to the Claverings, his first duty was to look after their property and interests. At the same time he was free to look out for private business opportunities, as did most agents who, by the nature of their work, were privy to useful information. A clever and ambitious man would also realise that in the frenetic world of coalfield rivalries, alliances did not last for ever and that it was preferable, in the course of pursuing the Claverings' interests, not to make too many enemies.

Carr seems to have become involved in the coal trade in his own right along with a long-term friend and partner William Barras. In 1709 he and Barras took an interest in the collieries of Fawdonsfield and Ridingfield. These were well-established collieries when they were referred to as belonging to Sir John Clavering at the time of the plans for the first "Regulation" in 1708. Carr and Barras are mentioned as paying rent for these collieries but what is most likely is that they contracted to work the pits for a year at their own cost in return for an agreed sum per ten of coal won. Barras appears to have been an "undertaker" who took on such contracts and Carr would have had a good idea of the proportion of coal to be extracted from these collieries under the "Regulation", while he may even have been aware of plans for the Bucksnook wagonway, which greatly improved the prospects for these pits.

In 1710 Carr found himself very much in the eye of the storm of the North East coal-trade when he became manager of the Claverings' Stella colliery. This was not one pit but a combination of Clavering collieries, which mixed their coals for sale. Clavering Stella is often referred to as belonging to Sir John Clavering but in fact it was mainly in the hands of the Claverings of Chopwell and James Clavering of Greencroft had an interest in it too. As relations between Sir John and the Regulation worsened, William Cotesworth and Henry Liddell were keen to keep on good terms with James Clavering, while Henry Liddell married Anne Clavering of Chopwell in 1711. John Carr replaced Sir John's close associate and fellow mine-owner Thomas Brummell as manager of Stella, a move that was approved of by Henry Liddell.

Finding a market for Stella coal, which was not always of the highest quality, was a constant problem, especially as Stella seems to have put coal on the market beyond the share allocated to it by the Regulation. Some of its production had to go as pan coal to the salt-pans of Shields, while much was off-loaded at low prices on the London market. As Henry Ellison wrote to Cotesworth in December 1710, "By last post I wrote to the Captain [George Liddell] and as J[ohn] Carr has the menagem[ent] of Stella, I should think the pan coal workers might be easily brought to an understanding both as to price and quality, which could not be done while Brummel was concerned."[8]

John Carr seems to have enjoyed the respect of Henry Liddell for another reason than his capability as a colliery manager, his staunch Hanoverianism. No doubt Carr's family background with its puritanism and support for the parliamentary cause and for the Commonwealth predicated that he would be a Whig. As a youth he attended the Presbyterian chapel at Swalwell and, although he later had a family pew in the parish church at Whickham, he continued to attend the Hanover Square chapel in Newcastle, which, under his friend and relative Richard Rogerson, moved from being Presbyterian to Unitarian. After George 1's accession Liddell wrote to Cotesworth enclosing a copy of, "..his Maj[esty's] most glorious speech to his Parl[iament], which after reading must desire you will give Pow a groat and send it with my humble service to Tom [Shafto] off Whickham, honest Frank [Baker], Carr and Barras..."[9]

By the late 1720s we find Carr and Barras referred to as the grieves or farm bailiffs of Robert Cotesworth, William's son and successor.[10] Carr both worked for a number of employers and for himself. He acted as agent to the Wortley Montagues and had interests in collieries at Gibside. Towards the end of his life he sent a note to his son Ralph asking him to seek out a Mr Leaton in Newcastle and persuade him to pay him £100 made up of colliery rent of £87.10 and wayleave rent of £12.10.[11] This Mr Leaton was almost certainly John Leaton, son of Anthony Leaton. Father and son were the viewers of the Gibside collieries, first for the Montagues and then for the Bowes.[12]

If John Carr had a multiplicity of interests in the coal trade in the Whickham area, he was not a man to stick to one type of mining or even just to mining. Throughout his life he had a number of diverse business interests. In 1711 he and three partners, John Richardson of Crossgate, Jonathan Maughan of Wolsingham and Miles Sidgewick, were granted a lease by Lord Thanet, "to work mines of lead and lead-ore at Knock and Milburn Fell in the county of Westmoreland". Sidgewick was to oversee the working of the mines but he absconded with £500 of the partnership's money. The other partners persevered and acquired a new twenty-one year lease from Thanet by which the rent was to be one-fifth of every fifth ring (a"ring" was a measure of 8 cwts), or £1.8s for every ring due to the landlord until a smelt mill was erected, after which the rent was to be one pig of lead in every six smelted. The partnership appears to have continued for the length of the lease, being mentioned in two superseded wills of Carr's in 1727 and 1728.[13] John Carr was to become very close to Lord Thanet, becoming his agent and adviser on coal and lead-mining matters and according to John's son, Ralph, saving Thanet's family thousands of pounds by his expert advice.[14]

A further lead-mining venture of Carr's was his stake in lead mines on Alston Moor. As we have seen, most of these mines, once the property of the Earl of Derwentwater, were leased by the Greenwich Commissioners to Colonel George Liddell in 1736. Carr was one of those who took some of the minority of shares that Liddell allowed others to take as working partners. He had two shares in the Peatstack Hill mine and a further two shares in a group of other mines.[15] Although this was a small share of the overall enterprise in which Liddell retained some seventy-five per cent of the ownership, it was for Carr quite a substantial investment. A paybill for a number of mines at Christmas 1738 shows the total wages for all the different categories of workers, the pickmen, the labourers and the washers, to have been £1133 and there were four pay days a year, at Ladyday, Midsummer and Michaelmas as well as Christmas.[16] Carr was responsible for one eighth of this bill though, as this seems out of proportion to his share holding, it is probable that he and the other working partners took responsibility for wages, while Liddell took care of the other expenses.

But John Carr's business interests extended well beyond mining. He became involved in shipowning and had sixteenth shares in the "Francis and Anne's Content", 270 tons, the "Providence", 200 tons, and the "Dairy Maid", 160 tons, which were all Scarborough ships, and also a share in a keel on the Tyne. Ownership of ships was usually divided into 64ths as a way of spreading the risk and John Carr's quarter share in these vessels suggests that he was a managing rather than merely a subscribing owner. Such owners were more than just sleeping partners and made the day to day decisions as to the employment of their ships. Whereas during the seventeenth century most colliers trading from the North East had been owned by men in London, Ipswich or Yarmouth, there was a general trend in the eighteenth century for the pattern of ownership to move northwards, first to Scarborough and then to Sunderland, Newcastle and Shields.

Towards the end of his career, he became much involved in the timber trade with the Baltic ports in partnership with Charles Atkinson, a Newcastle hostman or coal-fitter. The outward cargo in the "raff" trade, as the timber trade was known, was usually coal and sometimes grindstones, which suited Carr's and Atkinson's other interests.

Carr's involvement in the "raff" trade was presumably technically illegal under the "foreign bought and foreign sold" regulations of the Merchant Adventurers for one whose membership of that body had ceased. Carr, however, acted with his partner, Charles Atkinson, who was indentured in 1726, the same year that the two began trading, and was admitted to membership in 1727. To judge by the Newcastle Trinity House Primage Account books, Atkinson (and Carr) conducted a steady, if not spectacular, trade. Between September 1729 and June 1730 incoming cargoes consigned to Atkinson were:

Date	Ship	Cargo consigned to C. Atkinson.
Sept. 11 1729	George	Several parcels/pieces raff.
March 3 1730	Darwan	13 3/4 tons merchandye.
April. 3 1730	Darwan	6 3/4 tons timber.
May 8 1730	Hopewell	A cargo of raff.
June 1 1730	Hopewell	A cargo of raff.
June 1 1730	Darwan	16 tons timber.
June 10 1730	Darwan	7 1/2 tons merchandye.[17]

Atkinson, like Carr, was a man who found the restrictions of the old monopolistic societies irksome. In 1703 he and six other hostmen were hauled up in front of the society for:

> ...aideing and assisting gentlemen owners of coles not free of this Society who confederate with the lightermen and buyers of Coles in the Citty of London to the ruine and prejudice of the hoastmen and Coale trade in Newcastle.

Atkinson and the other offenders were suspended from their privileges as free hostmen for three months. They sought, however, the opinion of the Attorney-General, Edward Northey, as to the powers of the hostmen's charter and, when he advised that the society was not entitled to the sole loading and disposing of coal on the river Tyne, brought writs of mandamus against the hostmen's company.[18] The corporation supported the Hostmen's Company but, probably realising it was on uncertain ground, the company did not take further action nor enforce the suspension. The case was a sgnificant milestone in the slow diminution of the hostmen's privileges and the onward march of free trade. But, if the end of the power of the Newcastle companies was in sight, it was still strong enough to make membership of them necessary and, as we have seen, Atkinson became a boothman Merchant Adventurer in 1727.

With such diverse business activities, John Carr prospered, bought the estate of Dunston Hill and supported a large family. His marriage to Sarah Wynne seems to have provided him with a town house in Gateshead where he lived for part of the year and he soon took the opportunity of expanding his land holding at Dunston

Hill. He extended the estate in 1713 and 1714 with land purchased from Cuthbert Ellison (of the Lintz Green branch of the Ellison family) and William Grey. The house itself was of modest size but had a spacious hall and impressive double staircase. John Carr shared the contemporary interest in landscape design and appears to have planted the trees on his estate with great care. More than a century later, his great-grandson, Ralph Carr (later Carr-Ellison), who was a considerable expert on natural history, commented: "The arrangement of the park and grounds at Dunston Hill, which he is known to have laid out, shews great taste and a knowledge of forestry far before his time".[19]

Dunston Hill (by Harriet Carr)

Between 1701 and about 1720 John Carr's wife Sarah bore him twelve children. It is a reflection of the high mortality rates of the early eighteenth century that by the time of John's death at the age of seventy-two, he had outlived, not only his wife, but six of his children. It is also indicative of the extremes that make up estimates of average life expectancy that two of his children died in infancy or childhood, five in their twenties while three, Margaret, Katherine and Ralph, were to live to the ages of 86, c.80 and 94. Jane Carr, the eldest child, and her brother George, were the only members of their generation to live to near the average life expectancy of the period, dying at or around forty.

What is also noticeable is that only one of John's children married during his lifetime and only three ever married. Although letters and diaries of the period point to considerable affection within marriages, there can be little doubt that marriage remained as much a matter of economic alliance as of affection between the partners. Within polite society, men required dowries from prospective wives, while women, or their parents, required wealth or the prospect of it from putative husbands. Jane Carr married John Widdrington, a member of a junior branch of the noble family attainted for their part in the 1715 rebellion. This young attorney must have had reasonable prospects, while John Carr may have been able to give a suitable endowment to his eldest daughter. Early marriages for John's sons were probably out of the question, for they had their way to make in the world and, whether the problem was a lack of money for dowries or a lack of prosperous suitors, the only other daughter to marry, Katherine, did not wed until she was about forty.

John Carr had prospered and was in comfortable circumstances as his family grew up but his business, depending as it did on his own connections, knowledge and acumen, could not really be considered a "firm" to be inherited.[20] His wealth and estate were insufficient for his sons to become country gentlemen looking after the estate or for him to place them in upper class professions like the church and the law or for him to buy them commissions in the army. Their future lay in trade and commerce and it is noticeable that none followed the path of their father's main activity and became colliery viewers or coal factors but were entered on the traditional path to business life via apprenticeships. It was fortunate that one son, Ralph, was to display a remarkable aptitude for business and was to build upon his father's mercantile interests and connections.

John's eldest son, another John, was apprenticed to a Merchant Adventurer, George Headlam, in 1720, but died before he could be admitted to the Company. William found himself under the tutelage of a member of the Gateshead Saddlers' Company, beginning his indenture in May 1722. None of John's sons was, of course, eligible for admission to the Merchant Adventurers by patrimony as he had himself ceased to be a member and so Ralph Carr, like his brother John, was indentured in October 1728, in his case to Mathew Bowes, Merchant Adventurer and Boothman. George was sent to London and was apprenticed to a London lighterman, the equivalent of a Newcastle fitter. There was some uncertainty as to what to do with Benjamin. George Carr, writing from London, recommended to his father that his brother be apprenticed to a brewer, "...for there's none that fails and the prentis fee is not large".[21] Benjamin was in the event indentured to a Newcastle Merchant Adventurer, a Mercer called Michael Bland, in February 1733. At the time of his enrolment seven months later, he was set over to William Leighton but after the deaths of both Bland and Leighton, he was set over to his brother, Ralph, in July 1739.[22] By 1741 we find him trading on his own account, importing five tons of iron on the *Unity* in March 1741.[23] He died two years later, just failing to complete the ten years apprenticeship necessary for admittance to the company as a full Merchant Adventurer.

These Carr brothers were an adventurous bunch, by no means eager to make quiet and solid progress in the commercial world of Tyneside. William had an interesting but somewhat chequered career. He gave up his apprenticeship in Gateshead and we next come across him in the army of the King of Denmark. He had taken a ship to Copenhagen, probably one of his father's, got drunk and enlisted, an action he seems to have immediately regretted. John Carr was prepared to pay for his release but thought the £40 the Danes demanded a bit steep. Even after William had served his three years, the Danish army were still asking one hundred dollars or *rigsdalers*[24] before they would let him go. John Carr requested the aid of the influential Colonel Liddell and wrote to his son, Ralph, that the Colonel, "has been speaking to Lord Harrington about getting Will released".[25] The Colonel was as good as his word and soon Lord Harrington, Secretary of State, was writing to Walter Titley, Charge d'Affaires at Copenhagen:

> *I send you the enclos'd memorandum at the request of Colonel Lyddal. You will see it relates to a young man of the county of Durham, who was inlisted when drunk, and has been detained above three years in the Danish service. I must desire that you will find out this young man, and that you will examine into what is alledged concerning him, and do him all the good offices in your power towards obtaining him a free discharge.*[26]

That a Tyneside coal factor and merchant like John Carr was able, via his connections, to enlist the personal intervention of a Secretary of State is revealing. Eighteenth century society was based on a web of relationships and on patronage, deference and obligation; a pull on the right string by even a minor member of the network brought results.

Walter Titley discovered that the Danes were not entirely in the wrong, for William had managed to enlist for only three years, instead of the usual twelve, by promising to pay his officer one hundred dollars when the term was up. In addition to this debt, Carr owed an alehouse keeper seventy dollars. Titley reckoned that:

> *...about thirty pound will clear him; and his father perhaps had better pay that sum at once than continue him a weekly allowance, as I find he does thro' the hands of a merchant. This is a constant expense to his family, and only serves to keep him in such a way of life as will neither improve his manners nor understanding.*[27]

John Carr must have paid up because the errant William was soon home. As John wrote to Ralph Carr, then in Amsterdam, in November 1737: "Your poor bro. Will is come home but promises again he'll be very good. Pray God enable him to be as good as he promises."[28] Will was, however, to die, shortly before his father, in 1738.

In the early seventeen-thirties both Margaret Carr and her brother George were in London. They were both staying with a Mr Threlkeld at the Dial off the Strand and Margaret may well have accompanied her younger brother as companion and steadying influence at the beginning of his apprenticeship. Her letters to her brothers show that she was both humorous and endowed with common sense.[29] George does not, on the evidence of a letter of December 1731, appear to have been enamoured of his master and, when he found that due to the master's negligence he had extra time to serve, commented that, "...the worst Is to serve him so much the longer".[30]

It says much for the trading links between London and Newcastle that during the 'thirties so many of the Carr family were in London or were planning to go there. When Ralph was there in 1737, his brother Benjamin wrote enviously from Newcastle, "this dull place", asking for news of Ralph's doings in that "exciting place".[31] George Carr did not finish his apprenticeship in London, however, but due to the influence of Mr Emmerson, a wealthy merchant of Newcastle descent, who was a director of the East India Company, he embarked for India in 1736 where he worked for the next decade. He was back in England by the mid seventeen-forties and was rich enough to underwrite a shipping venture at his brother Ralph's request but the lack of further mention of him in Ralph Carr's papers suggests he died shortly afterwards while still in his thirties.

For one's children to die before one is a sad misfortune for a parent although it was a common enough occurrence in the eighteenth century, and John Carr's last years must have been much saddened by the death of half of his children. As he sat in his pew in Whickham Church, under which one daughter was buried, and contemplated the early deaths of six children, his faith, which was basically Unitarian, would no doubt have reconciled his mind though perhaps it was too intellectual a creed to comfort his emotions. He may well have found satisfaction in the promise of his son Ralph, at once the recipient of his business advice and religious guidance.

Ralph was as restless as his brothers and, when his apprenticeship still had two years to run, he was granted permission to travel overseas and set out on an extended tour of some of the commercial centres of Europe. The letters he received from his father demonstrate that his travels were occasioned by a serious determination to broaden his horizons and investigate commercial opportunities, though a young man's desire for adventure was probably a further motive. Although John was opposed to his son's going abroad on the grounds of his supposed poor health (Ralph had a persistent cough as a young man even though he was to live to such a ripe old age), he quickly appreciated the possibility that the knowledge gained and the contacts made on such travels could help expand his own trade in the Baltic and North Sea ports.

Even before Ralph left England and was staying in London, John was corresponding with him on business matters, advising him to caution their friend Emmerson about the risks of going into iron manufacturing: "...as Crowley's people can out do any in this country". In the same letter the thoughtful father told his son he was sending him mild beer (8 doz) and a pair of pistols "which I wish may come in time for flash mob one day".[32]

In a period when travel was difficult, arduous and dangerous, Ralph visited Paris, the north of France, Flanders, Holland, the Baltic cities and the newly founded capital of Russia, St Petersburg. His father was obviously very worried about his son and wrote to him in St Petersburg: "Considering you have a bad cough and have no strong constitution, pray whenever you write give an account of your health otherwise I shall be doubt of it". If he had known that Ralph had thrice ecaped from burning houses in the Russian capital, where wooden houses made conflagrations a constant risk, he would, no doubt, have added even more emphasis to the following advice:

> *Pray fail not to keep close to your duty to God Morning and Evening be*
> *thankful for preservation throw every day and protection every night and*
> *recommend youself to the care of heaven to keep you back from all sin*
> *and all dangers.*[33]

That Ralph's travels had a serious purpose and that he was already considered to have good judgement in business is revealed in another letter to him in St Petersburgh from his brother-in-law John Widdrington enquiring, "whether you think your stay there will be of any considerable advantage to your business". He added a warning that Ralph should not return home via Dunkirk as there was plague there.[34]

Six months later John was in Amsterdam and received a letter from his father full of business matters, which shows that the father was already relying upon his son to make contact with trustworthy foreign merchants. When doing business with far-off ports honest partners were even more vital than they were at home.

> *I hope you keep a journal and take notes as much as time will allow of*
> *everything worth your observation as also the names of the chief and safe*
> *traders and that you be very safe in dealing abroad everywhere because*
> *many have been undone by bad correspondents that set out very hopefully*
> *and with good stock.*

He went on to advise him to see some of the best trading places in France and to find out where there was a demand for lead and coal. These commodities might be Carr's and Tyneside's stock in trade but both father and son were prepared to contemplate more exotic items: "I enquired ...about the difference of Indian and Russian rhubarb which he makes very little difference in, but saith that from Turkey is accounted the best of em all".[35] Rhubarb was at this time still valued for its purgative rather than its culinary qualities and was a relative newcomer to the British Isles, having been introduced from Russia just over a century previously.

On his return to Newcastle Ralph finished his apprenticeship and was admitted to the company of Merchant Adventurers in July 1738, paying £5 in order to qualify two months before his ten years indenture was over. He had to tread carefully with the company in view of his father's defunct membership and because he had been trading on his own account. He seems indeed to have had goods imported for him as early as 1730 as the *Jane and Sarah* brought 5 1/2 tons of merchandise into the Tyne for him in July of that year[36] and to have continued throughout his apprenticeship, even while abroad, in breach of the company's regulations. If John had not allowed his membership of the company to lapse he would have saved his sons a great deal of trouble, as they could then have become Merchant Adventurers by patrimony instead of having to embark on ten year apprenticeships. As it was, Ralph had to watch out and John Carr warned him that the Merchant Adventurers would be "more particular with you than with others". He became a hostman the following year and was thus a full member of Newcastle's influential societies before his father's death. By that time he had already established himself as an active trader both in his own right and in association with his father and had expanded the latter's mercantile and shipping business.

John Carr, "the Patriarch", died in December 1739 at the age of seventy-two. Ralph later asserted that he was, "strong and healthy till 70 when he got a violent gravel or fault in the kidneys. But was actually killed by a quack violent medicine recommended by an old dotard, Dr Coteworth of London". Ironically the doctors were to be blamed for Ralph's own death sixty-seven years later. The attention of doctors was not an undiluted blessing in this period.

John Carr's will made provision for his unmarried daughters Margaret and Katherine who were left £700 each and for his sons George and Benjamin who similarly gained £700 legacies. Jane's children, John and William Widdrington, received the same sum. To Ralph, who was named sole executor went, "all my...funds, effects and real and personal estate".[37]

What all John Carr's copyholds, leases, shares in ships and other investments amounted to we do not know. That the estate of this coal factor, investor in lead mines, shipowner and timber merchant would be a complex inheritance is certain and it seems likely that he bequeathed to Ralph, not only a small estate and gentleman's residence, but a fortune of several thousand pounds.

References

1. The Carrs of Bishopwearmouth were also descended from the Carrs of Hetton and shared with the Carrs of Dunston Hill a common ancestor in William Carr of Woodhall near Hexham, who later moved to Hetton. The research of Grant Carr-Harris into the history of the Bishopwearmouth Carrs corroborates the connection of the Eshott and Hetton Carrs with William Carr of Woodhall. Mathew Carr, anchorsmith of Sunderland (1693-1757) and Mathew Carr of Ryhope JP (1729-79) came from the Bishopwearmouth line from which Lord Carr of Hadley, Home Secretary 1972-4, is descended. Grant Carr-Harris, *Ancestry of the Carrs and Cunninghams,* (Unpublished 1970; in the possession of Lord Carr).

2. Richard and his son John were the only Carrs mentioned in Abigail Carr's will. In that year, 1729, Richard, who died in 1734, was apparently a prosperous Newcastle merchant and John was in the East Indies. Little is known of Nathaniel's career; he died in the same year as his eldest brother, 1739, and seems not to have had children. A further brother, William, seems to have died in infancy and nothing is known of the sisters, save their names, Mary, Margary and Dorothy.

3. David Levine and Keith Wrightson, *The Making of an Industrial Society. Whickham 1560-1765.* (1991).

4. There were three branches of the Clavering family in the area: the Claverings of Axwell, of Chopwell and of Greencroft.

5. See Section 1, Chap.3.

6. Its opening was the scene of a Quixotic incident. Sir John Clavering and the vicar accompanied a wagon-load of punch down the way and Sir John, who

may have drunk too freely of the cargo, mistook a herd of cows for opponents come to pull up the rails and led a charge against the beasts.

7.   A feature of this society was the number of formidable women who concerned themselves in the coal trade. Both Anne Clavering of Greencroft and Lady Clavering were to be reckoned with, as was Lady Bowes.

8.   Henry Liddell to William Cotesworth, Dec.16, 1710. Liddell-Cotesworth Letters, Surtees Society, Vol. CXCVII, (1987) p.17.

9.   *Ibid*, 22 March, 1715.

10.   Hughes, p.129.

11.   John Carr to Ralph Carr, 1735. Carr-Ellison [Hedgeley] Mss., Northumberland Record Office 855, Box 4. The Carr-Ellison Mss. are made up of two separate collections catalogued as NRO.855 and NRO.165 (ZCE), the former are mainly papers of the Carr family transferred for safe-keepimg to the Record Office in 1974 and the latter, largely relating to business, financial, legal and estate matters, deposited by Dudding and Co., the Carr-Ellison Estate Agents in 1965. Each reference to a new or different sequence of documents is identified by the Box number in which the sequence is catalogued.

12.   *The Making of an Industrial Society*, p.66.

13.   Family of Carr, p.40-41.

14.   In 1790 John Carr's grandson, John, and Lord Thanet's grandson met in Vienna and became friends. (see Chapter 12). John's father, Ralph, wrote to him, telling him of this earlier connection and of Lord Thanet's gratitude as a sign of which he sent two fat bucks annually to Dunston Hill. *Family of Carr*, Vol. I, p.41.

15.   R. A. Fairbairn, *The Mines of Alston Moor*, (1993) pp.21-22.

16.   Pay bill for Alston Lead Mine, Christmas 1738. Carr-Ellison Papers, Box 2.

17.   Newcastle Trinity House Primage Account Books. Tyne Wear Archive, GU/th/109/5, 1729-41.

18.   *Extracts from the Records of the Company of Hostmen of Newcastle upon Tyne* by F. W. Dendy, Surtees Society Vol. CV, 1901,pp.160 and XXXV.

19. *Family of Carr*, Vol I, p.39.

20. As Richard Grassby has pointed out in respect of seventeenth century merchants ("English Merchant Capitalism in the late seventeenth century", *Past and Present* No. 46, 1970),

21. George Carr to John Carr, Dec. 9, 1731. Carr-Ellison Papers. NRO 855 Box 4.

22. *Newcastle Merchant Adventurers*, Vol. II, p.353.

23. Newcastle Trinity House Primage Account Books, March 24, 1741 Tyne Wear Archive GU/TH/109/5.

24. The English tended to refer to many continental currencies such as Danish *Rigsdaler* or the German *Thaler* as dollars.

25. John Carr to Ralph Carr 12 March 1737. Carr-Ellison Mss. NRO 855 Box 4.

26. Lord Harrington to Walter Titley, 4 March, 1737. Quoted in *Family of Carr*, Appendix VI, p.215.

27. Walter Titley to Lord Harrington, 23 April, 1737. *Ibid p.216.*

28. John Carr to Ralph Carr 14 Nov. 1737. Carr-Ellison Mss, Box 4.

29. A teasing letter to a brother, probably Benjamin, 29 Nov. 1733, tells of a dream she'd had of his marriage to a supposedly wealthy widow whose fortune turned out non-existent and goes on to warn against hasty marriages.

30. George Carr to Ralph Carr, 9 Dec. 1731, Box 4.

31. Benjamin Carr to Ralph Carr, 24 April, 1737.

32. John Carr to Ralph Carr, 8 April 1737. "Flash mob", in this context, probably meant thieves.

33. *Ibid*, 24 May, 1737.

34. John Widdrington to Ralph Carr, 24 May 1737. Widdrington added this note to a letter from John to Ralph which was addressed c/o Messrs. Cramond and Timmerman, St. Petersburg.

35. John Carr to Ralph Carr, 14, Nov. 1737.

36. Newcastle Trinity House Primage Account Books, 9 July 1730.

37. *Family of Carr*, Vol. I, p.217.

Chapter 10

Ralph Carr (1711-1806): His Business Life

Ralph Carr (1711-1806)

"...a Merchant has the most anxious time which can never be lessened while he thinks it worth the following...I can safely say I spent nearly Forty years of my Life in Slavery and often had the Mortification of seeing the very best concerted plans Overturned by a Variety of Untoward Accidents".

Ralph Carr

Ralph Carr was a remarkable man. His career demonstrates, not only his considerable business acumen and sound judgement, but the opportunities that were available to one with such gifts and some capital in the dynamic world of North-East England in the eighteenth century. In the history of his family, Carr's career marks the transition from merchant to country gentleman, though he himself always retained more of the outlook of the former than the latter. In the wider context, his life demonstrates the social fluidity of Northumberland and Durham in this period.

The view that the English elite was an "open elite" has recently been challenged[1] by historians and it is true that a successful merchant like Carr did not, though he acquired much land as well as wealth, become a peer of the realm or even a knight or baronet. There were, in any case, less than two hundred English peers until the last decades of the century; a new peerage like that of Ravensworth was unusual and came to the Liddells in 1747 after a century and a half of increasing prosperity, consolidated status and political influence, while the peerages granted to Lords Eldon and Stowell at the end of the century were in the special class of legal peerages. What we have to consider is the substantial number of North-East merchants, lawyers, land agents and coal-mine owners, who made their way into the ranks of the landed gentry in the course of the seventeenth and eighteenth centuries.

Edward Hughes considered that, "… a double revolution was in progress in the north in the first half of the eighteenth century-the disappearance of the old gentry on the one hand, and the rise of a new ruling class on the other-a change none the less revolutionary in its effects because its processes were as silent as leaven".[2] Hughes exaggerated the degree to which older and often catholic families were squeezed out, though many of them were. If some families were unable to withstand the vicissitudes of religious discrimination and an unfamiliar and more liberal economic climate others survived. For every decapitated Radcliffe or over mortgaged Heron or Chaytor, there were many Riddells, Charltons and Haggerstons who retained social prestige and substantial wealth. There was, nevertheless, plenty of mobility both upwards and downwards.

Where we find upward mobility it rarely took the form of a leap in one generation from merchant status to that of aristocratic great landowner but was more often a process over several generations by which families achieved parish gentry status and moved from thence to join the county elite. The successful businessmen who sought the station and security that possession of a country seat could bring, purchased in the first instance houses and estates which gave gentry rather than great landowner status. The greater number of new families, such as the Ridleys, Whites, Blacketts and Cooksons, made their way to their great houses and substantial estates at less than breakneck speed. The Carrs' progress was a cautious and gradual one.

Ralph Carr inherited a small but pleasant country house and estate and a few thousand pounds. At the end of his long life he was a considerable landowner and the sum of all his wealth and possessions must have been around £200,000. To put such a figure into perspective, a great landowner like the Duke of Northumberland had in the early nineteenth century an income of around £100,000 a year and a skilled craftsman an income of perhaps £1.10s a week. Carr was not, however, a man of great social ambition. He did not, he declared late in life, aspire, to found "what is called a family". He became a Justice of the Peace for County Durham, a sure mark of his accepted social status but, greatly respected and influential though he was, he did not aspire to greater positions such as those of sheriff or deputy lord lieutenant. He was always more the merchant in his attitudes than the country gentleman despite his considerable landowning.

If his father's business interests had been wide and various, Ralph's were more so. He was less concerned in mining ventures and did not have his father's intimate knowledge of that industry, but he inherited mining investments, controlled way-leave rights and continued to have shares in both collieries and in the Alston Moor lead mine. His greatest interest in the coal trade was, however, in the shipping and export of coal. This was not an age of narrow specialism in business and Ralph Carr was a consummate businessman who was prepared to deal on his own behalf, to invest, to insure and to lend. Colonel R.E.Carr depicts the width of his many interests as follows:

> *It included operations that would now be carried on by shipowners, shipbrokers, underwriters, general merchants, commission agents, bankers and, we might almost add, marine store- dealers. Nothing seems to have been too large or small for him.*[3]

He was, in short, a true merchant adventurer.

Hanover Square by W H Knowles (Gateshead Public Library)

His principal place of business was in Hanover Square, Newcastle, where his partner and nephew John Widdrington lived. He also had another business address at the "Head of Side" (the top of the Side, the narrow road that made its way up from the Guildhall to between St Nicholas's Church and the Blackgate of the castle) and a warehouse in the Close (a continuation of Sandhill by the riverside).

His most consistent interest was the one which he had prepared himself for during his year of travel in 1737, the trade between the North East and northern Europe. He had obviously made good contacts, especially in Amsterdam, and in his first decade in business after the completion of his apprenticeship established himself successfully as a trader in general merchandise to Baltic and Low Country ports. His knowledge of the Baltic must have been especially useful as the mid-eighteenth century witnessed an important change in the timber trade. In the first half of the century, British traders had tended to deal with Norwegian ports and only after this time did it truly become a Baltic trade to ports like Riga, Memel, Danzig and St Pertersburg.

The list of the commodities he dealt in includes: coal, iron, timber, butter, corn, flax, hemp, tar, grindstones, glass, spirits, wine, salt, whale-oil, lead, litharge, alum, copperas, cutlery and sailcloth.

Besides the trade between the Tyne and the Baltic and continental North Sea ports, Carr's ships and cargoes made their way up and down the east coast of Britain. Two cargoes landed at Stockton-on Tees give some impression of the variety of goods he traded in. The Customs Port Books record that on April 20, 1752, the *True Briton* with John Hobson carried for Ralph Carr: 2 pipes brandy (Qty. 326 galls.), 5 tons cordage, 15 cwt anchors and 2 tons cast iron. On July 6, 1752, an open boat (master, John Robson) arrived, carrying for Ralph Carr: 10 pipes Spanish wine (Qty. 1235 galls), 1 cask cider (Qty. 10 doz. bottles), 2 half hogsheads of brandy, dyes and glassware.[4] Spanish wine was worth £25 a pipe and was, Carr asserted, "much used at Bordeaux and Boulogne for mixing with the weaker clarets, as it has the acidic claret taste. The mixture is mostly sent to Ireland".[5]

He was naturally much involved in the coal trade with London, the greatest market by far for Tyneside coal,[6] and had business links with Hull and Whitby, while he did a great deal of trade with Edinburgh via the port of Leith. His connections in Amsterdam were to take him into the trans-Atlantic traffic and into shipping to and from New York, Boston and Newport, Rhode Island.

Letters to Carr from Joseph Paxton, his head clerk and office manager, give us a clear impression of the extent and variety of his mercantile activities. In the August of 1751 Carr was in Scarborough and Paxton kept him informed in detail as to the progress of the business:

> *The sloop for Dover took in a good many bottles more than Mr King expected so that she was not filled up till Tuesday last when the invoice bill of loading for 2311 dozen and 5 Cha. of coal was forwarded to Mr Minet, the amount is £222 2s & therefore the blank bill you signed must be cancelled and I have drawn another which may lay till you return...Capt. Bristow did not get his ship off the ground till Wednesday, Yesterday he took on 4 keels of coals, with 10 Cha. of grindstones; all the other things went down this morning and tomorrow he will clear out. Mr Caygill has given a credit for what money he wants & by next Post I shall send him the invoice, the Captain has left sufficient room for the goods to be shipped at Hull.... The 12 Chalders of coal for Messrs Brown and Godenus was put on board off Capt Shadforth and an account of the cost transmitted them...There was another letter last post from Mr Stephenson of Hamburg ordering two or three cargoes of coals, if ships of 12 to 15 keels can be had at £5 or £5.10 freight. I have therefore desired Mr Durham to be looking out for two such vessells and as price of coals are fallen at London he doubts not of getting them at £5.5 or under. if so I will load them with Mr Silvertopp's small coals and dispatch them.[7]*

Paxton's letters[8] record an astonishing amount and considerable variety of business: outgoing cargoes loaded included, as well as the staples of coal and grindstones, bottles, lead, litharge, iron, and salt and their destinations ranged from London to Cognac, Hamburg, Rouen, Nord L'Orient and Riga. This was two weeks business!

In 1746 Ralph took on his nephew, John Widdrington, as an apprentice. John was the son of his sister Jane and her husband John Widdrington, an attorney. John was given permission by the Merchant Adventurers' Company to travel abroad "for his improvement" in 1753. His letters home testify to the fact that he did indeed travel for improvement and that he had a considerable interest in the arts. He wrote from Holland to Isabella Carr, Ralph's newly married wife and sent her harpsichord music.

Music and Painting have each many friends in this watry land ...Messieurs Biscops and Brothers (private collectors) have laid out upwds of £30 thousand Pounds in Pictures-China-medals-Japan and Filigree work-shells etc., each sort so excellent of its kind & at once excited both surprise and pleasure.[9]

He otherwise served out his time with his uncle as his master and in 1755 he was admitted to full membership of the company. The following year he was made a partner in Ralph Carr & Co. In 1774 the name of the firm was changed to Carr & Widdrington. Widdrington, although a full partner in the firm, was always in effect the junior partner and it is significant that, after Ralph retired from the business in 1784, it declined rapidly without his guiding hand.

A letter from Ralph Carr to his partner casts considerable light not only on his business practices but on those of the generality of merchants in the shipping business:

> *I have often blamed myself that I did not explain to you and the rest in the counting house my motives which were always justifyable to myself, tho perhaps they might at sometimes not appear so to you for the mode of making out Invoices and Accounts of Sales. It is an undoubted truth that Every Factor acting upon Commission Business only must soon be undone, if he had not far more than 2% Commission it never was supposed that any man would be so mad as to receive out of the way consignments...and to be accountable for the full price such lumber happens to be sold at, no goods are ever sold for money down, you must give some decent time and even then receive off puts, if sold on Six months credit it is most frequently Nine or Twelve ere you get it, and too often be a Total or partial loss, A man would be a fool who did not deduct more than the Interest for any supposed time with a proper*

equivalent according to the risque you apprehend for the Del Credere and if you retail those Goods you are conscientiously entitled to the Retailors profits for you could either buy or import them yoursself & make the same or more advantage by so doing...

This was, he argued, the practice followed from "Petersbrough down the whole Baltock to Hamburg". It is clear from the letter that much of the problem was due to a shortage of specie which made credit the basis of trade and that things changed after 1760 "owing to a much greater plenty of money & the many banks". A considerable markup on goods beyond the ostensible commission was, no doubt, common practice but it is revealing that Ralph Carr was discreet enough only to belatedly reveal his methods even to his partner.[10]

Despite the great variety of its trading activities this merchant house was only one of Carr's many business interests. He was not a man to be content with one sphere of activity or be locked into a single partnership but was constantly on the outlook for new opportunities and investments.

He was one of the subscribing and managing owners of the Newcastle Whale Fishing Company founded in December 1751.[11] The company established a whale oil yard on the south bank of the river in 1752. No doubt this involvement in the Greenland trade followed naturally from his existing interests in the distribution of whale oil. He maintained his interest in the Newcastle Company until its original whaler, the *Swallow,* was lost in the Arctic in 1766.[12] Whaling was a risky business and Ralph Carr was involved in the insuring of whalers. In 1768 he informed the Dunbar Whaling Company that he had arranged insurance for three of their vessels to cover the voyage to Greenland and back for £1090, 98% to be paid in case of total loss, at a premium of £179. 12. 6d.[13] Ralph had, himself, some interest in the Dunbar Whaling Company but had largely divested his stake in it by the time of its bankruptcy in the early nineteenth century.[14] It had, he wrote at the age of ninety-three, been "ill-managed".[15]

If trade and shipping were his core business in the seventeen-forties and fifties, his creative business brain and knowledge of expanding markets led to his involvement in almost every possible aspect of economic life from the lending and insuring that underpinned and lubricated business life to the manufacturing of some of the articles in which he traded.

He, in partnership with John Cookson and Richard Ellison[16] of Thorn in Yorkshire and partner-manager Jonas Brown, opened an Alum works at Saltwick near Whitby. Carr put £4,000 into this business in the late 'fifties. Even the best of businessmen have their failures and the firm consistently lost money over three decades before it was wound up in 1789.[17] A number of letters to John Cookson cast some light upon the firm's failure. There were allegations about the works manager, Trattles, and Ellison too came in for some criticism to which he responded by urging the partners, "...not to revile one another but to take the most prudent steps we can to get quit of a bad bargain"[18]. Perhaps the main problem was the low price for alum. As Jonas Brown wrote to Cookson, "...neither Saltwick or any other allum work in the Kingdom -were or can be advantageous unless the price was always fixed at £20 per ton and upwards".[19] The partnership tried to hold out for such a price but this merely made matters worse.[20]

As we have seen, John Carr had had a share in lead mines at Alston Moor which were largely owned by Colonel George Liddell who had secured, against the competition of the London Lead Company, long leases on most of the mines there and in the Derwent Valley. This enterprise did not prosper and in 1744 George Liddell's executors decided to wind it up. Liddell's expectations of production had been optimistic and heavy expenses had been incurred, not only with the mines themselves, but in building a smelt mill at Nenthead and a refinery at Team Valley. Some seams worked by the company were almost worked out, attempts to find new seams had been unsuccessful, and the price of lead was low. Ralph Carr had been for carrying on and had lent the company over two hundred pounds. The company seems to have been wound up with a negligible loss and Carr's money was repaid.[21] The company's mines and smelt mills were bought up by the London Lead Company in 1745.[22] R.A.Fairbairn comments that "an unfortunate consequence of the failure of the company was the loss of confidence by Newcastle investors in the Alston Moor lead mines".[23]

Although he does not appear to have been involved in coalmining itself, as opposed to the trade in coal, he was well aware of the intricacies and problems of that industry. As he extended his Dunston Hill estate he found himself in possession of land valuable either for mining or wagon ways. As he wrote late in life to his younger son:

> *The Bishop Prince Palatine and absolute Lord of the Manors of nearly the whole County of Durham which are almost entirely copyholded of him and showed the coal in Dunston Hill (save my freehold part) belongs to him -yet neither he nor his tenants can work it till they first agree to pay what I choose to demand for liberty to build fire engines and lay wagon ways upon my copyhold lands.*

Carr had close links with Scotland and many business interests there. He had an investment in a glass works in Glasgow from which glass was exported to the American colonies and became a Freeman of the City of Glasgow. The British

Linen Company was another firm in which he was a "proprietor". This was a Scottish company set up by the Board of Trustees for Manufactures with the aim of improving the linen industry. It provided short-term credit to spinners and weavers and helped to market the finished products. Its backers included two of Scotland's most enterprising and infuential men. One was Lord Milton, a minister for Scotland under George 11, whose remarkable mother had secretly gone to Holland, taking weavers with her, to learn the Dutch technique of making fine linen, and then set up mills in her native Saltoun; another was John Coutts, an Edinburgh merchant and banker, who was an important and close businesss associate of Ralph Carr. Out of the British Linen Company was to develop the British Linen Bank, Scotland's third public bank.

Carr was also interested in the linen trade from the point of view of a shipper. In 1741 he imported a considerable quantity of flax: 20 bales on the *Friendship* in January, 40 bales on the *Anna* in May, 34 bales on the *Blagdon* in November and an unspecified amount on the *Anna* in December.[24] In September 1741 he wrote to Richard Thompson who was based in Amsterdam and much concerned with the Baltic trade: "Flax is a scarce article here tho does not advance in proportion to the prices in the Baltic and the difficulty of getting it home..."[25]

One of the goods Carr was most involved in buying, selling and transporting was that oldest and most basic of commodities, corn. In the first part of the century the North East exported increasing quantities of corn as did Britain as a whole, though there were years of poor harvests when, as in 1740, much grain was imported. Among the reasons for this were a stagnant population between 1720 and 1745, agricultural productivity, a booming continental demand as the Baltic increasingly ceased to fulfill its traditional role as the bread-basket of Europe, and the bounty the government paid on corn exports. As well as from southern England, much of this corn came from the east coast including Scotland, which in particular provided barley, rye and oats.

The North-East corn trade certainly owed much to agricultural improvement and for perhaps the only time in its history the region was an exporter of corn. The Act of Union had consolidated peace and law and order on the border and thus encouraged farming while the more commercial and scientific approach to agriculture which characterised the period found a ready acceptance in some parts of the region. By mid-century these developments had resulted in increased productivity and new roads, such as the "Corn Road" from Hexham to Alnmouth, enabled corn exports to be easily transported to the coastal ports of Alnmouth and Cambois ("Cammus"), near Blyth. Much of this corn was sent to Holland for both internal consumption and re-export, though some was sent to southern Europe, while the London market was an essential channel for both home and foreign sales.

London was the centre for the wholesale market, first at Bear Quay and, after mid-century, at the Corn Factors' Exchange at Mark Lane. Carr maintained close links with the London dealers, chiefly according to one authority to supply them "at times when the difference between home and overseas prices did not encourage export".[26] He supplied the London market, exported on his own account and took commissions for overseas buyers from such diverse quarters as France, Spain, Portugal and the north coast of Africa.

Carr worked closely with the firm which was possibly the biggest player in the corn market, the Coutts brothers, John in Edinburgh and James in London, who had established a network of factors throughout Scotland and England to supply their export trade. They had agents at Aberdeen, Dundee, Yorkshire, East Anglia, South Wales and in Northumberland and exported and imported corn between European ports from Ireland to the Baltic. As well as corn, they dealt in salt, beans and timber and indeed almost any cargo that would show a profit.[27]

John Coutts of Edinburgh and Ralph Carr had much in common. Neither had come from nowhere but had rather built upon the fortunes of successful fathers, even if they far outpaced the success of the previous generation. Like most businessmen of their time, they did not stick to one specialised line of business but few can have followed up so many opportunities as they did. Accomplished merchants, both soon appreciated that it was not just the movement of goods but the financial network that facilitated it that created profit. They traded in numerous commodities and understood their markets well; in parallel and often in alliance they took the small but significant step from being merchants, who took, gave and arranged credit, to becoming bankers as well as merchants.

By 1741 Carr had become a considerable exporter of corn[28] and was in regular correspondence with John Coutts in Edinburgh about the price of oats in Scotland and Tyneside. In late August 1741 he thought that Coutts had bought at too high a price, ten shillings a quarter, and wrote to John Coutts, "I should not be fond of buying at that price".[29] A week later he had changed his mind:

> *[I]…would be willing to have a cargo or two if could be shipped in 14 days at or around 10 per Qr. I am of opinion oats will be at or around that price a while after but till the Harvest be quite finished and the corn all gathered the farmers will not set about thrashing so briefly as to reduce the price.*[30]

In his import and export trade with Holland he dealt, among others, with his agents, T.M.Liebenrood in Rotterdam and J.A.Crop in Amsterdam, and with the resident British and Anglo-Dutch merchants, Anthony Simpson, a relative of the London firm Messrs.J. and T. Simpson, and the substanial and extended Hope family, Thomas and Adrian Hope in Amsterdam and Archibald and Isaac Hope at Rotterdam., among others. Things did not always go smoothly and there was an angry exchange of letters with Anthony Simpson in September 1741. Carr had sent Simpson a cargo of coal and Simpson had sent oats in return, that Carr found great difficulty in disposing of at a decent price: "I shall suffer by the cargo and therefore must expect your exert and help in dropping off the coales to the best account to attone for the loss which I must say is entirely owing to your acting quite contrary to orders". The oats, he declared were "such miserable stuff"; they had got wet before being put on the ship. Simpson had also been late in shipping the cargoes of oats and rye so that Carr had missed the time of highest prices and would lose £150 by this.[31] Whether Carr did actually lose by this transaction is doubtful as the high price of cereals, which he had foreseen in his letter of September 1 to John Coutts, continued and such was the local shortage that the export of corn from Newcastle was prohibited.[32]

Trade was a diversified matter and varied according to the seasons while the same ships carried numerous cargoes. Thus coal, wet and frozen in the winter, would be a favoured cargo in summer months, while corn was more profitable before the spring, when cargoes from the Baltic began to arrive in Holland once more.

The eighteenth century merchant required a private intelligence service and often had news of wars and peace before the newspapers or even governments. Wars disrupted trade, created shortages and led to shipping losses but, like bad harvests, they could bring bankruptcy to the ill-informed and opportunities to the man who knew what was happening. When, in 1741, Sweden declared war on Russia with ominous implications for the Baltic trade, Carr wrote to Richard Thompson:

> *[I] would be glad to hear what advice you have about the Sweeds whether or no they take any of our ships. I hear from Gottenburg that a ship from your place laden with cloath was taken...but expected shd be released. My last advice from St Petersburg made no mention at all of the War or any appearance of it.[33]*

In November 1759, Lord Ravensworth, who had early intelligence from the Admiralty of the defeat of a French fleet at the battle of Belle Isle, passed on the news to Ralph. In March 1761 he sent him a confidential letter suggesting that peace with France was imminent:

> *Supposing in the course of your great traffick abroad, that the conclusion of this war may make great alterations, I therefore take this opportunity*

> *to communicate to you that I have very great reason to believe there is at the juncture the prospect of a peace...*

Ravensworth's optimism was in the event unfounded and the war continued.

By the time of the Jacobite Rebellion of 1745 Carr was already a successful merchant who, as well as trading successfully with northern Europe, owned part shares in several ships and insured ships and their cargoes. He had also begun to act as a bill broker, that most essential function in the commercial world when there was as yet no nation wide banking system and there was a permanent shortage of currency. Carr's role during the 1745 rebellion demonstrates both his loyalty to the Hanoverian dynasty and how firmly he was established in the most influential and secure financial networks.

Members of the Coutts family were his most valuable contacts in the world of finance and banking. The Edinburgh firm of Coutts and Co., with whom Carr did considerable business, developed, as we have seen, from a merchant house into a merchant bank, no big step, for, before the coming of a national banking system, the provision of credit and the cashing of bills was part of the normal trade of many merchants. Coutts had taken this process further than most and two sons of the founder, John Coutts, Thomas and James, had by the 'forties moved to London and set up Coutts' bank in the Strand. Carr was to find his contacts with members of the Coutts family invaluable in developing, not only his trading interests, but his role as a bill broker, which was eventually to lead to his becoming a banker himself. This relationship with the Coutts family was to be of special importance during the 'forty-five.

The possibility and then the fact of a Jacobite rising posed both political and business problems for John Coutts. He had been Provost of Edinburgh in 1744 and was on good terms with George II's Scottish ministers in London, Lord Islay and Lord Milton. Coutts was to all appearances a committed Hanoverian, though Edna Healey has suggested his sympathies were with the Pretender and he certainly had Jacobite relations. He was, she suggests "torn between his Whig masters and his Jacobite relatives".[34] As a businessman and banker the rebellion posed obvious worries. His kinsman, Archibald Stuart, who was now Lord Provost, wrote to Lord Minto "the noise...about a rebellion has frightened everybody from parting with money. As they suspect there may happen to be a run on the banks, which must infallibly distress evrybody in this poor country".[35]

Ralph Carr wrote to John Coutts late in August;

I...would have you agree with Dawson [an agent or factor of Coutts's] to go back to Alemouth [Alnmouth] for ships are scarce here, it will not be possible to procure 310,000 in English coin even at this place in as hard time. I never knew it more scarce owing to our Colliers bringing no money with them from London....I had this week a large sum to pay for Dutys and had some difficulty to produce guineas. London bills are likewise plentiful however banknotes at three days sight may negociate more readily. you may send me up for £1000 or £1500 drawn on Bills of 100 to £200 & on above a week often they come to hand. you may send a messenger up shall endeavour in that time to convert them into English money. It will be enough to carry at once & then can advise you what can be done.[36]

On September 15, at a time when Prince Charles's armies had enjoyed considerable success and had taken Dunkeld, Perth, Dundee and Stirling, he again wrote to John Coutts:

You may be quite easy about your Gold, for should the Highlanders come this length it is easy to put it out of their way, but I apprehend they will not be allowed to cross the Firth nor have they any encouragement for so doing as so few are ready to join them. However the sooner I am cleared of it the better.[37]

A week or so later, after General Cope's defeat at Preston Pans, he had changed his tune and wrote to Alexander Coutts in London:

I forwarded you a packet by last post from Mr John Coutts which was brought me by his servant from Allanbank...I doubt not but ere this you've heard of Sir John Cope's defeat owing to the scandalous behaviour of the Dragoons who deserted without firing a shot and got to Berwick. We are in the greatest consternation not knowing but they may march here; this makes London bills not to be had almost on any terms, the people would give a premium as everyone is remitting away what they have.[38]

The dangerous political and military situation obviously posed great difficulties for merchants. These included: the blockade of Scotland, instituted by a Treasury order allowing no ships to clear for Scotland and which was intended to prevent arms and munitions falling into Jacobite hands; the threat from French warships and privateers[39]; and the problems for shipowners and masters caused by the pressgang. The shipping business became encumbered by government regulation, while the dangers from French warships put up insurance costs and necessitated a convoy system. In a letter to one of his Dutch business associates, Liebenrood of Amsterdam, Ralph Carr refers to having to wait for permission from the government to ship goods to Holland and added,"...we have never any ships go from here with any other convoy than the coal fleet". All the vessels in the coal fleet were armed. Convoys cut down insurance costs on voyages to Newcastle as well. When Carr was asked to insure the *Royal Oak* for a voyage from St. Petersburgh to the Tyne he offered to half his price if the vessel sailed with a convoy.[40]

But the crisis enabled a confident Hanoverian like Ralph Carr to both demonstrate his loyalty and make his mark as a financier with connections with the highest circles in both banking and government. In 1745 he was directly advancing money to army officers against drafts on the Pay Department in London and also paying out sums to local gentlemen who had themselves advanced money to the army against similar drafts. Thus he paid out £2,500 to commanding officers in Newcastle and reimbursed Matthew Ridley £500 and then £200 for two orders drawn at Berwick in September by General Cope on the Paymaster General.

He, together with John Coutts, was also able to speculate in the corn required by the army, though he was very critical of the way the army supply department handled its purchases:

> ...the people in Northumberland are going mad with their oats owing to Gomez Ara [the Government Commissary] sending among them. I persuade myself the army would be better and cheaper supplied if they would admit of an open trade.

He also thought that many of the government officials were more interested in lining their own pockets by selling the best grain to private dealers in Scotland and keeping the poorer corn for consumption by the soldiers.[41] He and the Coutts brothers combined to buy up great quantities of corn, storing it at Alnmouth, Cambois, Hartlepool and other ports until it could be sent to Scotland.

Early in 1746 Ralph Carr was involved in a very considerable financial transaction. Maberly Phillips recounts how, in 1746, as the Duke of Cumberland's army advanced on Scotland, Carr, between February 11 and March 7, remitted £30,000 to Scotland for the troops-in one sum of £20,000 and five of £2,000. Cumberland himself only stopped at Newcastle for a few hours on January 28 so that it is unlikely, though possible, that he personally commissioned this transaction. The army command foresaw that credit would be difficult to come by in Scotland and that without hard cash the army would have difficulty in paying the troops and getting supplies. The government was therefore in the market for loans and Ralph Carr, with his banking connections, was able to raise this very substantial sum.[42]

That Ralph Carr did indeed transmit such large sums of money to Scotland at this time is certain but there is an alternative theory to that put forward by Phillips as to its use. The Royal Bank of Scotland, not unnaturally, suffered a crisis of confidence during the rebellion and John Coutts was a director of that bank. According to Edna Healey, the Royal Bank drew £2,000 in gold on the Bank of England made payable to Coutts in Newcastle. Coutts, himself, absented himself from Edinburgh during part of the period of crisis, staying at Allanbank Banks close to the Border. Carr may have arranged to have this money sent on to Scotland.[43]

Either or both these accounts may be correct, as there could well have been a number of transactions, for Carr was in communication with London and Edinburgh bankers throughout the crisis and, realising the government's need and the profit to be made, was able to provide money where and when it was needed. In December he had written to John Coutts in Edinburgh about the continuing shortage of currency for the payment of troops: "When Mr Wades army lay here they drained this place and as trade is much at a stand many of their bills still continue on hand, I have them myself for a considerable sum."[44] On February 4 he wrote to the bankers Messrs Middleton in London acknowledging the receipt of their letter of January 30 announcing the dispatch of £2,000 by carrier.[45] Middleton's Bank was clearly acting as the London agents for the Royal Bank of Scotland at this time and was to eventually pass into the hands of James, John Coutts's son, and become Coutts Bank of London.

Ralph Carr's political loyalties and his business interests were thus able to go happily hand in hand and, if John Coutts had secret Jacobite loyalties, he disguised them well and his business decisions suggest certainty in the victory of the Hanoverian establishment. The episode, indeed, demonstrates the confidence that Carr and the country's leading finance houses had in the government's ability to put down the rebellion. There were few men in the North, however, who could have raised large sums so quickly and there can be no doubt that in doing so he rendered the government a singular service. Carr's reward lay not just in a percentage for his efforts and risk but in his enhanced reputation and standing as not only a loyal but a most capable subject.

The Atlantic Trade

Despite this spectacular financial coup and the continued development of his bill-broking activities, the cornerstone of Carr's business life continued to be the trade with northern Europe and the Low Country ports in particular. The relations between Carr and a number of Amsterdam merchants were usually cordial and based on mutual trust and confidence and it was almost as a by-product of his Dutch connections that he moved into the trans-Atlantic trade.

The loss of the erstwhile New Amsterdam to the British almost a century previously had not ended the connection between Holland and New York and there was a brisk trade between Amsterdam and the British colony. The Dutch sold the colonists German linens, Bohea and Hyson tea and various manufactured goods and bought logwood and rice in return.

The problem, which the Dutch merchants faced, was that British government regulations forbade, as a result of mercantilist policies, direct trade between foreign countries and British colonies. The European goods, that the merchants exported to New York, had therefore to be landed in a British port and receive Customs clearance before proceeding across the Atlantic. This was where Ralph Carr came in. He could facilitate their commerce by looking after their shipments, usually on American ships, when they used Newcastle as the British port they had to call at on their way to America. He could see to it that their papers were in order, smooth the way with British officials and ensure they got Customs clearance. In return he secured his important connections with the Dutch and made a modest profit from his commission.

William Roberts has argued in his essay, "Ralph Carr: A Newcastle Merchant and the American Colonial Trade"[46], that Carr entered the trans-Atlantic trade as a favour to his Dutch business associates. This was undoubtedly one of his motives and, although the traffic between Amsterdam and Newcastle was a lucrative affair for both Dutch and English traders, Carr's part in opening up the trade with the British colonies to his Dutch associates did serve to make them more dependent upon him. There were also, however, positive advantages for the Newcastle merchant: even if Carr's profits from the transactions were small in relation to those made by the Dutch, they were worth having; he was an almost compulsive businessman, who snapped up small profits even while he made big ones; and he hoped that the small sums he made from the American trade would eventually become substantial.

It is true that Carr's part in the expanding Atlantic trade gave him comparatively modest profits from his important role, though they were not negligible and Roberts is too dismissive of what must have amounted to a profit of over a thousand pounds a year. As he charged the standard 2.5 per cent, he gained between £25 and £250 a shipload, depending upon the size of the ships and cargoes involved. The ships would spend two or three days in the Tyne, Carr would see to their documentation, forward copies of the invoices to New York and draw a bill on the Amsterdam merchant for his remuneration. He would make some extra profit by making up a full cargo, for the ships were rarely full, with "ballast" commodities which he sent on his own account. Coal was the most common "ballast" cargo but he also shipped glass, grindstones and anchors.

Such cargoes didn't make great profits and could present problems; coal exports required bonds signed by the ship's master, which were only released following receipt of a certificate of importation from the customs officer of the colonial port. Carr often experienced difficulty and delay in getting the certificates sent back to him. A more serious problem was that he found himself conniving at a certain amount of smuggling. The Dutch merchants would send a ship to the Tyne with a small cargo for New York on which duty would be paid and a large consignment for some foreign port, usually St Thomas in the Virgin Islands. Carr realised that in fact the bulk of the cargo would be unloaded in New York and began to worry that the Customs officers would get suspicious. He was, after all, the man who paid the duty and who would be held responsible. He wrote to Adoniah Schuyler and Henry Cuyler, owners of a thirty-five ton sloop, after one such transaction in which they had carried a cargo for Anthony Simpson of Amsterdam, which officially consisted of three parcals of cloth for New York and a great quantity of goods for St Thomas:

> *I wish our friend Mr Simpson had considered the matter better; for I am afraid the Commissioners will have some suspicions when they see this report, for your ship should either had no goods for New York or at least half the cargo, however I hope all will come safe to hand.*[47]

All in all Carr was providing a considerable service to his Dutch friends and the New York merchants and ships' masters. His influence and knowledge made him invaluable when it came to matters of salvage and either extracting ships from the hands of privateers or getting compensation for them. Carr was, himself, not averse to dabbling in privateering. He had an interest in the Newcastle Whaling Company's vessel, *Dolphin*, which took out letters of marque during the Seven Years War. Thus, he was in a position to give good advice when the Boston merchant Ralph Inman sent a cargo on a ship under the command of a Captain Jones which was impounded by the French at Dunkirk. He wrote in February 1749, "Captain Jones's ship has been condemned. This is greatly to the advantage of all involved as the insurers will have to pay...if he had been released you would have had a bad account of the cargo and no damages would have ben recovered from the Captain". A month later he was able to tell Inman that the underwriters had paid up.[48]

Ralph Carr was thus going to a great deal of trouble and taking some risks to facilitate a trade in which he had only a small share of the profit. The "small" profits do however need to be seen in the context of the profits and risks of shipowning. Carr had, for instance an eighth share in the *Molly and Jenny*, which cost £1637 to build and fit out and made only about one hundred pounds profit in her first two years.[49] In contrast the Atlantic trade provided a modest but steady income. It is not surprising, nevertheless, that he began to look around for more profitable cargoes than the ballast ones he usually loaded on ships bound for the colonies.

Much of the New York-Amsterdam trade was carried by American vessels and in a letter to Henry and John Cruger and Nathaniel Marston, owners of the ship, the *Dragon*, Carr set out his wares:

> *I shall carefully observe your orders for anchors and grindstones...I shall at all times be glad to receive your commands for any article you may wish from hence, we have sundry articles here which can answer well with you, and I ship great quantities yearly for all parts of America, as crown glass bottles and all sorts of glass wares, sheet lead shot all sorts of woolens which we have from the makers , particularly Leeds cloths, Kendall and Wakefield and Halifax manufactures, rugs, blankets. We have also factorys erected for coarse and fine checks and Osnaburghs from 5 3/4 to 8d per yard and there is a bounty upon them of 1 1/2 per yard, which brings them very low and they are made to great perfection. I am just now shipping a large quantity of both for Boston. We have also Crowleys and other factories for nails, edge tools and every kind of iron ware, coarse felt hats and coarse earthenware, both which go to your place.[50]*

As Roberts has demonstrated, Ralph Carr was consistently unsuccessful in his attempts to sell northern manufactured goods to America. There seems to have been nothing wrong with the goods he offered. The Osnaburghs were a type of coarse linen specially made with the American market in mind, for the colonists had been accustomed to buy coarse German linen. Carr, as we have seen, had an interest in the British Linen Company, which marketed this product, and he claimed to be able to undercut the prices of the German product. He probably could, especially as there was duty to pay on the German linen shipped from Hamburg and Amsterdam.

The response was disappointing. He got a couple of orders for earthenware but it proved unsuitable for the New York market and another two for linen but they were not repeated. The bulk of the thirty-six shipments he dispatched to New York between 1749 and 1761 were cheap bulky goods.

His trade with New England ports was similarly largely a matter of making up with ballast cargoes shipments sent by other merchants. In this case the other merchants were from London and Hull. Again he tried to interest New England merchants in more profitable cargoes and did succeed in carrying on a more varied trade with New England. He also began to receive goods such as tar, mahogany and whale oil from Boston merchants.

As Carr wrote to the Boston merchant Ralph Inman, he could supply:

> *...all sorts of Woolens and have manufacturies in the Neighbourhood of all kinds of ruggs, Blankets, Kendal Cottons and variety of striped woolen goods. also checks and Coarse Hats... Borthwick Sail Cloth and Vitry- and a Coarse sort of Norwich Goods, Oakum and old Junk are good articles to fill up empty room.*[51]

In similar vein he wrote to William Bowdoin, this time itemising, "Coals, Lead, Shot, Sheet Lead, Grindstones, Bottles, Glass of all sort, Anchors, Edge Tools, Nails etc." He went on to suggest that Bowdoin sent him a cargo of tar: "Tarr always sells here better than at Hull or London, the sort fitted for this market is the thick Yellow Tarr and the greatest demand for it is in August and September."[52] His trade with Boston was he claimed already extensive: "I have had cargoes from your neighbours Messrs Wendell, Hutchinson, Inman, Quincey, Cooper etc. and they always found the goods I sent on return well bought and to their satisfaction."[53]

The trade in tar was encouraged by the government which paid a bounty on Tar imports and Carr received at least three consignments of tar between 1749-51. One of these from Bowdoin consisted of 978 barrels of tar as well as 4,800 barrel staves. Carr sent him a cargo of Scottish linens and various North-East products in return. Unfortunately, Bowdoin objected to Carr's handling of the transaction. The tar was sold on credit, the bounty bill sold at a discount, which was the usual practice because the Treasury was always tardy with its payments, and the return cargo paid for out of the proceeds. Bowdoin sent no more consignments.

A further two way transaction in 1751 saw Carr receive a consignment of tar from Ralph Inman and Thomas Gunter and send in return a cargo of local products and Scottish linen worth £424. Inman was largely satisfied with the goods but Gunter complained about the price of the Scottish Osnaburghs and the packing and handling charges.[54]

When American merchants visited Newcastle Ralph Carr found it easier to persuade them to take consignments of his merchandise. Thus Samuel Engs, a Boston merchant, visited Tyneside in 1751 and he, together with Stephen and William

Greenleaf, received a cargo of goods worth £210. It was a similar personal contact with an American visitor which resulted in a disastrous deal with William Fletcher, also from Boston, to whom Carr sold and shipped twelve and a half tons of merchandise to the value of £951 when Fletcher visited Newcastle in 1750. The Boston merchant remained in England until the spring of 1751 and paid promptly for the goods before ordering sail cloth, lead, linens, cottons and glassware to the value of £333. Carr was never to receive payment for this latter order and an increasingly angry correspondence dragged on for years. Carr wrote to Fletcher in August 1752:

> *I am really quite tired out with writing to you year after year upon this same disagreeable subject and am sory your repeated promises which only pass for words of course, however, I shall wait until the Fall for their accomplishment & no longer.*[55]

Fletcher continued to send vessels to Carr for coal and other bulky cargoes and paid for these by bills on London merchants. Undoubtedly Carr could have seized the ships Fletcher sent him, but he refrained from doing so until it was too late, for Fletcher, greatly in debt, absconded to the Dutch colony of St. Eustatia in 1755. Carr had, of course, good Dutch connections, and with the aid of the Hope brothers of Amsterdam, was able to get the Governor of St Eustatia to put pressure on Fletcher. As late as 1761, Fletcher had still not paid and was offering to pay twelve shillings in the pound on a debt then increased by interest to about £500.

Clearly the American trade went far from smoothly for Carr. There was a profit to be made with the ballast cargos, from the commission he made for his services in clearing the goods of Amsterdam merchants, and from the few cargoes of tar and naval stores he imported, but his efforts to export more lucrative cargoes came to little.

William Roberts has argued that Ralph Carr's failure to sell more north country manufactures in the American market was due to his caution: "Carr was simply unwilling to assume any appreciable risk in the colonial trade, either by extending long-term credit to his correspondents or by sending goods to them on his own adventure". Carr did, in fact, occasionally give credit but Roberts is basically correct. Carr thought the quality and price of his goods sufficient to make them attractive to North American merchants but those merchants were interested in dealing on credit and were able to get generous terms from British merchants in other British, especially West Coast, ports. As Roberts demonstrates, the real money was to be made by sending consignments of goods to colonial correspondents and allowing them to sell them on his behalf. Nor was Carr interested in joint ventures. He turned down an offer from Gulian Verplanck of

New York and Daniel Crommelin of Amsterdam to take a third interest in a vessel that would have sailed between Amsterdam, Newcastle and New York with Carr and Crommelin providing the outward cargoes. His future brother-in-law Christopher Scott took over the share proposed for him.

The world of the eighteenth century merchant was one beset by risks: bad debts, dishonest correspondents, shipwrecks, pirates and privateers. Ralph Carr, who was doing well from the European trade and already moving via bill-broking towards becoming a banker, must have seen no reason to stake his hard-won fortune on the undoubted possibilities of financing exports to the colonies.[56] He was able to supplement his profits by looking after the interests of his Dutch associates and by providing ballast cargoes but his efforts at selling more expensive and manufactured goods were too tentative and cautious to bear fruit.

In considering Ralph Carr's involvement in the Atlantic trade a "failure", William Roberts judges his record against those merchants who were foremost in that trade and fails to take sufficient account of the way his trade with the colonies fitted in to his wider business interests. He failed to become a major trader in the export of the most profitable commodities but carried on a steady and rewarding trade with the colonies, a trade which lasted far longer than the period covered by the two letter books which form the basis of Robert's study. Ralph Carr continued to be involved in the trade with the American colonies right up to the beginning of the War of Independence, as we can see from his continuing correspondence with such merchants as Ralph Inman, Thomas Hutchinson and Philip Livingstone.

Clearly the Tyne's trade with the colonies was considerable, for, when the British government in 1765 sought to compel all shippers trading between British and American ports to provide bonds of £2,000 as a surety against their carrying tea, brandy or other contraband goods, the refusal of the Newcastle merchants to comply brought the Tyne's colonial trade to a standstill. Carr wrote to Livingstone:

> *This port was more affected by the £2,000 bonds than any other in England as we load out a far greater number of ships & it being absolutely agreed by all people in Trade here not to comply with them, we could no more break through it than any single person with you could support the Stamp Act- but you, Sir, certainly don't consider Fatal consequences that must have attended us and our employers if we had once compl'd with such bonds . In less than twelve months we should have been a million deep to the Exchequer, which is worse than an inquisition, in bonds for a parcell of Tarrs who wd be sure to smuggle...*[57]

Soon the troubles that would lead to war were making trade difficult and Ralph Carr was writing to his old associate Inman, "We dare not venture to ship any [glass and earthenware] least the humour still prevails against all English commodities". A few months later he was complaining to Inman that the colonists resisted every British tax without ever considering how they would contribute towards, "the millions of debt England is loaded with, and taxed to the very teeth to pay the interest of, and which was actually expended in the sole defence and support of the Colony".[58]

Carr's correspondent Thomas Hutchinson was a person of some importance in the history of Massachusetts and indeed America. A leading merchant of the colony and a man who devoted his life to its public welfare, he rose to high office but suffered because of his loyalty to the crown. In 1765, when he was Chief Justice and thus had responsibility for enforcing the trade laws even though he was personally opposed to the Stamp Act, his house was wrecked by a mob egged on by the middle class tradesmen, known as the Sons of Liberty. His was the tragedy of an intelligent loyalist, who could appreciate the fatal combination of dictatorial language and timorous action that marked the policies of Greville and Townshend and who could sympathise with many of his fellow colonists' complaints while condemning the extreme responses of the radicals.

He became Governor of Massachusetts in 1771 and was at first, as a native born man with long service to the colony's interests, popular. Carr, who had a long-standing dispute with him over a minor commercial transaction, had nevertheless never allowed this to sour their personal relations and he wrote to him in May 1773, agreeing to accept £35 in settlement of the dispute and congratulating him upon his policies as governor: "We most sincerely wish you every felicity, and hope your unwearied endeavours for the peace and prosperity of England and the colonies will meet with deserved success".[59] Unfortunately, when opposition to the Townshend duties was at its height, Benjamin Franklin passed to Hutchinson's opponent, Samuel Adams, stolen copies of letters that the Governor had written to the government several years previously. Franklin did not wish the letters to be made public but they were published with a selectivity and some twisting which made Hutchinson appear an enemy to Massachusetts. His authority was compromised just before the event known as the Boston Tea Party, shortly after which Hutchinson was recalled to England to face an enquiry. He wrote to Carr after being cleared by the enquiry: After the most cruel calumnies and Slanders I am happy in receiving from the King as full and explicit an approbation of every part of my conduct as perhaps has ever been given to any servant of the Crown".[60] Ralph Carr replied promptly:

Honorable Sir, Your much esteemed favour of the 2nd Inst. gives me great pleasure, as it confirms your safe arrival from a place where even your life was in Emminent Hazard, & the highest approbation of his Majesty must be thought by every man in Old England no more than what your uniform conduct highly merited, am glad to see so great a number of the most respectable and dispassionate in New England are of the same sentiments.....As it materially concerns our trade here, permit me Sir, to request the favour of your sentiments whether you think New York and the Colonies so far South as Carolina will joyn with Boston in stoping all Imports and Exports, shd they be so mad as to put this scheme into Execution, I suppose they wd neither receive the Goods sent out nor load our ships back. Perhaps you will soon have some authentic accounts as to this particular, and your communicating them would be a very singular favour done to, Sir, your most obedient Humble Servant...[61]

When the British retaliated to Boston's decision to stop trade with England by closing the port of Boston completely, Carr managed to continue trading with Massachusetts by sending ships to Salem. He thus managed to continue to trade with the colonies up to almost the point of final rupture of their relations with Britain. In 1774 he wrote to John Alsop a New York merchant on business matters, concluding with his wish for "the restoration of that harmony betwen Great Britain and the Colonies which is essential to the intersts of both". Alsop was at that time attending the First Continental Congress at Philadelphia of representatives from twelve of the colonies and Carr's wish was not to be realised.

The Old Bank. The First Provincial Bank in England

During the 'forty-five rebellion, Ralph Carr had, as we have seen, been able to be of considerable service in providing gold for the Hanoverian cause in the north of England and Scotland. His success in this enterprise demonstrated his acumen, his wealth of business contacts and the trust men were prepared to place on his word. In raising the money he depended greatly on his important banking contacts, John Coutts in Edinburgh and Alexander Coutts and his partner William Campbell in London.

Some ten years later, Ralph Carr founded his own bank and the historian of Northern banking, Maberly Phillips, has discerned a direct link between the achievement of 1745 and the establishment of the Old Bank in Newcastle: "So well did Mr Carr carry out the commission entrusted to his charge, that after the country had been restored to quietness, Mr Campbell suggested to him the suitability of his forming a bank in Newcastle which he subsequently accomplished".[62]

Ralph Carr was peculiarly well qualified to undertake the role of banker. As a general merchant with a myriad of interests he knew the economy of the region inside out. He knew the shipping business, the coal trade and the agricultural economy intimately. His assessments of the probity, ability and wealth of local merchants, coalowners, farmers and even landowners were to be valued. He was well travelled and had useful contacts in continental and American ports as well as in London, Hull, Edinburgh and Glasgow. He had also carried on a bill-broking business from the beginning of his career.

In 1755 (the exact date is uncertain but it is not later than August), Ralph Carr in association with Matthew Bell, John Cookson and Joseph Airey set up the Old Bank in Pilgrim Street. They were a formidable combination: Matthew Bell was a member of a family which owned much land at Woolsington and Ponteland, he had married the daughter of Richard Ridley of Heaton Hall, was a coal fitter and was prominent in the civic life of Newcastle; John Cookson came from a wealthy industrial dynasty and owned a glass-works at Close Gate; while Joseph Airey came from a numerous and influential nonconformist family. The site was suitable for a bank in terms of historic associations as it was close to the junction with Silver Street, the old name of which was Jews' Gate. The bank thus stood upon two layers of banking history, the time when most of the essentials of modern banking were provided by the Jewish merchants of that quarter and the more recent past when silversmiths had provided banking services.

Although Carr had three partners, his was the initiative as his account of its formation makes clear:

> *[It]...being my Hobby Horse and solely begun by myself, on Mr Campbell's recommending my beginning a Bank at Newcastle and to take his nephew, the present rich banker, Thomas Coutts, as my first apprentice, and after three years as a partner, for their father, my worthy friend John Coutts, Esq., had beg'd me to be a father to his four sons, this accident gave me the first notion of a Bank, and it proved to be advantageous to us and of the utmost service to the country, till too many others started up.*[63]

The coming of provincial banks was an important step in the development of the British economy. We have seen something of the difficulties and risks merchants had previously encountered in their transactions with different parts of the country, while even gentlemen of means had to find cumbersome ways of providing themselves with money when travelling. Maberly Phillips has made out a convincing case that the Old Bank was the first proper provincial bank in England:

> *This I claim to be the first regularly constituted country bank in England...They adopted all the branches of a regular banking business-opened drawing accounts, received money on deposit, discounted bills, and issued drafts on their own agents.[64]*

There were a number of merchant houses throughout the country that carried out banking business but they did so as part of and in the same premises as other branches of trade.

Although the bank had already been operating for several months, the formal partnership agreement between Carr, Cookson, Bell and Airey was not drawn up until January 1756. Its capital at this date was small, each of the four partners putting £500 into the concern. But this was really only the nominal capital, as there was unlimited liability and its real capital was the total wealth of the partners, all men of substance. According to the *Newcastle Courant* of 23, August 1755, "notes are issued from the Bank established in this town by a company of Gentlemen of Character and fortune which will be of infinite advantage to this place and County".

Confidence in the new bank was soon established and its notes widely accepted. The announcement in February 1757 that the Collector of Excise would accept the bank's notes in payment or give cash for them was an early indication of its soundness. Soon Northumberland landowners were ordering their tenants to take payment in the bank's notes[65] while in 1771 meetings of merchants in Newcastle and Sunderland voted to accept the notes of either the "Old" Bank or its new rival the Exchange Bank.

Bank notes were a great easement of the continual shortage of coins as well as being much more convenient to carry and transport, but they brought with them the danger of forgery. Originally all the notes issued by banks were from a single plate, the amount and the name of the person to whom they were issued being filled in by hand and for sums above a pound this practice was retained for many years. The Old Bank had its plates made by a London printer. Mathew Bell, in a letter to Carr, then in London, asked him to get a plate made for twenty shilling notes to the following specifications: "One pound in the body of the note, and the twenty shillings at the bottom, are both intended to be in the like hand that the sum is wrote in in the notes of the Bank of England, and a Scrawel in the left hand".[66] Even so, forgeries occurred and in 1765 there were instances of counterfeit notes belonging to the Old Bank and the British Linen Bank being in circulation.

At the end of its first full year of operation, the bank had issued notes to the amount of £17,648, had fifteen depositors whose combined balances came to over £10,000, had itself £11,502 in the bank of Vere, Glyn and Halifax and £505 with Coutts, cash in hand came to about £3,000 and there was one overdraft for just under £1,000. The profit for the year was £1,017.19s.7d. The bank's progress can be seen in the figures for 1771: notes issued amounted to a value of £82,000, there were forty-two depositors (one of which had £16,000 in the bank), twenty-one overdrafts (one for £6098) and the profit for the year was £3,705. By 1776, the bank's record year during the time of Ralph Carr's involvement, the totals in the balance sheet were £278,708, the profit was £5,712, while the list of customers reads like a roll call of all those most prominent in Newcastle and county society.

In 1768 competition emerged, when Aubone Surtees and Rowland Burdon opened what became known as the Exchange Bank, and in 1772 the Tyne Bank owned by Messrs. Baker, Shafto, Ormston, Cuthbert and Lamb opened for business.

The ownership of the Old Bank had already seen some changes. In 1762 or 1763 Joseph Saint became a partner and, after Airey's death in 1770, Carr's nephew, John Widdrington, took his place in 1771.The firm was now known as Bell, Cookson, Carr, Widdrington and Saint and the capital was divided into eighteen parts, the three old partners retaining four shares each and the two new partners getting three shares each. Saint and Widdrington, probably because of their lesser stake, were bound to attend to the daily business of the Bank without extra remuneration.

As Cookson and Carr were both partners in the Alum works at Saltwich, there was a considerable overlap between the interests of that company, which banked with the "Old Bank" and those of the bank itself. At one time the Alum Company was some £13,000 overdrawn and was sitting on a large stock of alum that it could not sell at a decent price. Ralph Carr told Cookson he would furnish what cash he could spare and lent the bank £2,000 and then other amounts against the company's overdraft. A satisfactory outcome to this matter seemed to have been achieved when the stock of alum was sold to Sir George Colebrooke and Carr confidently expected to be repaid the £5,000 he was now owed. A run on the bank, however, meant that his money was needed and it was used by Cookson and Widdrington in London to support the bank's credit. Colebrooke then defaulted on further payments for the allum. In 1771 an unsigned document, set out the position: "Mr Carr has always looked upon his money as advanced", the bank was now in a position to pay him back, Carr needed the money and should be paid.[67]

In 1775 there was a further reshuffle with Bell, Cookson, Carr and Widdrington being allocated seven shares each and Saint four, the latter having to attend to the bank's daily affairs without extra remuneration. Clearly Widdrington had put additional capital into the partnership. John Cookson and Joseph Saint both died in 1783 and in 1784 a new partnership was formed with Bell, Carr, and Isaac Cookson

(John Cookson's son) as the senior partners with four shares each, Widdrington in an intermediate position with three shares, and James Wilkinson and Thomas Gibson as the junior partners with one and a half shares each and responsibility for day to day business.[68]

By this time Ralph Carr was tired of banking and he withdrew from the Old Bank on 31 December 1787. A new partnership consisting of Sir John Eden Bt., Sir Matthew White Ridley Bt., Isaac Cookson, John Widdrington, James Wilkinson and Thomas Gibson was formed and the bank's name was changed to Sir John Eden, Sir Matthew White Ridley, Cookson, Widdrington & Co.

Exactly why Ralph Carr gave up his share in the bank he founded is not clear. He had made money out of the enterprise, some forty thousand pounds over thirty-two years, though this was a modest return when we consider the financial risk involved. Mrs Caroline Twistleton, his granddaughter, thought that he withdrew from the bank because of "over-caution". She wrote: "…he unfortunately withdrew in this year as later it made the fortune of several families and became very prosperous. His nephew John Widdrington became a partner in it in 1787."[69]

Ralph was indeed a cautious man in the sense that the good gambler is cautious. He knew that business involved risks and, though in general he sought to minimise them, he was prepared to put his money on a favourite when he had studied the form carefully and had made up his own mind. He thought banking was becoming too risky as more people moved into it.

At times he regretted having much of his capital tied up in the bank when it might have been earning more elsewhwere: "The Bank has also made many thousand pounds by the interest on money in their hands, for I most absurdly charged them with no interest for a good many years". On another occasion he told of not being able to get his money out when he wanted it:

> *Too often have I lost many thousand pounds by having large sums in their hands and often wanted to buy stock or other advantageous purposes. They could not pay me on the peace with America, of which I had early intelligence. This prevented me buying stock to the amount of 12 to £15,000, by which I evidently lost, as I shewed to them, circa £6,800 for on examining their discounts then in 1785 with Mr Gibson, we found Discounts of near a hundred thousand pounds Intirely locked up and they could not pay me, and the same has repeatedly happened. I always had large sums in the Bank and Messrs -----&-----were generally greatly in Debt to the Bank, and were in fact the cause of my Loss.*

What probably precipitated his departure was the appearance of another competitor bank, Davison Bland & Co. By 1790 this bank had losses of £2,151 after two years trading and this inaugurated a difficult time for the region's banks[70] and may well be taken as confirmation of Carr's judgement.

In truth he was sick of his partners and desired no more partners.

> *Having from this time quitted the the Bank and turned over my share to Sir John Eden and Sir Matthew Ridley, for if I had continued a banker it should have ben on such terms so as to have taken in no other partners, nor were they necessary, as my fortune alone of near a Hundred Thousand Pounds was a sufficient security to the Publick as not being under settlements"...I calculaye I have at this day made more than Forty Thousand Pounds by my concern in the Bank, but now that so many Banks are begun here and everywhere the business is spoiled, and must be attended with daily hazard, and their competitions disgraceful. I must wish my nephew J.W. was clear of it.[71]*

He wrote with the pride of the independent entrepreneur, with a little sideswipe at entailed aristocratic and gentry wealth. He distrusted the judgement of his partners and, though he liked his nephew and old business partner, John Widdrington, and had in fact been instrumental in introducing him to the bank, he had become doubtful of his business judgement. Widdrington, a cultivated man who was an early President of Newcastle's Literary and Philosophic Society, lived beyond his means. He was getting deeply into debt but continued to maintain an extravagant life-style: "Of all the indolent, thoughtless spendthrifts I have ever heard of J. Widdrington has astonished me the most".[72]

In that the "Old Bank" throve for many more years, Ralph Carr can, indeed, be seen as having left it precipitously, but, if his foresight was too long sighted, it did perceive the banking collapses that were to come and many provincial banks collapsed. The Old Bank continued to be prosperous well into the next century, becoming known as Sir Matthew White Ridley and Co. When the Bank of England set up in Newcastle in the 1820s, Isaac Cookson boasted that it was hardly necessary as Newcastle banking was so sound. Yet, shortly afterwards, following Sir Matthew Ridley's withdrawal, the Old Bank became insolvent.

Ralph Carr had, nevertheless, performed a considerable service for Newcastle and assisted the expansion of the economy of the region in acting as the father of northern banking.

Tithe Farming[73]

The prosperity and the expansion of the North East economy in the eighteenth century owed much to coal and to a burgeoning trade in manufactured and consumer goods but its motive power, like that of the economy of the nation as a whole, remained agriculture. Ralph Carr had, as we have seen, been active in the corn trade since early in his career, and his familiarity with the economics of agriculture led to what was by far the most advantageous bargain he struck, his acquisition from Merton College, Oxford, of the right to collect the Great or Rectorial tithes of Embleton and Ponteland. The lease of these tithes was passed on to Ralph's son and grandson and remained in the family of the Carrs of Dunston Hill for some eighty years, greatly to its profit.

Tithes were an ancient clerical privilege by which the church was entitled to a tenth of the produce of the land. Great tithes were held by rectors. A *rector*, in the word's ecclesiastical usage, is a parson or incumbent whose tithes are not impropriate. His position is thus superior to that of a *vicar*, who originally acted in place of the rector or was the representative of the religious community to which the tithes had been appropriated. Vicars were later simply incumbents of parishes in which the Great Tithes were impropriated or appropriated, though they usually had lesser tithes in addition to their glebe lands.

Most rectors were thus clergymen and incumbents who collected their own tithes but the positions of incumbent and rector could be separate and the rector be a corporate body or a layman. With the Henrician Reformation, many rectorial tithes previously held by religious houses passed to the crown and from thence into the hands of laymen (the Ellisons were the impropriators of Jarrow). In the case of Embleton and Ponteland it was a corporate body, "the Warden and the Scholars of the House of the College of Scholars of Merton in the University of Oxford", which was the rector and also had the right of presentation to the livings.[74] Ponteland gives the clearest example of the division of roles between rector and vicar, for adjacent to the Church of St. Mary were both a rectory and a vicarage.[75]

It was Ralph's marriage to Isabella Byne in 1758 that gave him the opportunity to purchase the lease of the Embleton and Ponteland tithes. Her father, the Reverend Henry Byne, who had died in 1732, had been a Fellow of Merton College and Vicar of Ponteland. He seems to have been the lessee of the rectorial tithes at Embleton and Ponteland as well as the Vicar of Ponteland. He was, indeed, often referred to as "the Rector" and, with his vicar's living together with his rectorial tithes, must have been a wealthy man.

Although a new vicar, Dr Robinson, was appointed to the living on the Reverend
Byne's death, Mrs Anne Byne continued to live at the Rectory and she and her
daughter were living there when Isabella became engaged to Ralph Carr. The
Rectory, as well as various cottages and adjacent fields, went with the great tithes;
the Vicarage was where the incumbent lived and was itself endowed with some
vicarial or lesser tithes as well as glebe land. After Byne's death, the tithes of
Embleton and Ponteland were leased by Merton to the Hankey family[76] but Mrs
Byne clearly maintained a residual interest in them and it was upon her death in
1769 that Ralph Carr acquired the lease. He had, however, to purchase it from Sir
Joseph Hankey, paying him the very considerable sum of £8,700. This was to prove
a wise investment.

Tithes were unpopular and difficult to collect while local knowledge was needed to
estimate accurately the yield and value of harvests. It therefore made sense for
Merton College to let out the tithes of these distant parishes. The system they
adopted was to let them on a twenty-one year lease with, if everything was
satisfactory to both parties, the lease being renewed every seven years for a further
seven years. This seven year cycle enabled the rent for the tithes to be assessed on a
sliding scale against the price of corn. The corn tithes were by far the most valuable
of the great tithes, although the Ponteland tithes in particular were extensive,
including as they did "Corn and Grain Wool Lamb Turnips and Potatoes" instead of
the usual great tithes of corn, hay and wool.[77] The tithe-owners were further
protected by a system of "fines" exacted from the lessee or "tithe-farmer" at the
time of renewal which reflected any great variation in the value of the tithes. The
fines varied more than did the annual rents and, in the circumstances of the
eighteenth century, the movement was uniformly upwards. Nevertheless, the system
had disadvantages for the college as for others who rented out tithes: the margin of
profit that went to the tithe-farmer was considerable and the introduction of a profit-
taking intermediary between farmer and tithe-owner must have contributed to the
unpopularity of this ancient tax. As Ralph Carr appreciated, however, the tithes of
Embleton and Ponteland promised considerable profit to a capable man.

The annual rent paid by Carr, as by his predecessor, Hankey, was modest, around
£200 a year, and, indeed, it only varied slightly with the price of corn. As late as
1810, Ralph's son, John, was only paying £270, though the following year the
college estimated the annual value to be nearly £5,000.[78] What they did adjust was
the amount of the fine to be paid at the septennial renewals of the lease, raising this
as the price of corn increased. Thus when Hankey first took over the lease in 1733
he paid a fine of £274, in 1748 he paid £431-15-0 and in 1755 a meeting of the
college council decided to put the fine up to £1,000.[79] As in 1762 the college valued
the tithes at £600 a year and was prepared to accept about £8000 over twenty-one
years for them, it would appear that there was, even on the college's own valuation,

a profit of over £5000 to be made by the lessee over the period. But how accurate was the college's valuation? It was almost certainly a gross underestimate otherwise such a large sum would not have been paid when the tithes changed hands.

The college did make half-hearted efforts to get a realistic valuation. In 1744 it provided Dr Robinson, the Vicar of Ponteland with five guineas to enquire into the real value of the great tithes but clearly little had been done by the time Ralph Carr became involved.[80] Some idea of the college's competence in this matter can be glimpsed from the college council minute of 2 Sept. 1769 when it was stated that a valuation could not be done on the Embleton and Ponteland tithes as the season had advanced too far and the harvest had made some progress.

> *It is agreed that the college will accept the usual fine of £1,000 for the present renewals (the lease to commence from Michaelmas 1769) and that Mr Ellison[81] be desired at a proper season to employ Mr George Dale of Hebburn near Newcastle to visit the said Rectories and to make and return to the college a true and fair estimate of the same distinctly - and that in order thereto Mr Ellison be empowered to communicate to Mr Dale an abstract of the particulars of those Rectories granted in the lease.[82]*

The lease to Sir Thomas Hankey was accordingly renewed for seven years for a fine of £1,000; although Carr purchased the tithes about this time it was not until the next renewal in 1776 that Merton formally leased them to him.[83] Although the annual value was now estimated by the college to be £800, it was not until 1790 that the fine was raised to £1,200.[84]

The tithes were a source of great profit to Ralph Carr but their collection was a troublesome matter. Ponteland was close to Dunston Hill and to Carr's usual place of business, Newcastle, but Embleton (or Emildon as it was often referred to in the eighteenth century) was quite remote. With the Ponteland tithes came the Rectory, other buildings and land but at Embleton there was no building or land available to him, a major difficulty should he seek to collect the tithes in kind instead of money. Not surprisingly he often sub-let the collection of the Embleton tithes or came to temporary arrangements with local landowners as when in 1783 he accepted an offer of rent for a seven year term for the tithes from Charles Grey.[85]

Tithes, as has been noted, were unpopular and, indeed, they became more so as the century wore on and as farmers became more prosperous and agricultural yields increased. Landowners and farmers resented them and doubly so if they were nonconformists or catholics. In general it may be said that rectorial tithes weighed more heavily upon farmers and vicarial tithes upon cottagers and even the rural poor. In extreme instances vicars, often themselves rather poor, sought to extract tithes from the cottage gardens of indigent villagers[86], while there were even instances of attempts to draw tithes on acorns and fallen apples.[87] At Ponteland the vicar's small tithes extended to such moduses (*modus decimandi*) as one penny in lieu of tithes of wood burnt, one and a half pence for a calf and one for a farrow cow instead of the tithes of milk, while sixpence was taken as the tithe on hens.[88]

Throughout the eighteenth century, the cultivation of new crops gave rise to disputes as to whether they were subject to tithes and, if so, who owned such tithes, rectors or vicars? It says much for Ralph Carr's determination and perseverance that at Ponteland, he won the argument as regards turnips and potatoes. The vicar, Dr Snowden, declared in June 1773, "...that the tithes of turnips and potatoes though vicarial are not customary there", while at the same time the college expressed the hope, "...that tenant and rector will find some way of resolving their dispute about tithes of potatoes and mustard seed".[89] As the agreement over the commutation of tithes for the township of Ponteland of 1841 shows, however, Carr must have won at least so far as potatoes were concerned as the rectorial tithes were held to be: "Corn and Grain Wool Lamb Turnips and Potatoes"[90].

As is often the case, the richer tenants could be more troublesome than the poorer. One farmer who held land both within and outside Ponteland parish resented making the smallest tithe payment and annually would move his ewes to tithe-free land just before lambing; the lambs being born he would drive them back again, having escaped the lambing tithe.

At Ponteland, however, things seem generally to have gone fairly smoothly. There does not seem to have been a need to resort to the original method of exacting payment, "drawing" every tenth stook of corn, every tenth rig of potatoes or every tenth lamb or fleece, a system which was increasingly avoided and which was expensive and time-consuming. Carr lived close enough to go Ponteland before harvests and, with the aid of valuers, make an estimation of the likely valuation of the crops. Usually he was able to arrange terms with the farmers and he would collect the tithes in person. Thus, on August 15 1782 it was rent day at Ponteland and Ralph Carr went there "as usual".[91]

Embleton was much more troublesome. There he had to rely much more on an agent and the farmers there were often reluctant to agree terms. Sometimes, as we have seen, Carr sub-let the tithe collection but on other occasions he had, despite the difficulty of the enterprise, to collect in kind. In 1777 he had to instruct his agents to draw the whole of the Embleton tithe.[92] After he had collected from several farmers in kind the rest submittd and came to agreements as to payment. That a local tithe collector could be much more effective than someone who lived at a distance was shown in 1794 when Carr, having turned down the tenants' offer of £651, sub-let the tithes to a local farmer, ready and able to draw them, with the result that the tenants had to pay this person twice as much to prevent him from doing so. Carr recorded: "I hope this will make them honester. They are a sad set of people". The next year the tenants meekly paid Carr £822.[93]

The owners of tithes tended to do rather well out of parliamentary enclosures as land was usually allotted to tithe owners in lieu of the tithe income they lost as a result of the enclosures. At both Embleton and Ponteland however the common land enclosed was subject to vicarial rather than rectorial tithes so that it was the vicars and not Carr who benefited in 1744 and 1761 respectively from allocations of land by the Commissioners. Carr unsuccessfully made a claim when Rennington and Long Houghton commons were divided but the villagers denied ever having paid tithes to Embleton.

The agricultural prosperity occasioned by the French and Napoleonic Wars greatly increased the value of the Embleton and Ponteland tithes and began a period of hard bargaining between the Carrs and Merton College. In 1797 the tithes were valued at £960 per annum and the fine was put at £1,200.[94] Between 1800 and 1801 a spectacular leap in the price of corn took place so that the combined Embleton and Ponteland tithes yielded £2,376 in 1800 and £3,491 the following year. Despite the fact that the rent for the tithes had been agreed at the usual modest figure of £200, Merton College, having calculated that wheat was selling for the fantastic price of 25s a bushel or 200s a quarter, asked Carr to pay £500. Wheat was certainly fetching unheard of prices in 1801 with an average of 119s a quarter[95] but, as Ralph protested, Merton's estimate was nonsence and prices were, in any case, lower in the north. Nevertheless, he paid up, as well he might, for his tithe-farming was more profitable than ever. Merton asked for what was, in the circumstances, only a modest increase in the fine to £1,440 at the 1804 renewal[96] and in the last year of Ralph Carr's life, 1806), the tithes brought in £4,290, a net profit of at least £3,500.[97]

As well as, what was in effect, a sort of tenant right to the tithes, Carr had a number of cards to play in any dispute that threatened to end with the college refusing to renew his lease. In 1774 he noted:

> *Dr Hoadley, the late Bishop of Winchester, has a certain fixed annuity of £30 per annum out of the tithes as a descendent from one of the old proprietors…but in case I or my successors should have more Fine demanded than is thought proper to be complied with, or that by any other accident the Lease should fall in to the College, I asked Sir Thomas and Mr Chaplain Hankey what then became of the annuity? They said it*

> *would be lost to Dr Hoadley and his sequels, Else he should manage*
> *about it with the College, and when that high fine was demanded and no*
> *renewal for twelve or thirteen years, the Bishop in several of his letters*
> *said he should lose his annuity if matters were not accomodated, and he*
> *took a great deal of pains to bring the Warden and fellows to compliance*
> *and was of the utmost service to the Hankeys.*[98]

Clearly rights to the rectorial tithes belonging to corporate bodies could become encrusted with barnacles in the shape of the claims of the descendents of previous proprietors. In June 1822 the college authorised the Bursar to tell Ralph's grandson that they would indemnify him if he resisted the claims of a Mr Griffith to an annuity of £30, "as after a careful examination of the old leases...no trace of any such annuity can be found".[99] In the case of Bishop Hoadley, however, the annuity was more of an assistance than a burden and, indeed, the Hankeys had refused to buy him out, even though he was prepared to accept a modest price, preferring to retain his interest and influence.

Carr could also have embarrassed the college if they had refused a renewal in that they had negligently allowed the Vicar of Embleton over a period of fifty years to collect the tithes of lambs and wool, though these were properly rectorial and were as such included in Carr's lease and he believed he could have demanded compensation. There was never, however, any great crisis in Ralph Carr's relations with the college though his son and heir, John, was not to have such smooth dealings with that society.

Ralph was perhaps lucky as he entered into contracts with the college at a time when the church and many ecclesiastical and corporate bodies were just beginning to become more businesslike in their attitude towards their property and their income from it. His "luck" was perhaps good judgement in that he may have realised that Merton would only awake slowly to the potential of the tithes while agricultural prosperity would produce profits enough to keep the college satisfied and allow him even greater rewards. Even Ralph, however, could not have foreseen the enormous rise in agricultural prices occasioned by the French Revolutionary and Napoleonic Wars and the consequent increased revenue for tithe-farmers. The very size of those increases was enough, however, to alert Merton to what it was missing out on and Ralph's son and grandson were not to enjoy such large profits.

Of all Ralph Carr's business ventures, the renting of the Embleton and Ponteland tithes was the most risk-free; it was also one of the most profitable and he seems to have made as much from it as from the infinitely more risky venture into banking. This must have suited him for he was a cautious man as we have seen both with his involvement in the North American trade and with his decision to quit the Old Bank when he did. Had he been less cautious or more greedy he might have become richer. Alternatively he might have lost his hard-won fortune.

Hedgeley Hall in 1892 by Thomas Hope McLachlan

As his active business career drew to a close, Ralph Carr purchased land, always a secure investment, but one that was increasing in value in this period. Apart from their material value, landed estates provided pleasure and status. The main purchase was High and Low Hedgeley that had belonged to the Carrs of Eshott, remote cousins of the Dunston Hill Carrs. Thomas Carr, son of a junior scion of this family, who had emmigrated to Georgia earlier in the century, inherited, through a series of disinherited heirs and heirless inheritors, the bulk of the Eshott estate. Returning from America in 1771, he found himself translated from being a tax-collector in Georgia with an income of some £150 a year to a country gentleman with land worth some £1,500 a year. He lived as if he had several times that very respectable income and, after two decades of extravagance and display, was bankrupt with his lands mortgaged to his solicitor, Thomas Adams of Alnwick, who foreclosed on them. In 1784 Ralph Carr bought the Hedgeley property from Adams and set about enlarging the house, adding a north wing, and extending the gardens.

Hedgeley, close to the Breamish Valley and the Cheviots, must previously have been very remote from Newcastle but Ralph Carr purchased it just at a time when turnpike roads were to make the journey by carriage easier. Its idyllic setting, with towering hills to the west and the coastal plane stretching to the east, made it a perfect country seat. Ralph and his son John made extensive alterations to the house which, over time, was to become the family's favourite residence.

A few years later he bought the Prendwick estate, half of it from the heirs to his son-in-law, Charles Byne, and half from a Mr Alder. This was a sensible purchase as Prendwick is only about six miles south-west of Hedgeley, but at a time of agricultural prosperity and rising land values, Carr had to pay dearly for it. The valuers thought it worth £10,000 but Ralph had to pay £12,500 at an auction. Mrs Carr thought, "people do not know what to do with their money". The matter obviously resulted in some bad feeling between the Carrs and the younger Bynes and Isabella Carr wrote to her younger son: "Throughout this whole business your father has not only been honourable but friendly to them, and if they think otherwise they are devoid of common sense".[100]

About the same time as he purchased Prendwick, Carr bought Bygate Hall and Lumsden from the Bells of Woolsington. This property was bought for his younger son, Ralph, but, as the rental was worth only £563, Ralph jnr. was obliged to sell it back to his father upon his marriage and the property eventually went with the rest of the landed property to the eldest son, John.[101]

Within a few years of his retirement from business Ralph Carr had thus converted much of his merchant wealth into land. He was thus a considerable landowner just as the wartime boom in agriculture, which did so much for his tithe income, began a rapid inflation in the price of land. He was also in a position to leave his eldest son John that which more than anything gained respect and social position, inherited land.

Although he was a most capable businessman with a shrewd insight into the workings of the economy of his day, he had not enjoyed business. As the quotation which begins this chapter suggests, he considered that a merchant has "the most anxious time" and that he had spent nearly forty years "in Slavery and often had the Mortification of seeing the very best concerted plans Overturned by a Variety of Untoward Accidents".[102] Part of the problem was that cautious, shrewd and honest as he was, he realised that too many of those one had to depend on in business were rash, gullible or far from honest. Although in the nature of his business life he had often to depend on others and engage in joint ventures, this usually made him uneasy and not without reason. Eighteenth century business depended upon trust to a remarkable degree, being without the security of modern banking or insurance and with a legal system which gave a far from ready resolution of problems. Trustworthy himself, generous and a good judge of character, Ralph Carr was, nevertheless, all too well aware of the dangers present in every transaction. He was by inclination something of a lone wolf in his business life. At the beginning of his career, he worked quite closely with his brother-in-law John Widdrington, who was his legal advisor as he had been to John Carr. He also occasionally cooperated with his other brother-in-law Christopher Scott of Hull in business ventures. More importantly he was for many years in partnership with his nephew, the younger John Widdrington, both in his merchant house and, along with John Cookson, Mathew Bell and others, in the "Old Bank". But he came to view John Widdrington as rash and improvident, while the experience of unsuccessful ventures such as his whaling investments and the failure of the alum works impressed upon him the dangers of relying upon the management of others.

Having made a fortune of some hundred thousand pounds, Ralph retired from active business life as a merchant and banker in his early seventies with some relief. His tithe income and land purchases were yet to make him richer but he was free to enjoy his private world with his young family, for he had married late in life. His business career had been remarkable both for its success and for the variety of his interests. If, by the time of his retirement, the Merchant Adventurers of Newcastle had become a largely honorific body, few Adventurers in the heyday of that society could have had such a good claim to the name as Ralph Carr.

References

1. See Lawrence and Fawtier Stone, *An Open Elite? England 1540-1880*, (1984).

2. Hughes, p. XVIII.

3. *Family of Carr*, p.46.

4. Stockton-on-Tees, Custom House Port Books, 1752, PRO E190/252/1. I am indebted to Dr A. Barrow for these references.

5. *Family of Carr*, p.67. Colonel R. E. Carr also refers on the same page to a letter to Messrs. Herries in London from Ralph Carr, telling them that two pipes of white wine that could not be sold are being returned "after filling them up with raison wine". The wine trade was ever one in which *caveat emptor* applied.

6. Along with all Tynesiders, he felt that the London coal-dealers took an undue share of profit and in a letter to George Silvertop, a pit-owner, he wrote: "Sorry I am that there is a single penny decline in coals or advance in measure; it can answer no good purpose to any one beside the coal buyers at London". Ralph Carr to George Silvertop, 10 Feb. 1768.

7.   J. Paxton to Ralph Carr 9 Aug. 1751.

8.   *Ibid* and 11 August 1751.

9.   J. Widdrington to Mrs I. Carr, 30 April, 1754, Box 5.

10. Ralph Carr to John Widdrington, undated.

11. Other managers were John Stevenson (master mariner), John Simpson (merchant), Ralph Soweby (coal fitter), George Colpitts (coal fitter), Mathew Bell (coal fitter), John Cookson (glass maker) Aubone Surtees (coal fitter), Robert Carrick (merchant), Peregrine Tyzach (glass maker) and George Headlam (shipbuilder). Anthony Barrow, "The North-East Whale Fishery 1750-1850". Ph.D. thesis, Newcastle Polytechnic 1989, p.93.

12. Information provided by Dr. A. Barrow.

13. Family of Carr, p.67.

14. The full name of this company was the East Lothian and Merse Whale Fishing Company. It was established at Dunbar in the same year as the Newcastle company, 1751-52, and John Cookson with whom Carr often associated in business enterprises also had an interest in it. Barrow thesis, op cit., p.93.

15. Ralph Carr to Sir Alexander Kinloch, 21 Aug. 1804. Carr-Ellison Mss. NRO 165 ZCE Box 32.

16. Richard Ellison does not appear to have been a relative of the Ellisons of Hebburn. He founded the bank of Smith, Ellison & Co. of Lincoln.

17. The Alum works must have appeared quite an attractive investment. A major problem for the alum industry along the north Yorkshire coast was the difficulty of transportation but Saltwick with its small cove had better loading facilities than were avalable to most of the alum works along this coastline with its high cliffs. See Peter Barton, "The Alum Ships", The Dalesman, March 1969.

18. Robert Ellison to John Cookson, July 10 1781. NRO. 855 Box 4.

19. Jonas Brown to John Cookson, 28 July 1782.

20. Robert Ellison to John Cookson, 15 Feb. 1781.

21. Nicholas Walton (Walton was Lord Ravensworth's Agent) to Ralph Carr 11 Sept. 1744. The executors of George Liddell owned 65 shares, Mr Lowther 7, Thomas Airey and Robert Ellison 5 each, John Airey and Mr Hinton 3 each and Messrs. Hicks, Hall, Gilpin and Carr 2 each. John Carr had owned an eighth of the previous company but the company of which Liddell was the principal investor was a much bigger concern so Ralph Carr's two shares do not necessarliy indicate a smaller investment.

22. See Athur Raistrick and Bernard Jennings, A History of Lead Mining in the Pennines (1965) and R.A.Fairbairn, the Mines of Alston Moor, British Mining No. 47.

23. Fairbairn *Ibid*, p.21.

24. Newcastle Trinity House Primage Account Books, 1741.

25. Ralph Carr to Richard Thompson, 5 Sept. 1741. Carr-Ellison Papers NRO 165 ZCE 10-14.

26. David Ormrod, English Grain Exports and the Structure of Agrarian Capitalism (1985), p.40.

27. *Ibid* and W. Forbes, Memoirs of a Banking House (1859) p.7.

28. In 1741 Carr imported into the Tyne 227 lasts of corn (a last=10 quarters=80 bushels) and 20 bags of barley. Newcastle Trinity House Primage Account Books, 1741.

29. Ralph Carr to John Coutts and Co., 25 Aug. 1741. Carr-Ellison Mss., NRO. 165 ZCE 10-14.

30. *Ibid*, 1 Sept. 1741.

31. Ralph Carr to Anthony Simpson, 24 Sept. 1741.

32. During the summer of 1741 Carr imported a considerable amount of corn: 50 lasts on the *Lark* 24 June; 50 lasts on the *Elizabeth* 3 August; 10 ½ lasts on the *Elizabeth* 14 August; 40 lasts on the *Newcastle Packet* 14 August; 15 lasts on the *Newcastle Packet* 29 August; and 20 bags of barley on the *Newcastle Packet* 28 September. Newcastle Trinity House Primage Account Books.

33. Ralph Carr to Richard Thompson 5 Sept. 1741.

34.   Edna Healey, Coutts and Co. 1692-1992. The Portrait of a Bank (1992) p.72.

35.   *Ibid*, p.69.

36.   John Coutts to Ralph Carr, 29 August 1745, ZCE 10-16.

37.   Ralph Carr to John Coutts, 15 Sept. 1745.

38.   Ralph Carr to Alexander Coutts, 24 Sept.1745.

39.   Even after the rebellion was over French privateers continued to be a problem. In 1746 the vessel, Culloden, in which Carr had a fourth share, was captured by the Dunkirk privateer, the Louis. The vessel, worth about £220, was ransomed and Carr who handled the payment of the ransom got a commission of 2 per cent from his fellow owners, though he must still have lost by the incident. With his wealth of continental contacts, he must have been good at handling such matters and in the same way looked after the payment for the release of the Margaret of Kirkwall and again received a commission.

40.   Ralph Carr's Account Book. Undated.

41.   Family of Carr, p.64.

42.   See Maberly Phillips, A History of Banks, Bankers and Banking in Northumberland, Durham and North Yorkshire (1894) and Family of Carr p.64.

43.   Edna Healey, Coutts and Co. 1692-1992. A Portrait of a Private Bank.(1992) pp.72-75. See also "A very great public convenience: the origins of banking in County Durham" by John Banham, Durham County Local History Bulletin, 1994, No. 52.

44.   Ralph Carr to John Coutts, 13 December 1745.

45.   Ralph Carr to Messrs Middleton, 4 Feb. 1746.

46.   William I. Roberts III, Ralph Carr: A Newcastle Merchant and the American Colonial Trade", Business History Review (1968 Autumn).

47.   Ralph Carr to Adoniah Schuyler and Henry Cuyler, 22 July 1749. Quoted by Roberts ibid.

48. Ralph Carr to Ralph Inman, 17 Feb. 1749 and 13 March 1749. NRO 165 ZCE 10-14.

49. Bills and Accounts. Carr-Ellison Papers.

50. Ralph Carr to Henry and John Cruger and Nathaniel Marston, 26 June 1750. Quoted by Roberts, "A Newcastle Merchant".

51. Ralph Carr to Ralph Inman, 17 Feb. 1749.Carr-Ellison Mss, ZCE\10\14.

52. The Tyneside demand for tar was occasioned by the heavy pounding the hulls of colliers took when coal was loaded in their holds, resulting in the need for constant caulking. August and September were months when the coal trade was slack and when the weather made it a good time to repair the ships.

53. Ralph Carr to William Bowdoin, 10 Feb. 1749.

54. Roberts, "A Newcastle Merchant", p. 282.

55. Ralph Carr to William Fletcher, 2 Aug. 1752.

56. He was in 1773 invited to speculate in another distant market. Messrs John and David Brown, merchants of Copenhagen, were old associates of Carr's and when, in 1772, David Brown was made Governor of all the Danish settlements in India he invited Carr to invest a few thousand pounds in a plan to send a ship with goods for the Indian market in the hope of "some extraordinary profits". The following year he asked Carr to lend him two or three thousand pounds for three or four years at 6% p.a. David Brown to R. Carr, 21 April 1772 and 10 Aug.1773., Box 4.

57. Ralph Carr to Philip Livingston, March 1766. NRO ZCE 10-23.

58. Ralph Carr to Ralph Inman, 12 April and 18 Nov. 1768. NRO ZCE 25.

59. Ralph Carr to Thomas Hutchinson, 12 May 1773, NRO ZCE 10-27.

60. Thomas Hutchinson to Ralph Carr, 2 July 1774.

61. Ralph Carr to Thomas Hutchinson, 8 July 1774.

62. Maberly Phillips, Banks, Bankers and Banking in Northumberland, Durham and North Yorkshire (1894) p. 177. Banks, p. 175.

63. Quoted in Family of Carr, p.70.

64. Phillips, Banks pp. 174-5.

65. A considerable advantage to the bank was that Carr's nephew and business partner, John Widdrington was from 1767 auditor to the Duke of Northumberland and would no doubt bank the rents he received from the Duke's tenants at the old bank. See John Banham, "Business Development and Banking in North East England 1755-1839". Sunderland University Ph.D thesis, 1997.

66. Matthew Bell to Ralph Carr, 6 Feb. 1768.

67. Document regarding Ralph Carr's Allum Investment. 1771. Unsigned but probably by Thomas Gibson.

68. The above is largely based on Maberly Phillips pp.178-9 but his account is contradicted in some particulars by that of Colonel R. E. Carr in Family of Carr, p.70.

69. "Family Memoirs" by Caroline Twistleton. A handwritten recollection of family members and events by Ralph Carr's granddaughter (Hedgeley Hall).

70. John Banham, "A very great public convenience", Durham County Local History Society Bulletin, 1994, No. 92.

71. Family of Carr, p. 74.

72. "Family Memoirs". According to the author, Caroline Twistleton, both Widdrington and his wife were very extravagant.

73. For a fuller account of Ralph Carr's tithe-farming activities see A. W. Purdue, "An Oxford College, Two Parishes and a Tithe-Farmer: The Modernisation of Tithe Collection", Rural History (1977) 8,1.

74. At Benton, also near Newcastle, Balliol College was the impropriator.

75. The rectory is an early eighteenth century red-brick house. Nothing is left of the vicarage which stood next door to it in the eighteenth century for it was replaced by the 1860s vicarage, now a private residence. In its garden stands the remains of a tower house, the residence of earlier incumbents.

76. The Hankeys were London merchants and financiers and were clearly well known to the Bynes. When Charles Byne wished to purchase of a troop of Dragoons, Sir Joseph Hankey advanced the £3,000 for the purchase (Charles Byne to Mrs Anne Byne 25 Dec. 1755). Ralph Carr had business dealings with the family. In January 1772 he corresponded with Robert Hankey about the latter's order for alum (Ralph Carr to Robert Hankey 4 Jan. 1772).

77. Commutation of Tithes Agreement for Ponteland, confirmed by the Tithe Commissioners, 17 April, 1841. NRO.

78. Warden of Merton College to John Carr, 10 Nov. 1810 and 3 Aug. 1811. Carr-Ellison Papers NRO 855 Box 6.

79. Collegii Mertonensis Registrum, Michaelmas, 1733, 1748 and 1745. Merton College Library. I am grateful to the Librarian of Merton College who allowed me to consult the register.

80. *Ibid,* 14 Aug. 1744.

81. Nathaniel Ellison (1737-98) of the Newcastle branch of the Ellisons was a Fellow of Merton and later a prominent clergyman in the North East.

82. *Ibid*, 2 Sept. 1769. The choice of a valuer from Hebburn was, no doubt, due to Nathaniel Ellison's connections with the Ellisons of Hebburn Hall.

83. *Ibid,* Michaelmas, 1776.

84 *Ibid,* Michaelmas,1790.

85. Charles Grey to Ralph Carr, 29 Sept.1783. Carr-Ellison Papers.

86. Pamela Horn, *The Rural World 1780-1850* (1980), p.154, quotes the instance of a Dorset vicar: "the vicar could be seen gazing over gates and peering into the dusty recesses of barns to discover the hidden sacks of apples or the pound bag of clover seed...".

87. See W. E. Tate, *The Parish Chest. A Study of the Records of Parochial Administration in England* (1960).

88. Provisional Agreement for the Commutation of Tithes in the Township of Ponteland; confirmed by the Commissioners, 17 April 1841. NRO.

89. CMR, 3 June 1773. The Revd. James Snowden was a Fellow of Merton. His notebooks reveal that, while at Ponteland he was relentless in pursuit of value from his tithes, which he went around collecting on horseback. Blackett of Wylam Papers, Northumberland Record Office ZBK. I am indebted to Mrs Barbara Harbottle for this information.

90. Communation of Tithes Agreement. *op. cit.*

91. Caroline Twistleton, "Family Memoirs"(unpublished).

92. This confirms the view of Eric J. Evans expressed in *The Contentious Tithe* (1976) that collection in kind remained a practice in the North East and was not confined to the North West, parts of the South and areas of East Anglia as Lord Ernle claimed in *English Farming Past and Present* (6th ed. 1961).

93. *Family of Carr,* p.83.

94. MRG, Michaelmas, 1797.

95. National Corn Prices are taken from J. D. Chambers and G. E. Mingay, *The Agricultural Revolution 1750-1880* (1966).

96. MRG, Michaelmas, 1804.

97. *Family of Carr,* pp.85-86.

98. *Ibid,* p.84. The difficult renewal referred to was probably that of 1755. The fine was more than doubled then but the college may have originally intended an even greater increase.

99. MCR, 6 June, 1822.

100. I. Carr to R. Carr jnr., 10 Dec. 1792. NRO 855 Box 6.

101. It was a good long-term buy because as the leases ran out rents could be raised and by 1804 it was valued as having an eventual rental (after the expiry of the leases) of £1,350. An overall valuation based on twenty years rental would thus have made it worth some £27,000.

102. Ralph Carr to Ralph Carr (his son), 30 April 1788. Letters of Carr Family (typescript) collected and arranged by Caroline Twistleton Vol.I 1780-1804. At Hedgeley Hall.

Chapter 11

Family and Social Life at Dunston Hill and Charlotte Square

Newcastle upon Tyne 1827 (from Dunston Hill) by J. W. Carmichael

A woman especially, if she have the misfortune of knowing anything, should conceal it as well as she can.

Jane Austen, Northanger Abbey

Ralph Carr was forty-two when he married Isabella Byne in 1753.[1] This was a relatively advanced age at which to embark on marriage but Ralph still had more than half his life ahead of him. He was, as we have seen, a cautious man and it is probable that he waited until his fortune and circumstances enabled him to be an acceptable suitor to a woman of some wealth and standing such as Isabella.

Much of his early life was taken up with establishing himself in business and with looking after the interests of his sisters, Margaret and Katherine. Jane, Ralph's elder sister had married John Widdrington, an attorney, and died in 1742. Their son, John, became Ralph's business partner. Margaret never married so Ralph had to make provision for her while Katherine did not marry until 1758.

Christopher Scott, a merchant of Hull and Aldbrough, married Katherine as his second wife. The negotiation between Scott and Ralph Carr as to the marriage settlement is a further example of how, although eighteenth century marriages were often based on affection, the financial basis continued to be not only important but overtly so. Marriage in most societies has been endogamous and dowries merely underline this. The suitor wrote to Ralph: "...I imagin'd your sister might have had some fortune fixed and knowing your natural disposition that if it was small, probably you might have added to it". He needed a dowry, he added, because he had the children of his first marriage to look after and otherwise, he gallantly avowed, would have married Katherine without one. "...None but an independent man can marry", he went on, "-supposing yourself in my situation. I appeal to your own heart if you think I act out of character."[2]

From the time he inherited Dunston Hill, Ralph began to expand the estate, buying a nearby house and nine and a half acres, a purchase that had probably been arranged by his father, in 1739. In 1750 he enlarged Dunston Hill itself, retaining parts of the old house and adding a west wing. The grounds were enlarged in 1750 by a diversion of the Whickham and Dunston turnpike. The improvements to and the expansion of Dunston Hill were to be followed, as we have seen, by the steady acquisition of land and estates in Northumberland. Land was not only the most respectable form of property, it was by far the safest investment.

By the time of his marriage Ralph was a man of means and a merchant who had a considerable reputation for probity and fair dealing. He was about to take the major step of launching the "Old Bank". The marriage was financially and socially advantageous, for the Bynes were a well established gentry family from Carshalton and the marriage brought with it the opportunity to "farm" the tithes of Ponteland and Embleton. We should not conclude, however, that this was not a love match, but rather that Ralph found a woman of some fortune that he could love.

A letter from his future brother-in law, Charles Byne, refers to the acceptance of his offer of marriage to Isabella:

> *According to your desire I spoke to my mother last night...and I need*
> *only tell you this particular, which are her own words, viz., that as to the*
> *circumstances it was her duty to have that examined and settled...I am*

> *ordered by her to acquaint you that as my sister agrees so does she...and*
> *my mother expects that you will send in your proposals to her in*
> *writing...I understand by "your proposals" she means a settlement. I*
> *doubt not but you'll concur...[3]*

His marriage to the daughter of a clergyman of the established church would have necessitated a change in religious affiliation, if that had not, indeed, already taken place. During most of his youth and young manhood, he was a Unitarian and a member of the congregation of the Hanover Square Chapel. He continued for many years to be a trustee of the chapel and was related to its minister, Richard Rogerson, through the latter's marriage to his cousin. Ralph's progress from dissent to the established church may well have been accelerated by his engagement to Isabella but it was in accord with the general tendency for successful men who acquired landed estates to become Anglicans. Even in Newcastle life there were penalties for those forthright dissenters who refused to make the gesture of occasional conformity demanded by the Test and Corporations Acts and Joseph Airey, Ralph's business partner in the "Old Bank" and such a non-conformist, was not numbered among members of the Corporation.

Ralph was a warm and affectionate man and his letters to Isabella from early in their marriage both demonstrate his fondness for her and capture something of the Tyneside accent and terminology that must have marked his speech. In 1756, after nearly three years of marriage, he addressed her as "My Dearest Woman" and went on:

> *I did not propose writing before next post but having thine of the 3rd inst.*
> *I cannot leave it unanswered tho have only time to tell Thee I am well*
> *and that it rejoices me to hear thou art so -Indeed my Rube I am glad to*
> *find thou hast fixed a date for coming home to me, I scarce can say how*
> *much I miss thee both day and night...[4]*

In another letter of the same year, he wrote from Newcastle: "My Dearest Lass, I have been in pain for thee ever since we parted...". He went on to tell her how he gave up society to write to her yet sought to tease her by describing the delights that were available to him should he choose them: "I will not tell thee one word how joyously I pass my time. At present I happen to be alone Indeed & for the sake of writing your Ladyship I have declined out of hearing a most agreeable Concert in the next room Consisting of a great variety of performers of which three women singers and an Eunoch are chief".[5] The middle-aged merchant was much in love but was able to tease.

It was some seven years before their first child, Isabella, was born in 1760 and she died in infancy. It is clear from the letters to Isabella Carr from her brother Charles that she was in poor health in her early married life and he warns her against the administrations of doctors, recommending the waters of Bath instead.[6] There may well have been miscarriages and some doubt as to whether they would be able to have a family.

Between 1763 and 1771, however, the couple produced their family of four children: Annabella (1763-1822); John (1764-1817); Ralph (1768-1837; and Harriet (1771-1848). Few children can have enjoyed so happy and fortunate a childhood as the two sons and two daughters of Ralph Carr and Isabella. It is clear from the letters exchanged between children and parents and between the children themselves that Ralph and his wife created at Dunston Hill an environment at once secure, loving, and creative. The letters give the historian an insight into the domestic life of this late eighteenth century family. Affectionate describes, not only the relationships between husband and wife, the couple and their children and the brothers and sisters, but those within that wider "family" that in the period still included the servants.

Isabella Carr had had the conventional education of a woman of her station, the daughter of a clergyman from a gentry family. She had accomplishments, was a good harpsichord player and was skilful at drawing. If her main interests in life were her home and family, she retained an independent spirit within that domain, quite prepared to disagree with her husband on domestic issues or on the subject of her relations. The successful running of a large household required skill and character. Mrs Carr's household account book for the year 1795 has survived and demonstrates both the complexity of her responsibilities and her care in managing them. It includes the amounts of grain (wheat, oats, barley and beans) from Ponteland used in the kitchen, George Hudson's (the coachman and groom) expenditure on oats for the stables, and items such as land tax, the taxes on the servants' houses and on the coach, tradesmens' bills, a tithe rent to Mr Grenville (Vicar of Whickham) and servants wages, the whole amounting to £983-2.5d.[7] A big house was indeed a major part of a local economy and much esteemed for the employment and custom it provided. Dunston Hill ran smoothly, provided the context for fulfilling family life, was a warm centre for the entertainment of neighbours and visitors and was a place of refinement and culture. This owed much to Isabella Carr.

Ralph Carr was a man at ease with himself. He fulfilled his ambitions by making a considerable fortune, which he lived long enough to enjoy, marrying a woman whose companionship he valued and raising children whom he was proud of and who remained close to him when they became adults. He had the respect of local society and had the friendship of many who had achieved powerful positions at a national level but, unlike many who have risen in the world, was quite content with the station in life that came naturally to him and did not seek to advance socially by conspicuous expenditure.

A conscientious citizen, concerned both for the welfare of the poor and for law and order, he took on the duties of a Justice of the Peace for County Durham. He was most charitable towards the poor of Dunston and Whickham but bewailed the rising poor rates, which he blamed in part on the increased number of ale houses which lured the poor into intemperate habits:

> *The Poor Sess at Dunston Hill cost me more than £50 per annum including the sums I subscribe for their relief at different times and £5 or more given them at Christmas   Also to a list of them who are weekly pensioners & over and above a very great number that come daily to the door,-it is lamentable to see the profligacy of the age...*[8]

Welford comments that:

> *...severe as were his strictures upon the drinking customs of his day, and the poverty and misery engendered by them, he was a liberal contributor to the wants of the deserving poor. He was one of the founders of Newcastle Infirmary, a generous supporter of local dispensaries, the Lying-in hospital, and kindred institutions. Every week for some years he gave to forty-eight persons-twelve from each of the four parishes of Newcastle-sums varying from 1 s. to 2 s. each, while he dispensed unlimited bounty to wayfarers at his own door.*[9]

He was not appointed to the positions that substantial gentry filled as Sheriffs or Deputy-Lieutenants. His relatively humble origins, his continued commercial life and dissenting background may have stood in the way of any ambitions for such offices, but it is probable that he eschewed them. As we have seen, there was no great gulf between merchants and gentry on Tyneside but rather a series of graded steps by which, at a decent pace, urban wealth moved to broad acres. In his forties Carr was embarking on his banking career and still needed to increase his fortune by concentrating on his business activities. He remained, in any case, much more the merchant than the country gentleman in his social and moral attitudes, even when his many influential connections and ample wealth and land would have enabled him to bear the port of the latter.

The Carr children were lucky, not only in having parents who were both wealthy and loving, but because their births corresponded to a period in which childhood and the indulgence of children became fashionable. As the historian of an aristocratic family of the time has written:

> *In the 1750s, England was at the beginning of a love affair with children and with domesticity that was swelled by and in turn fuelled an outpouring of sentimental novels, paintings of sweet infants and happy family groups and books of advice about raising and educating children. Visitors to great houses noticed children everywhere; they were spoiled, deferred to and adored.[10]*

As we have seen with the upbringing of Henry and Hannah Ellison's children in the 1730s and '40s, happy childhoods and loving relationships between parents and children were by no means unknown earlier in the century and the idea that parental affection has not been a constant throughout the ages is deeply suspect. But certainly the theory and to a lesser degree the practice of bringing up children have changed over time, not necessarily in a linear way. Among the upper orders of Georgian society, the influence of the notion of sensibility and of Rousseau's *Emile* resulted in some odd and eccentric practices[11] but it made life for many children more relaxed, less strictly disciplined and happier.

Ralph delighted in the company of his wife and children. When in London in 1767, he wrote regularly to his wife describing his visits to the theatre, his glimpses of the King and Queen and his social and business engagements. After an account of a visit to the British Museum, he went on, "…and yet I assure thee I shd. have far more pleasure in examining John's and Annabella's collection at Cross House" and he concluded "…give my Little Angels some Kisses for me, my heart yearns after thee and them".[12] On a subsequent stay in London he wrote: "I am rejoiced to hear of my Queen Annabella's and King John's behaviour. Tell them I have found out a most famous toyman, but he will make nothing but for very good children".[13]

Cross House by W H Knowles (Gateshead Public Library)

The principal setting for family life was Dunston Hill, now a substantial mansion which was further enlarged in 1782, but the family did not live there all the time for they had also a town house in Newcastle. During the early years of the marriage this was the same Cross House in Westgate Street, where Ralph had lived as a bachelor, but around 1770 Ralph purchased a terraced brick house with simple classical details in the newly built and fashionable Charlotte Square. This was the town's first formal square and its three sides of tall houses surrounded a garden in the London manner.[14] No doubt Ralph needed a Newcastle residence to be close to his businesses for, although, today, Dunston Hill is only some ten minutes from the centre of Newcastle by motor car, it would have taken an hour or so by carriage and longer in winter when the roads were muddy. During the winter months the family lived in Newcastle. Few of the county families of the day migrated to London for the season but, rather, spent winter in Newcastle. Even the Montagus at Denton Hall, only a couple of miles from the city centre, had a town house in Pilgrim Street.

The landed gentry and prosperous merchant families mingled in a polite society but until late in the century Newcastle had little in the way of places of public entertainment for respectable society, while fashionable clothing and many luxuries had to be acquired from London. Early eighteenth century social life for persons of quality was, apart from some coffee houses, Springwell Gardens (a local imitation of a London pleasure garden) and the civic banquets which punctuated the cycle of civic life, the Assizes, and the inauguration of the Lord Mayor and Sheriff, still essentially private; a round of card parties, masques, musical evenings and balls in the drawing rooms of town houses, though for the sportsman there were race-meetings and cock-fights, while the hunt still met in the centre of the town. After a civilised evening in a candle-lit drawing room, guests would make their way through unlit streets guided by servants holding lanthorns. Yet even Mrs Elizabeth Montagu of Denton Hall, lioness of London literary salons, who had felt on journeying north with her husband to take up their North-East inheritance that she was moving from light to barbarism was pleased enough with what she found. In 1760 she wrote to Lord Lyttleton:

> *I am actually an inhabitant of Newcastle, and am taking out my freedom, not out of a gold box but by entering into all the diversions of the place. I was at a musical entertainment this morning; I have bespoke a play for tomorrow night, and shall go to a ball, on choosing a mayor on Monday night.*

She did however complain that conversation was limited, as it "always turns upon money".[15]

Like many provincial towns, Newcastle acquired in the late eighteenth century the infrastructure for an expanding polite society. Shops, tailors, dressmakers and milliners increasingly provided fashionable goods and luxuries, which hitherto had only been available in London. The 'seventies were significant years in the development of Newcastle life. Society was moving up from the riverside and Charlotte Square was at the very centre of the fashionable world. Just round the corner, the Assembly Rooms, designed by William Newton, the same architect who built the square, went up in 1774-76 and provided concerts and dancing. A Philosophical Society was founded in 1775, the Theatre Royal opened in 1778, while circulating libraries, such as Sand's in the Bigg Market, ensured that Newcastle society should not be without the latest novels. The Carr family thus moved into Charlotte Square just as the social and cultural life that could be enjoyed by Newcastle's elite was richer and broader than ever before.

Childhood was shorter for boys than for girls and by the age of eight John, and then young Ralph, Carr were away at boarding school. Annabella and Harriet remained at home to be privately educated and enjoy to the full, as they reached their late teens, the social and cultural life of Newcastle. The early life of Annabella Carr points to the advantages and disadvantages of a young woman of good family in this period.

Annabella Carr (1763-1822)

If the education of a girl of such a family was not seen as a preparation for public life, this could hold advantages as well as deprivations for the intelligent. Education for males was rigorous but could be regimented and unimaginative while that of females could result in mere superficial polish but could, alternatively, produce well-educated women. Girls were expected to achieve some accomplishment in music and painting, to master some French, and often some Latin, be able to write an amusing letter and show some acquaintance with at least the popular novels of the day. Writers in later ages, in which the great majority of the population fail, despite a state education system, to emulate such standards, have often loftily dismissed them as mere "finish" and have not paid sufficient attention to those women who were well-educated by any standards. The very unstructured nature of the education of the daughters of the well-to-do meant that the intelligent girl with able tutors or governesses and with access to books could follow her intellectual interests with a freedom denied to her brothers. Such a girl was Annabella Carr.

Although the boundaries between the sexes were clear enough in respect of male and female duties, rights and expectations, there was not in the late eighteenth century that sharp divide between separate mental spheres that the early Victorian period was to insist upon. The cult of sensibility was beginning to erode the more robust eighteenth century attitude to life, to encourage women to display sensitivity and modesty, and even to shun physical exercise, but there was a long way to go before the modesty, prudishness and ignorance of the world's ways, which young Victorian women were expected to at least feign, became *de rigeur*.

The upbringing of Annabella and Harriet Carr gave them an amount of freedom, physical, social and mental, that would have horrified a future generation. As Annabella's niece, Caroline Twistleton, put it: "Her indulgent parents allowed her at the early age of 17 and 18 to go where she chose and invite whom she chose". Thus, Annabella rode into Newcastle to attend concerts or lectures or to visit friends, became an accomplished musician who was also deeply interested in the sciences and in literature and invited home, not only friends from gentry or leading merchant families, but musicians and literary acquaintances. All appear to have been welcome at Dunston Hill and Charlotte Square.

Annabella had perhaps the makings of what the second half of the eighteenth century referred to as a "blue-stocking" but it must be remembered that that term did not originally have the purely derisory implications it later acquired. It was applied to a group of intelligent women who held receptions for both men and women in London drawing rooms where literary and philosophical topics were discussed. The "Queen of the blue-stockings" was Mrs Elizabeth Montagu who, as we have seen, spent some time at her house, Denton Hall, and mixed with Newcastle society. She was acquainted with Ralph Carr and may have provided the young Annabella with a model of female intelligence. An admirable aspect of Annabella Carr, however, was her ability to combine her intellectual pursuits with a fondness for balls and parties, a delight in "hoops and gowns" and an expertise in flirtation.

The Carr's urban base in Charlotte Square enabled this remarkable young woman, at once belle of the ball and stern analysist of an inadequate lecture, to be launched on Newcastle society. Caroline Twistleton, Ralph Carr's granddaughter and eager listener to the reminiscences of her father and aunts, recounted:

> *My Grandfather, Ralph Carr, had a mansion in Charlotte Square Newcastle whither himself and his family repaired before the winter set in, and much sociability and gaiety was thus attainable, many of their country neighbours also making it their winter headquarters-as a perusal of Annabel Carr's (my aunt's) journal will fully prove, the Carr family in Charlotte Square scarcely passed a day without guests and as in 1782 there was an encampment in the neighbourhood many were their military*

acquaintances and guests. The fashion in those days was to pay and receive visits in the "forenoon". Dinner was at 3 or 4 o'clock (and the Tea at 6, I conclude) and the most sociable meal was supper to all of which guests came with and without invitation- at a Guild assembly with dancing the Charlotte Square party stayed till 2 o'clock on Jan. 14 1782 and on the 26 Jan. they were 15 at dinner and 13 at supper. March 26 a concert of twelve performers took place at Charlotte Sq. "a great deal of company" and on April 20th there were 15 musical performers and 30 or so with their own party and 16 stayed supper & May 21st 13 dined besides their own party.[16]

Annabella was the oldest of the Carr children and by 1780 was sixteen and fully able to enter into the pleasures of Newcastle society. Her entry into that society was clearly an enormous success. She was immediately in great demand as a partner at the balls in the Assembly Rooms. As the dances were long country dances one did not have many partners in an evening so that to be asked by a gentleman to dance was a marked compliment.

In October 1780 she wrote to her brother John, a year her junior and away at school:

At the Election Ball (Newcastle Assembly Rooms) I danced with (to use Papa's expression) the Baronet Williamson who I also dined with last Monday, so that I should not be greatly surprised if you should hear a former report circulated you...This particular attention to your humble servant was noticed by the whole room and people are apt to put wrong constructions on behaviour so public...I forgot to tell you that Bowes[17] very politely asked me to dance with him at the last Guild Assembley as did Lord Lindores and Baron Norton [son of Lord Grantley] but I was engaged to Williamson -this is ostentation but it is to let you know I'm in fashion with the Beaux at present.

As the novels of Jane Austin have made us all aware, nothing so contributed to the gaiety of a neighbourhood, brought romance into the hearts of young women and put mingled hopes of successful marriages and fears of unsuitable attachments into the minds of their mothers, than a regiment encamped in the vicinity. From 1781, for most summers of the decade, there were militia camps at Stella, a short distance from both Dunston Hill and Newcastle. The officers encamped there were to greatly enliven the lives of many young women of quality, among them Annabella, and to have their relatively light military duties relieved by a constant round of parties and balls and the company of eligible young women.

Annabella was much in demand and was at the centre of the social whirl as the militia entertained the local quality and they in return invited the militia officers to their houses, to concerts and to the Assembly Rooms. For an attractive young woman this round of pleasure had a serious aspect for within it marriages were made.[18] Lord Lumley, the heir to the Earl of Scarborough, who was an officer in the militia, was an early potential suitor who paid great attention to Annabella, though she clearly felt that his deportment on the dance floor left something to be desired:

> *On Wed. we went to the assemblies and I danced with Lord Lumley. He dined with us twice in the course of the week but is amazingly worse in his dancing, much more ridiculous than ever - tho his attentive polite behaviour makes up for every deficiency.*[19]

Annabella's musical interests were always evident and she seems to have acted as a the promoter of her favourite musicians within her social circle:

> *On Wed. morning we were at Noserre's concert...several people sent me one, two, three and four guineas to give Mr Noserre amongst whom were Lord Adam Gordon and Lord Lindores.*[20]

The pace set by the hectic social round would have taxed all but the most youthful and hardiest of constitutions:

> *On Thursday Harriet and I went to the Review. My Mama and cousin (Miss Sarah T.Scott) thought it too early to rise. I can say with truth there was no one person missing I ever saw or heard of in this country, besides hundreds of strangers.*

> *There was after the review, a public breakfast given by Lord Adam (Gordon) and the officers in the Mess-room, which did not contain half the company at once- so as one party left it another went in, so everybody got a breakfast at last. We luckily were in the first set. Lady Mary Lumley, Harriet and I got next the Duchess [the Dowager Duchess of Atholl, had married Lord A.Gordon; she and her husband were constant visitors at Dunston Hill].*

> *We then came home- (my Papa was at Ponteland)- and had Monsieur Noser [Noserre, the professional musician], Mr Milner, Wallace, Captain Rudyard, Sir Thomas Clarges, Mr Beilly, of the East York (who plays very decently) to dinner-and in the Afternoon had the band and a little concert.*

Mr Webbersley was our violincello, and acquitted himself with great eclat. Our audience consisted of Lady Williamson, Lady and Miss Clavering, Mrs and Miss Reed, Miss Peareth, Lady Ridley, Messrs. Ridley and Ellison, Lord Lindores, Captain Callaghan (a Performer), Lord Lumley, Captains Stanhope, Hill and Ditmas. We played till near ten, when we all went to the Assembly

My cousin, Miss Scott[21], danced with Lord Lumley. I introduced him to her, and it was particularly obliging of him to dance with an utter stranger on hearing me say she had not got a partner.

Lord Scarborough remains very indifferent; the whole of the family are at Lumley [Castle] and we expect to see them very soon.[22]

By the beginning of 1782, Annabella was eighteen and had already "been out" for two years. She now dressed in the latest fashions of the day. On the 3rd of January, she "had her satin try'd on" and "had her hair dressed for the first time by William".[23]

By the summer, the militia regiments were once more encamped at Stella but this year it was Lord Lindores, rather than Lord Lumley, who figures in her diary as her most attentive companion:

May 8th. Lord Adam and Lord Lindores called before I went out. I put on my summer clothes this day.

11th May. Lord Lindores called.

18th. Mrs Atlee (milliner) came to speak about hoops and gowns.

21st May. Colonel Mrs Maisters and Captain Sykes, etc., in all 13 strangers (besides our family dined.

22nd. Met Lord Lindores and rode awhile with him.

23rd. Lord Adam and Captain Fane came.

Nothing came of the particular attentions paid to Annabella by Lords Lumley and Lindores. Her niece Caroline Twistleton commented that, "somehow she mismanaged and trifled with her good fortune, for she never married". Perhaps there was a disappointment for Mrs Carr and her daughters spent much of the summer of 1782 at the spas of Harrogate, Scarborough and Buxton with the hope this would "quite reinstate them" after "a dreadful winter". Yet as there was much rebuilding at Dunston Hill that summer, extended stays at fashionable spas were understandable enough.

In a letter to her father Annabella gives a lively account of the fashionable company at Harrogate. This was the hey-day of the Spas; the obligatory attendance at the Wells was accompanied by excursions and sightseeing, music and balls. Her references to her health and to her obedience to instructions as to "not heating myself-and *scarcely* ever used the long trot on Horseback" suggest, however, that she had been ill.[24]

By the autumn the family was back at Dunston Hill, close enough to Newcastle for a good horsewoman like Annabelle to enjoy the more cerebral aspects of its cultural life.

> 20th October 1782. I rode to the lecture upon Mechanicks by Clark.
>
> 22nd. To the lecture with my papa. Dr Rotherham upon the centre of gravity. Clark also explaining his clock.
>
> Nov.23rd. Played with Miss Stowe all the morning. Messrs. Faulkner, Avison, Earl, Carr (three curates), Barnett dined. Mr Grenville came in the afternoon. We play'd and danced. It passed very pleasantly.
>
> Dec.4th. Rode to Clark's lecture on wheel carriages.
>
> 14th. Mr Grenville drank tea. We did not play at all. It pass'd very badly on account of my papa ill.
>
> 18th. To the lecture on Hydrostaticks and the doctrine of fluidity.
>
> 21st. To the lecture on water engines and pumps-not very pleasing tho' laughable.
>
> 23rd. Mr Grenville came when I was out but rode home with me from Redheugh.
>
> 24th.To the lecture on syphon water etc.[25]

This was certainly a more serious routine than that enjoyed with the militia officers. One is relieved to note that, after the Christmas Eve lecture on syphon water, Annabella had her hair dressed on Boxing Day, "and it was a long time in dressing", to go to dinner with the Claverings at Axwell Park. Her attendance at lectures was punctuated by visits from Mr Grenville, who was Vicar of Whickham.

He was a mainstay of the musical ensembles she put together, accompanying her harpsichord with his violincello, and clearly a suitor but, as with Lumley and Lindores, marriage did not follow the romance or flirtation.

Annabella Carr fits no stereotype. She was neither all hoops, gowns and ribbons nor all severe intellect. If her attendance at lectures on hydrostatics and mechanics might win the applause of a feminist historian, her enthusiasm for the round of balls and parties with aristocratic military officers would be less welcome. It is of course the stereotypes that are wrong and this was not a period that necessarily demanded of either men or women that they separate pleasures into mutually antipathetic categories, those of the flesh and of the mind. It is possible that with men she fell between two stools, too intellectual to enjoy for long the company of the merely fashionable and too much the lady of fashion to be content with a local clergyman. Certainly there would have been no pressure from her father to enter into a marriage she had doubts about, for Ralph Carr delighted in his daughters' company and was loath to lose either Annabella or her sister Harriet. Probably her marriage chances were spoiled by the ill-health that seems to have dogged her from her late teens. Her musical ability seems to have been considerable and in another age might have been her career, but her interest in science was also a serious study and in 1807 she was to publish her *Conversations on Chemistry*. All the intellectual topics of the day were of interest to her and she carried on a correspondence with the poet George Crabbe.

John Carr (1764-1817)

It was increasingly the custom of the English upper classes to have boys educated at boarding schools. An obvious choice for a man of Ralph Carr's means would have been to send both his sons to a major public school such as Eton, Harrow, Winchester or Westminster but he had a distrust of such schools, fearing their moral influence and disagreeing with their almost total concentration on classics.[26] His choice was to send both sons to a private school, Mr Croft's School at Beverley, John going in 1772 when he was eight and Ralph following when he was that age in 1776. John had the responsibility of looking after his little brother, which indeed he did most commendably and, when John went on to Oxford in 1781, young Ralph journeyed south with him. The father overcame his dislike of public schools and sent the younger brother to Westminster for four years preparatory to going to Oxford. John could look after his brother during the holidays and Westminster would provide Ralph with the thorough grounding in the classics which would enable him to shine at Oxford and go on to the career at the Bar which was already mapped out for him.

It must have been with a heavy heart that Ralph Carr saw his much loved sons off to school for he was an emotional man, who not only cared for his children but valued their company. From almost the moment of parting his perpetual complaint for the rest of his life was that they did not write regularly enough. Probably the parting with his son Ralph was the greater wrench. He was fond of and proud of John, who early showed himself to be remarkably mature and responsible for his years, but, as often happens, the younger son was treated more indulgently and was, a charming boy, the object of the entire family's affection. To Ralph he was "My dearest boy", "My Ralpho". Luckily John shared the universal fondness for Ralph and was ever the protective elder brother.

Ralph Carr (1768-1837)

John's letters home begin formally and respectfully as was the code of the age: "Dear Papa" or "Mama" giving way after he's about fifteen to "Dear Father " and "Dear Sir". The early letters tell of minor childhood illnesses and complaints ("had a little breaking behind my ear" or "had a hive on my arm") and of Ralph's progress: "We are both very well indeed and Ralph goes on very well with his schooling and will I think make a good dancer. I like fencing very well." The elder brother takes his responsibilities seriously. "...you need not be uneasy about Ralph eating bad fruit for I am sure he shall not to my knowledge and I am sure he wont for he is a very good boy".[27] Then there is the normal impatience for the holidays and the return to home: "Ralph is impatient to know when Thomas [a manservant at Dunston Hill] comes as I believe we break up 20th of next month".

Ralph was rather ill in the autumn of 1777 and John wrote to his mother: "As I am sure you and my Papa are very anxious to know how Ralph goes on, I have the pleasure to acquaint you that he is pretty well".[28] A note from Ralph was enclosed: "I have got into another room this morning, and I here the boys playing and wished to have joined them but Mrs Webster would not give me leave lest I catch cold".

It is improbable that Ralph Carr knew much Latin but he was ever ready to help with his sons' problems and sent John a translation of Terence for which he received the rather earnest reply: "...I am much obliged to you for the translation of Terence for I find it rather hard but I wont make an improper use of the translation".[29] He was not always perfect however and had to apologise for bringing his gun back to school without permission.

John was soon writing mature letters. In 1779 he gave his father an account of the riot at Hull in favour of Admiral Keppel

> *We have had great doings on Admiral Keppels account, and an effigy made of wood with gunpowder contained in the head, which was afterwards burn, to the disgrace of Sir Hugh Palliser: and also an illumination when a great number of people had their windows broken who would not put out lights.*[30]

In the same year he wrote dutifully: It gives me no small pleasure to sit down and write to a kind and affectionate father, who I know has my welfare at heart".

John was early aware of the ways of the world and the importance of property and money and when Dr Croft left his school to be replaced by Mr Jackson, a Fellow of Trinity, he commented: "Dr Croft had no sooner arrived at his new habitation than he married a young lady of £10,000 fortune as is reported..."[31]

He remained the exemplary elder brother always recounting news of Ralph: "Ralph you may suppose is counting the days before he will see little Harriet, he has writ her a long letter in a language unknown to any but themselves". Ralph and Harriet, the two younger children, were very close and shared a childhood world of common hobbies, jokes and even language. They shared a garden at Dunston Hill and later

Harriet took up taxidermy and Ralph would shoot birds for her to stuff, though Harriet, herself became quite a reasonable shot and told her dear "Bepe": "I went out shooting that night you went away and we got a partridge and a crow, my brother [John] 2 hares 4 partridge. I went out yesterday and we got a hare".

In 1781 both boys left Beverley, John to go to Christ Church and Ralph to Westminster. Both were exceedingly aristocratic establishments[32] and Ralph Carr may well have worried about the influences his sons would come under. Oxford was a place where young men often acquired the habit of heavy drinking and gambling and it was easy to run up debts there. Ralph was a rich man, but not in comparison to a great landowner, and spendthrift sons could have swiftly gone through his fortune.[33] Public schools had a reputation for violence, regular floggings, bullying and even riots and there was concern at Dunston Hill during Ralph's second term at tales of "battles" at Westminster but John reported, "that it is much left off and indeed there is no likelihood of it now as it only happens to new scholars".[34] Ralph Carr also worried that his younger son might, with other Westminster boys, get involved in the Westminster election of 1782.[35]

The letters to young Ralph Carr from his family have a very different tone to those to John, even allowing for age. "My Sweet Fellow", the father wrote in Ralph's first term," Be of good courage for sure I am thou wilt in a little time be equal to any of the class".[36] He told Ralph to let John know immediately he needed money, "...for money has wings in London & my Ralpho shall not be neglected if he wants any".[37] Isabella informed her son: "Harriet was transported at the sight of your letter and will carefully observe all you say about the garden. Your sisters send their most affectionate love to you and Harriet (who is a very good girl) a thousand good wishes".[38]

Ralph Carr escorted John to Oxford. He had made careful enquiries about the cost of living as a gentleman commoner and had been told that it would cost John at least £200 a year. This was a relatively generous estimate, and, provided fast company was avoided, was enough to enable an undergraduate to live comfortably. John exceeded his allowance, but not by too much, steering a course between his determination to live like a gentleman, with the expense that this entailed, and his cautious nature. In his first term he wrote home:

> *I have so far been excessively fortunate in every particular and I flatter myself something has been owing to my own behaviour. I see the effects both of a cynical reserve and foolish compliance in many instances already and I hope I shall persevere in my resolution of preserving a due medium....I wish my sister Harriet could see how snug I am at my breakfast in a morning after prayer....I hear much about the dishonesty*

of the people in Oxford but as I show no temptation by locking up everything, I am easy as to that particular.[39]

He later wrote, while brother Ralph was staying with him over the Christmas holidays:

Pray tell my sister that I am a better caterer than she may expect and that I think myself more intelligent in those affairs by far than she is. I have every utensil necessary for a Housekeeper and we live like Kings. Our dinner is almost invariably a roast fowl & some roast mutton, good tart & cheese.[40]

To keep up with others at an aristocratic college like Christ Church was expensive and a defensive note creeps into John's letters home as he seeks to justify his expenditure: "Most people keep a horse here but I think that if I let it alone till after I return here it may answer as well....My expenses so far have been perhaps more moderate than most the Gent. Commoners....Oxford in one thing or another is the dearest place except London".[41] Three weeks later, he wrote that: "I am obliged to be a little expensive in the point of cloathes for you must dress genteelly and neither of my coats that were made in Newcastle can be worn here. they are more like jackets than coats and anything of that kind looks very ill under a gown".[42] By the following year he clearly felt he needed to cut more of a dash. Lord Barnard, who had taken rooms above him, kept servants and horses and lived in great style and John felt that he too needed, not only a servant, but one who would do him credit: "I have done as long without one as I well can...I have every reason to believe that you will give me credit for not incurring any improper expense". He described his servant: "He dresses hair very well and will make a very good servant. A man out of the county would not be of half the use to me here".[43]

Expenses clearly mounted and by 1784 he was having to request extra funds: "My book says I have had £125-15-0d this year, if you will make it up to £200 now, I shall be a very rich man..." and (one month later, when he had already received £205) "...if you will be so good as to remit me £60, I shall have £34-5-0 ready against any emergency. I find my expenses very considerably increased..."[44] In his final year he spent some £400, a large enough sum but one that the shrewd father had probably expected. Emulation and caution had moderated each other.

Even as an undergraduate John kept abreast of the affairs of the world, what a position was worth, who could or should be helped to a position and who would inherit what. This was an age that knew the value of every post and felt no compunction about the use of influence. When Dr Bagot, Dean of Christ Church, became Bishop of Bristol, John reflected that, "I believe upon an average his late promotion will not bring him in above £500 per ann. The Deanery is reckoned at £1,200". He enlisted his father's help in getting a friend and member of a North East family, Mr Ord, a Merton fellowship and gave sage advice on how Ralph, who had a close relationship with the college via his rental of its tithes, might speak in the candidate's favour, while he also felt a gift of lobsters to the Dean would not go amiss. He also retained a close interest in what was going on at home wishing to know how Sir Thomas Clavering was and how Lord Ravensworth had left his estate.[45]

By the time John left Oxford in 1785, having taken his exams and passed his degree, his brother Ralph was already at Christ Church. The protective relationship between elder and younger brother was still in place and John wrote to his father about Ralph: "I beg you will not be under any apprehension about drinking for I believe this college to be much freer from that vice than any other. The society is too much mixed...for drunken people to get together without meeting as many who are adverse to it...scarce any wine to be met with here but the most nauseous mixture".[46] It seems improbable that this was true but it was, no doubt, what a father wanted to hear. Ralph Carr was, nevertheless, worried about his son Ralph and the temptations of Oxford life. He may have loved Ralph more affectionately but he clearly had greater faith in John's steadiness. When deciding that Ralph should go to Christ Church he had ordered, "on no account shall you be a Gentleman Commoner, they mispend far too much time in their rooms with each other" and intimated his worries about the dissipated life led by many undergraduates.[47] Ralph, who had established at Westminster a reputation as a classicist, was quite capable of entering Christ Church as a scholar but his father continued to worry: "On no account be seduced by any example to enter into the drinkings at Chambers after dinner".[48]

Ralph went on to have a distinguished career at Oxford and his academic ability could have led to considerable advancement there, though he would have had to take holy orders. By 1787 he had nearly finished his initial course of study and decided to take his degree, arguing that an MA excused two years residence at the Inns of Court. His father, having decided that his younger son was destined for a legal career, became impatient. "Taking a degree is not of the least use to you", he argued and "I grudge you spending another year at Oxford unless you could study law there which I doubt you can not, Every other study to you now is time mismanaged". But he could never say no to Ralph for long and continued, "I could possibly get you introduced to Dr Scott or his brother John [later Lords Stowell and Eldon]...". The Scott brothers had been recipients of favours from Ralph Carr when they were young. Sir William Scott was applied to and, acknowledging his debt to the father, used his considerable influence at Oxford on behalf of the son, who was elected a Fellow of Merton.[49] Ralph received his MA in 1792 and in the same year began reading for the Bar at Gray's Inn.

During the 'eighties the Carr family, partly to be near John and Ralph and also, perhaps, to give Annabella and Harriet a taste of London society, spent some time in London. They rented houses for the Season, at Dover Street in 1783, at 141 Old Bond Street in 1787 and at 2 Hanover Street in 1789 (six guineas a week). They clearly did the Season in some style. At Hanover Street they had a coach and horses and three men servants while, "Annabella and Harriet enjoyed several gaieties accompanied by their mother and brothers".[50]

For Mrs Carr and her daughters spring and early summer in London and the autumn at Harrogate became a frequent routine. The delight and the danger of resorts arose from the same cause, the mixed company. Spas had a constantly changing society as clusters of visitors came and went and were open to anyone who had money and could dress like a gentleman or a lady. This gave them a somewhat risqué reputation as the haunt of adventurers and the setting for unfortunate engagements. Harrogate abounded in the solid families of the northern gentry the Carrs knew well but a letter of Annabella's to her brother, John, describes, with wicked humour, the assorted society:

> ...the odd contrast of people that chance places by each other at table- Col Cousseau by a little man like the Rev Mr Hutton,- a great bluff sea captain by a youth just returned from the Grand Tour... [an] Irish officer who looks like one of the "four and twenty captains all in a row" and would if offended I daresay be no less ready to kick his adversary down stairs- a pert sprig of the law and a lethargic Leeds cloathier- a vulgar Liverpool merchant who is continually cracking his thumbs in time to something of a tune he hums & drumming upon the table with his fingers & a Col of the Guards-so perfumed & essenced that there is no coming near him uncontaminated. [As for the ladies]...her Grace of Chandos & her sister Lady Henniker rank in the very first class of Quizes- the former ressembles what Mr Allgood would be, if dress'd as a Lady...We have three or four very genteel Girls here- the rest have come for the purpose of shewing off feathers and flounces....

Her old flame Lord Scarborough was there but her comment was dismissive; he was "generally speechless drunk every night". Sadly, however, the ill-health that was to dog the rest of her life was already evident. She could not dance "as one of my legs has been so dreadfully inflamed & swell'd that I have not been able to walk without assistance it has passed for a sprain'd ankle..."[51] Although still only twenty-three, Annabella was to spend much of the rest of her life at Spas seeking cures rather than diversions.

By the late 'eighties, Harriet, the youngest of the family was a young woman and able to enter fully into the social life of Newcastle and of the Season in London. The playful girl, her brother Ralph's inseparable companion ("Tush"), who delighted in gardening, taxidermy, shooting and riding, had, like her sister Annabella, become both attractive and well educated. Whereas Annabella's interests encompassed music and science, Harriet's lay in fine art. It was, of course, usual for young ladies to have some accomplishments but Harriet's artistic ability went beyond the usual ladylike talent, while her work was informed by her knowledge of the history of art. Again like Annabella, whose health deteriorated after her triumphant entry into society, Harriet was delicate and incipient consumption threatened the outdoor girl who thought nothing of riding for many miles.

Harriet Carr (1771-1848)

One can only admire the fortitude with which the Carrs, like other families of the period embarked on long journeys by coach or on horseback along poor roads with often inadequate inns, though both were gradually improving. John and Ralph always managed to get back from Beverley for the holidays, a servant being usually sent to accompany them, but even when at Westminster and Oxford they would be home at least once a year. Christmas 1785 was spent at home and John and Ralph did not leave until February 2 encountering poor travelling conditions: "...snow increased upon us after we left Durham and the roads were extremely heavy. From Boroughbridge to Wetherby the snow had drifted so much that on each side of the path that was cut for a passage, it was up to the chaise door".[52] To transport the family to London for the Season was a major undertaking, especially as family in this sense included servants. Nor was such travel cheap, for John Carr calculated the cost of a journey to London for a single person at £18-15-0d in 1795.[53]

Servants made up a considerable section of society and even people with quite small incomes would have a servant, but a big house and a large number of servants were inseparable. The letters, memoirs and diaries of the period remind us that the well-to-do were rarely alone; there was always a servant, to help one dress, to wait at table or be one's travelling companion. They were as much part of a house as the very walls, furniture and gardens and without them the house would not have functioned. It would be wrong to think, however, that servants were seen as merely functional, for many decent families regarded them more in the light of retainers to whom they had obligations and sometimes saw them as friends.

Dunston Hill was a big but not a great house and there was no army of servants with a complex hierarchy, as would have been found in the houses of great aristocratic families, but some fifteen or so indoor and outdoor servants (two indoor manservants, a coachman cum groom, a cook and maids, two nannies when the children were young) under the authority of a butler and housekeeper.

There was a close relationship between the family and its servants. Mrs Carr's letters to her sons when they were away at school and university are full of news about the servants. She was particularly fond of her house-keeper and maid, Peggy, who was her aide and confidante while her children were young. She concluded a letter to her son John in 1771: "All the Servants present their love and duty to you but more particularly Peggy who loves you little less than I".[54] When Peggy left to get married, she was distraught: "I have this day parted with my servant and friend, who was married this morning (Sunday). To you who knew her worth, and what she was to me, I need make no remark on my loss or how I feel it".[55] When a manservant, Bart, was dismissed by her husband, she complained that it was "for a trifle" and that he had become "a very good servant". John was later to offer Bart a job as his manservant.

As in many households a remarkable toleration was given to the vagaries and failings of servants. Butlers were notoriously given to drink and butlers at Dunston Hill were no exception. Thomas Pulleine was one such and, according to Caroline Twistleton, "...he left my Grandfather's service I know not for what but can guess the cause". The family, nevertheless remained fond of him and took an interest in his fortunes. He must have been given a good enough reference for he got a position with the Duke of Northumberland at Northumberland House where unfortunately he was again found unsatisfactory. Poor Pulleine's appearance was clearly not up to the standards of a ducal household for as John related: "The Duke he says once named to him his want of side curls that his hair could not be properly dressed and that on the great days in London he would not be able to give satisfaction".[56] Pulleine got in touch with young Ralph who was at Westminster School and many attempts were made to help him. He eventually became a clerk in young Ralph's chambers when the latter had qualified as a lawyer.

A subsequent butler, George Taylor, or "Old George" as he became during his long service with the family, was "given to deep potations". He would often fall off his chair and once broke his arm doing so. There never seems to have been any question of sacking George.

The family's contacts with relatives outside the immediate family were regular, but not necessarily greater than those of a twentieth century family. Ralph Carr remained close to his surviving sisters, Margaret, who lived in Newcastle until her death in 1790, and Katherine Scott, who died in 1800, and to the latter's family. He was also, as we have seen, the friend and business partner of his nephew John Widdrington. All did not go smoothly with either the Widdringtons or Mrs Carr's Byne relatives. Fond though he was of John and Jane Widdrington, Ralph Carr considered, with some reason, that they were ruining themselves with their extravagance, while Isabella Byne's relatives caused Ralph Carr a number of problems.

Isabella had two brothers, Henry and Charles.[57] Henry died at Morpeth in 1760. His son Henry inherited the family's Carshalton property and his daughter, Anne, married John Skerrit, who later became a lieutenant-general. Charles Byne, Isabella's, other brother, married three times. His grandson Henry was involved in a law suit with his cousin twice removed, the other Henry Byne, over the Carshalton property. It was one of those law suits in which the period abounded, which ruined everyone but the lawyers, and its costs dissipated the family's remaining property. Ralph had a poor opinion of the thrice married Charles's son by his third marriage, another Charles, telling his younger son Ralph not to go to Carshalton while Charles Byne was there, "whose acquaintance I by no means wish you to make" and referring to him as "my perpetual plague C. Byne who is ruining himself and family by their shameful extravagance at Bath, London and every county in England".[58]

Despite such minor problems, Ralph Carr could, in the late 1780s, congratulate himself: he had wealth and position, a fine family, a companionable wife, a sensible and intelligent elder son, a promising younger son and two attractive and talented daughters. Though he did not know it, an Indian summer of contentment was yet to be granted to him.

References

1.   Colonel R. E. Carr in *Family of Carr* records the date of Ralph's marriage to Isabella as 1758 but a search of the register of St. Mary's Church, Ponteland, reveals it to have been on 29 Nov. 1753.

2.   In fact Christopher Scott seems to have had ample means. His first wife, a Miss Clark of York, had brought him a large fortune.

3.   Charles Byne to Ralph Carr, undated. NRO. 855. Box 6.

4.   Ralph Carr to Isabella Carr, 6 Aug. 1756.

5.   *Ibid*, Undated but probably late 1756.

6.   Charles Byne to Isabella Carr, 18 Sept. 1755 and 9 May 1756.

7.   Isabella Carr's Household Account Book, Dec. 1795.

8.   Ralph Carr, 1796. Quoted in *Family of Carr*, p.57.

9.   Welford, *Men of Mark* pp.493-494.

10.   Stella Tillyard, *Aristocrats. Caroline, Emily, Louisa and Sarah Lennox 1740-1832*, (1994), p.87.

11.   The poet and physician Erasmus Darwin refused to discipline his children at all, while the young Charles James Fox and his siblings were allowed to do much as they wished in the grand surroundings of Holland House.

12.   Ralph Carr to Isabella Carr, 11 Feb., 1767 NRO. 855. Box 4.

13.   Ralph Carr to Isabella Carr, 7 March, 1770.

14. Built by Willian Newton in 1770.

15. Quoted in *Eighteenth Century Newcastle* by P. M. Horsley (1971), pp.236-237.

16. "Family Memoirs" by Caroline Twistleton. In 1866 Caroline went to look at the Charlotte Square house but couldn't understand how this "miserable looking small dwelling" had been the scene of the parties described in Annabella Carr's journal. She concluded that "they didn't have so much furniture then and ladies' dresses were smaller". The house still stands, though somewhat dilapidated, and is a fine Georgian town house.

17. Stoney Bowes or Andrew Robinson Bowes was the winner, along with Sir Mathew Ridley, of the 1780 election in Newcastle. An Irish adventurer, he married the widowed Lady Strathmore whom he later abducted after she had left him. He was in the words later applied to Lord Byron, "mad, bad and dangerous to know".

18. Some indication of how marriages could often result from militia camps is given in a letter from Annabella's brother John to his father. John was at school in Beverley in 1779 and during the summer the Northumberland militia was encamped there. J. Carr to R. Carr 8 Aug. 1779: "Colonel Bell is going to be married in a very short time to a lady who has I am afraid spent most of her money on fine cloaths and has not I must say a good stock of beauty. Her name is Grand and her younger sister is also going to be married to one Redhead. In short there are 3 or 4 more ladies going to be married in a very short time all to gentlemen in your militia". These were very sophisticated observations coming from a fifteen year old boy.

19. A. Carr to J. Carr, Aug. 10 1781 NRO. 855. Box 6.

20. *Ibid.*

21. Sarah Isabella Scott was the daughter of Christopher Scott and Katherine, Ralph Carr's sister. She was known to the family as Sally Bell and was frequently at Dunston hill.

22. A. Carr to J. Carr, Aug. 1781.

23. William was a footman and he and the other footman Robert appear to have had the very useful accomplishment of being very skilful at dressing the hair of the ladies of the family.

24. Annabella Carr to Ralph Carr, July 8, 1782.

25. Annabella Carr's journal as transcribed by Caroline Twistleton.

26. The public school education of the day certainly had its limitations. Robert Ellison, who was sent to Eton earlier in the century, had, on being apprenticed to a banker, to be sent to Mr Footer's Academy to learn arithmetic, geography and modern languages.

27. John Carr to his father, Ralph Carr, 9 Aug. 1777. Medical advice in the eighteenth century tended to be as suspicious of the deleterious effects of fruit as that of the twentieth is enthusiastic as to its benefits.

28. John Carr to Isabella Carr, 26 Oct. 1777.

29. John Carr to his father, Ralph Carr, 28 Sept. 1777.

30. Admiral Keppel was cleared by a court martial for his failure to beat the French off Ushant in 1778 and the blame was attached to Admiral Sir Hugh Palliser. Keppel's acquittal was the occasion for riots throughout the land. Palliser was a supporter of the North government and Keppel was backed by the Whig opposition.

31. John Carr to his father, Ralph Carr, 15 Oct. 1780.

32. Christ Church had in the period 1780-89 a total of 75 peers or peers' sons as undergraduates, far more than any other Oxford College, while more of the peerage were educated at Westminster than any other school save Eton. John Cannon, *Aristocratic Cantury. The Peerage of Eighteenth Century England.* (1984) pp. 40 and 50.

33. Charles James Fox for instance had run up gambling debts of £140,000 by the time he was in his late twenties.

34. J. Carr to R. Carr, 28 Feb., 1782 NRO. 855. Box 4.

35. As Westminster had a large number of voters, elections there tended to be tumultuous and riotous.

36. R. Carr to R.Carr jnr., 22 Nov. 1781.

37. *Ibid*, 7 April 1782.

38. Isabella Carr to R. Carr jnr. 1781.

39. J. Carr to R. Carr, 14 Nov. 1781.

40. *Ibid*, 1 Jan. 1782.

41. *Ibid*, 1 Feb. 1782.

42. *Ibid*, 28 Feb. 1782.

43. *Ibid*, 26 May. 1783.

44. *Ibid*, 16 April 1784 and 16 May 1784.

45. Sir Thomas Clavering had been ill but did not die for another decade. Lord Ravensworth had no male heir and, if he had died intestate, the estate would have gone to his errant daughter the Countess of Upper Ossory. In the event he left the estate to his nephew, Henry Liddell, who also inherited the Liddell baronetcy. Mrs Montagu found this hard to understand. Sir Henry was a wild rake: "He amused himself with the exhibition of two Lapland women whom he imported. He collects all sorts of wild beasts; and his ale-cellars make beasts of men. It is strange that Lord Ravensworth should prefer such a nephew to his grandsons". Doran, *A Lady of the Last Century* (1873) p.335.

46. *Ibid*, 1 April 1785.

47. Ralph Carr to R. Carr jnr. 9 April 1785.

48. *Ibid*, 20 March 1786.

49. Sir William Scott to R. Carr, 5 April 1789 and to R. Carr jnr. 19 April 1789.

50. Caroline Twistleton "Memoirs".

51. Annabella Carr to John Carr, Sept. 1786.

52. J. Carr to R. Carr, Feb. 2, 1784.

53. J. Carr to R. Carr May 16 1795. The cost was made up of 1/- a mile to Newark and 13d thereafter and two nights at inns.

54. Isabella Carr to Ralph Carr jnr., 1791.

55.   Isabella Carr to John Carr, Feb. 17, 1792.

56.   R. Carr to J. Carr, Sept. 10 1791.

57.   Her two sisters died young from smallpox.

58.   R. Carr to R. Carr jnr. April 9 1785. This was the Charles Byne from whom Ralph Carr bought the Prendwich estate.

Chapter 12

The Grand Tour[1]

With extreme regret did we hear of the declaration of war, not that the vague threats of that wicked nation can strike the smallest dread into a British bosom...

Harriet Carr

Ralph Carr intended that his son John would inherit the bulk of his land and property. This was conventional enough for primogeniture had long ordained among the landed classes that the main estate went to the elder son and, as wealthy merchants purchased land, they tended to adopt the *mores* of the gentry. Primogeniture, together with entailment, was what kept estates intact over time. But Ralph was determined that his younger son and his daughters would be well provided for and indeed he was somewhat equivocal about founding an estate which the family would be connected with for generations. He stated that he had not "the vanity of making what they call a family". Yet, by providing John with an education suited to a country gentleman, giving him the means to divide his time between London and the north, and asking only that he begin to gradually learn something of the management of the family property he would eventually inherit, Ralph was indeed producing the head of a county family, who would have the background, acquaintances and culture fitting for a landed gentleman.

During the eighteenth century it had become increasingly fashionable for a gentleman to complete his education by travelling on the continent. The classic motive for continental travel was the post-graduate polish provided by the cultural education of the Grand Tour and it was this, together with a sense of adventure and desire for new experiences, that prompted John Carr to begin planning a continental tour soon after he left Oxford. Ralph Carr, remembering no doubt, the value of his own travels as a young man, was happy to support his son's travels. His only demand, in the event, was a steady stream of letters home, to which we are indebted for our detailed knowledge of John's experiences. An early plan for John to travel with his relative Henry Byne fell through, probably due to Byne's financial position, soon to be worsened by his family's legal wranglings. It was not until the summer of 1788 that John and a wealthy Oxford acquaintance, Richard Meyer, set forth for France.

In the spring and early summer of 1788 John was making arrangements for his travels which were intended to last one and a half years. He was eager to assure his father that he was being economical and that, though Meyer was rich, he was modest and thrifty in his habits. The beginnings of a tourist trade had already grown up: the travellers were able to buy a coach suitable for the roads they would have to deal with (it had been especially made for the Duke of Bedford when he had gone abroad three years previously); and arrangements were made with Sir Robert Herries, who had an extensive network of contacts with continental banking houses, for bills of credit which would await them at various towns along their route. They dispensed with the "bear-leader" or tutor-companion that many young men engaged but John did find a manservant with experience of foreign travel, turning his present servant, Stephen, over to his brother on the grounds that he would have been, "a very great encumbrance".[2] John and Meyer did not stint themselves, for even a second hand coach of a duke was a luxury purchase, but were generally sensible with their expenditure at the beginning as they were to be throughout their travels.[3]

They planned to spend some months learning French "in some proper part of France -Blois or Orleans" and in the end Tours was decided upon. They crossed the channel from Dover to Boulogne and were in Paris by mid June. Time in Paris, so John assured his father, was spent "in seeing the most striking public buildings" in the company of two temporary fellow travellers, who were "respectable" and members of the Society of Antiquaries.[4]

At Tours they took lodgings with a language teacher and stayed there for three months, their studies, according to John's letters home, punctuated only by meals until they ventured out in the cool of the evening. No doubt a provincial town provided little enticement to stray from study, but John was clearly concerned to give his father the impression that he passed his time as the latter would have wished.

John's early impressions of French cuisine were not favourable: "Their cookery is so very different from ours that I have not been able to eat two ounces per day - and as for their wine which is the only liquor we can procure to drink, it is so nearly allied to vinegar...".[5] He revised this opinion and, as they journeyed south after leaving Tours, described in glowing terms a meal at an inn in Rochefort:

> *...a couple of fowls fricassed and mutton chops - a young Turkey - red leg'd partridge flanked by seven ortolans for the second course and a large plate of excellent prawns with a handsome collation of fruit for*

desert, included they give you a bottle of a kind of claret which is the vin du pays and afterwards we treated ourselves with a bottle of vin de Bordeaux. Everything excellent of its kind...[6]

Once in the south of France, the travellers determined to do, what was relatively unusual and adventurous for tourists, to cross into Spain. John's fellow north-countryman, Henry Swinburne, had recently published an account of his travels in Spain, but the country was still considered somewhat inaccessible.[7] A voiture and four mules had to be hired at Perpignan and the party arrived at Barcelona five days later, having walked behind the mules most of the way. He found the Spanish much more to his liking than the French and was impressed by Barcelona and the Spanish vineyards:

"...conceive a hundred acres planted with red and white grapes, interspersed with Pears, Apples, Plums, Apricots, Cherries, Peaches, Olives, Pomegranets, Quinces, Pommes d'amour, Almonds, Oranges, Lemons, Mulberries, Walnuts, Figs, Chestnuts, Citrons..."[8]

John was to meet a great many English travellers in the south of France for both the fashionable and the invalid had begun to winter there for the warm climate. The travellers came across the young Prince Augustus (later Duke of Sussex), whose doctors suspected he was consumptive. John and Meyer enjoyed a varied social life, mixing with residents like Gouverneur Ellis and Abbé Raynal as well as with other tourists. As John wrote from Marseilles in February, "We do not associate too much with the English though we must meet some of them into whatever company we go". The English sought out a climate akin to an English summer and tended to flee the south at the approach of spring. By February 1789, John thought the weather, "...now warmer than one would wish it for pleasure".

They moved on to Lyon for the spring finding "troops of English passing through this place every day from the southern parts of france and Italy, the approaching hot weather having driven them to colder latitudes". Here they came across, a north country neighbour of the Carrs, Mr Clavering.[9]

At Lyon Meyer got word that his father was seriously ill and it was decided that, after a brief tour of Switzerland, he would return home. John, however, fell in with new companions, Mr Portman and his professional tutor companion, Mr Dillon, and it was with them that he journeyed on to Germany.[10]

John was much taken by his first impressions of Germany:

> *In entering the Palatinate at Gemmershein nothing can be more striking*
> *than the contrast between the two nations. From poverty and the*
> *ignorance of every real comfort of life you pass at once into a land of*
> *ease and contentment...the towns in Germany are as different from those*
> *in France, as Swallwell of smoaky memory is from Aubern, loveliest*
> *village of the vale...the* men are much stronger than French and the
> women are as fair as our countrywomen *and quite as well shaped as the*
> *French.*[11]

He was soon to find, however, that the roads of the Palatinate were to give no
warning of the dreadful uneven tracks he was to meet with elsewhere in Germany
and especially in Prussia.

An Englishman, with the right background and with letters of introduction, found
many doors open to him and dining tables set for him as he travelled. John and his
companions enjoyed the hospitality of British diplomatic representatives and both
British and foreign royalty and aristocrats. As he wrote from Berlin to his sister
Harriet: "...we have been living with the great ones of the land. We have been
dining with Princes and Dukes, and supping with Kings and queens...Is it not a
proud thing for our little island, my sister, that its inhabitants are distinguished
wherever they go...". The younger sons of George III were at this time travelling
and studying abroad. John had already come across Prince Augustus at Hières. At
Geneva he dined with Prince Edward (later Duke of Kent) and in Brunswick he
dined with both of them and Prince Adolphus (later Duke of Cambridge). The
princes were engaged in military and academic studies at the University of
Gottingen and John noted approvingly that they were " kept very close to their
studies and exercises ...they seem already to have profited from the strictness of the
people about them".[12]

They journeyed further east, finding the roads dreadful, through "forests and
commons where there was no appearance of wheel ever having been" and both their
carriages broke down between Dresden and Prague. Around Prague and Vienna,
however, John considered that the roads were "good as they are almost throughout
the dominions of the House of Austria".[13]

At Vienna John fell ill with the malarious fever that the Austrian Army had brought
back from its campaign against the Turks in Wallachia. For the modern traveller,
the thought of being taken ill when far from home is worrying, but for the
eighteenth century traveller it was a prospect to be dreaded. John was unable to
return home with Portman and Dillon, when they left Vienna in December 1789,

and was ill for several months. He was lucky both in the support he received from the British community and in the medical attention he received.

During his illness, he received visits from the British Envoy, Sir Murray Keith, and other British residents, whilst Lord Thanet, whose family had a long-standing association with the Carrs, going back to John, the "Patriarch's", time was living in the same house.

He relied for medication upon some English bark given him by Portman, which would have been much more efficacious than the bleedings most doctors would have prescribed. Bark contains quinine, though the drug was not to be isolated until 1820. Naturally, his family was very worried about him. His mother sent advice about his treatment, telling him not to take the bark at the onset of a bout of fever and consulted Dr Turton, a London physician who was favourable to the virtues of taking infusions of bark. Dr Turton also turned out to be a friend of the Emperor's physician, Dr Quarin, who, he advised John to consult if not entirely recovered.

It was not until the spring of 1790 that John was fit enough to set off for home. By this time European affairs were in disarray as a result of the French Revolution and Ralph Carr was much disturbed as to which route home his son should take. He advised him to travel via Germany and Holland and "avoid those districts which are now in arms". John took the suggested route and by late October had reached Rotterdam and was preparing to embark for England.

John's appetite for travel was undiminished by his experiences and by August 1791 he was busy with plans for a journey through revolutionary France to Italy to be made with his sister, Harriet.

Harriet who became twenty that year had grown into a talented, attractive and vivacious young woman. Aware of her beauty, she both enjoyed the advantages and surmounted with ease the contemporary restrictions of her sex. She rode well and, unusually for a woman of the period, enjoyed shooting. Clearly idolised by her family, she enjoyed cutting a fashionable figure and, pursued by males and emulated by females, being the centre of attraction. She was also, as we have seen, a talented artist, who painted, sketched and created medallions and friezes and had considerable knowledge of the history of art. Colonel R. E. Carr said of her in his history of the Carr family:

> *In figure she was petite, and as shewn in a water-colour drawing of her taken by Mr Thane in Florence in 1794, must at that time have been a most attractive girl. She is represented on a grey horse in a dove-*

coloured habit, with a wide hat (in the style of the Gainsborough's
Duchess of Devonshire) shading her brown hair and blue eyes.

Her health had, however, worried the family for some time, a troublesome cough seeming to presage consumption. Some time in a warm climate might, it was felt, might save her from an early decline.

John was, like all the family, very fond of his sister, though perhaps somewhat worried by her accomplishments. He had written to her from Lyon in 1789 recognising that she possessed greater attainments than the generality of young women but warning her not to neglect, "to give a proper share of attention to those more trifling accomplishments which from the usual education of women is all they can boast of...".[14] His letter was somewhat pompous, as he half recognised. Did he worry that too great a display of intelligence might frighten off suitors? Did he consider that the formidable mind and intellectual interests of Annabella had indeed had such an effect?

It was quite bold of John to consider a tour of the Continent, during which he would be responsible for his sister's welfare, for in 1791 the course of events in revolutionary France became ever more disturbing. "These are wonderful days", he wrote, "when we see Kings flying from their own subjects as though from their greatest enemies, and afterwards brought back in chains to their palace."[15] Certainly the revolution presented new dangers to the English traveller and Ralph Carr must have been very concerned for the state of his daughter's health to let her go. As Mrs Montagu wrote to her nephew, Matthew, in the autumn of 1789, urging him not to think of going to France: "...to go into a country to partake of the horrors of a famine or mix in the confusion of civil war would be very unbecoming your prudence".[16] Nevertheless, John and Harriet, accompanied by a manservant, Stephen, who had been rejected as unsuitable for the previous tour, and Harriet's maid, Dolly Bates, set off on their travels at the end of August.

The Carrs' journey to Italy took them through France and John had taken the precaution of having his coat of arms erased from his carriage before leaving England and he provided the party with "four national cockades which are to be our passport through France".[17] In the event the journey was uneventful and the party's progress was not hindered. John was able to report from Genoa:

> *Except being very strictly and we thought invidiously searched by the*
> *Customs house officers upon Mount Jura...we have nothing to allege*
> *against the French patriots. The children sometimes called us aristocrats,*
> *but those whose anger was to be feared let us pass very quickly.*[18]

The passage across the Alps presented different dangers. The Mount Cenis pass was not suitable for wheeled vehicles and tourists were carried over in a type of sedan chair. Although the brother and sister crossed, according to Harriet, "with the utmost ease and pleasure",[19] they did so just in time to avoid torrential rain and great flooding. "In the memory of the oldest man", wrote John from Turin, "nothing has been quite equal to the deluge in the plains, the Po runs through the streets".[20]

Once in Italy, they found themselves welcomed into society. If Harriet's health was their major concern, and their letters home are full of information and reassurances as to her cough and the progress of her recovery, Harriet did not allow her invalid status to spoil her enjoyment of new experiences. They attended the King of Sardinia's *Grande Chasse* as the guests of the British Envoy.

John had already had some experience of continental sporting mores from his time in Bohemia. There the *battue,* that was not to become fashionable in England until the late nineteenth century, was well established. John, a keen shot who was used to the English habit of going out with a few friends and dogs, was horrified by slaughter of a host of driven game and, with respect to a bag of 3,258 pieces of game slain by a party of eight in three days, wrote: "This gives one a good idea of their brutal manner of hunting in this country, and of the brutal taste that such butchery can entertain".[21] He was even more appalled by Italian customs but was delighted by Harriet's social success:

> ...both the King [Victor Amadeus III] and his son's wife, the Duchess of
> Aosta, spoke to Harriet as she had hold of Mr Trevor's [the Envoy] arm .
> It is a sight worth seeing but going hunting in a carriage does not answer
> to our idea of the Chase. At the death all the court is assembled by sound
> of trumpet, and Harriet had the compliment payed her of being presented
> with a foot of the stag.[22]

During the winter of 1791 and the spring of 1792, John and Harriet stayed at Florence, Naples and Rome, following a regime designed for the improvement of Harriet's health, the pursuit of her interest in Italian art, John's literary interests, and the enjoyment of a social life both in Italian society and amongst English compatriots. Harriet wrote to her mother from Florence, where they had journeyed via Parma, where she especially admired the Correggios, and Bologna:

> I dare not suffer myself to remember one picture as there are hundreds
> beyond description excellent; and it is a subject that I cannot speak
> reasonably on; suffer it to say that I scarce thought myself on earth and
> here I feel I shall lose my senses.[23]

Harriet was not just an admirer of paintings but an artist herself. In Lord Berwick's view, "she excelled all the Ladies in practise that are present distinguished", and much of her time in Italy was spent in copying from the masters or in doing sketches and watercolours. At the Uffizi she applied for a private room where she drew from the sculptures and painted a copy in miniature of Titian's Venus.[24]

In Rome they rode with Lord Cole and Sir Ralph Waller, and John commented in a letter to his father that Harriet, "has a very good horse, and is the admiration of all the Roman ladies who never venture out of their carriages..." There were many English artists in Rome and they naturally interested Harriet who was introduced to some of them by Henry Swinburne, the writer, who often accompanied John and Harriet on their morning excursions.

During the winter of 1791, Naples was full of English tourists. As John wrote from Rome: "Most of the English have taken flight for Naples which we are told is a second London. Prince Augustus goes there on Monday".[25] John's and Harriet's entry into Neapolitan society had already been prepared, for Sir Robert Herries had entertained them and Sir William and Lady Hamilton to dinner in London the previous summer, and the Carrs and the British Ambassador and his wife had again met in Genoa. In Naples Lady Hamilton sat to Harriet for a watercolour miniature; she wrote on the back of it: "Emma Hamilton, Naples Feb. 11, 1792. I had the happiness of my dear Miss Carr's company all day, but alas the day was too short".[26] The brother and sister were enjoying success among the smartest of expatriate society and the Italian aristocracy.

Italy signified music and opera as well as the fine arts. Neither Harriet or John were particularly musical but John diligently attempted to increase his knowledge of music and his appreciation of it in the interests both of self-improvement and so as to be able to write to his musical sister, Annabella, about her main interest. He was impressed by the Neapolitan opera and by the throng of musicians in a city where every theatre had its own orchestra. In comparison, he thought poorly of the Roman opera: "The circumstance alone of men playing the parts of women is disgusting".[27]

The Carrs' intention was to start for home in April 1792, but, like many English travellers, they found themselves unable to leave because of the approach of war. The habit of foreign travel had become so deeply ingrained in the English upper classes that, despite the French Revolution and the worsening international situation, Italy was full of British tourists in 1792. Although Britain did not enter the war that began with the French declaration against Austria in April 1792 until February 1793, John Carr was worried enough by May to decide to stay in Florence for the summer. "We have accounts that all the towns in the north of Italy are full of English who have stopd on the same account." Florence was, he considered, if they were to remain in Italy, "the most eligible place to take up our summer residence...". He had decided to stay another year, which would in any case be good for his sister's health, rather than run into danger.

Staying at Florence for the summer meant enduring the sort of weather the modern tourist looks for. They had to go out very early, "the heat being intolerable at eight o'clock in the morning"[28], and spent most of the day in the house. There was no shortage of English companions, for amongst those staying in Tuscany were the Bishop of Winchester, the Duke of Manchester, Lord Orford, Sir Horatio Mann and Lord and Lady Wright.[29] By the autumn the crowds of English people had increased. Nice and Savoy were now in the hands of the French, who were preparing to descend upon Piedmont. Italy as a whole, John felt was ready to welcome the French revolutionaries, but Tuscany was different for the Grand Duke was honoured and loved. "This country is a Utopia in comparison to the rest of Italy which is wretchedly governed."[30]

John and Harriet did not return to England until the autumn of 1794. It was by no means an unpleasant exile. "We have had a completely happy summer", wrote John in September 1792. Despite fears that the French might attack Rome, he commented in November on Harriet's popularity with the ladies of Florence, whilst in December 1793 he reported both that the French had sent the Pope an ultimatum and that Harriet was setting the fashion in Florence. They both were enjoying a lively social life to which the collection of visiting cards they brought home with them bears witness and Harriet was able to paint and explore art collections, while John followed his antiquarian interest in Italian literature.

Harriet accepted Britain's declaration of war in February 1793 like the good patriot she was:

> *...with extreme regret did we hear of the declaration of war, not that the vague threats of that wicked nation can strike the smallest dread into a British bosom but that their barbarous manner of making war may in other respects injure us severely. It most nearly concerns us who are abroad as it will render our return very difficult...We are at present inundated by French, escaped from Rome, most of them young artists and par consequence Jacobins who with their short-cut hair and high crowned hats ressemble tole grate the Oliverian Round Heads.*

John's worries were not solely concerned with his sister's health, which in any case appeared to have improved, and the difficulties of returning home. To be responsible for an attractive young sister, a fashionable woman and accomplished equestrienne, who was popular with both expatriate and Italian society, must have been at once a source of pride and something of a worry. Harriet obviously attracted men, though she was quite capable of eluding unwanted admirers; it was to escape the attentions of a Mr Basky that she requested the private room in the Uffizi where she could draw in peace.[31] There was, nevertheless, always the danger of a wanted but socially unsuitable admirer. Gossip about Harriet and some Italian suitor made its way back to Ralph Carr, and John had to write denying it had any substance. He had, he said, been careful to provide against any such possibility: "I have consequently been upon my guard that no young man should frequent our house sufficiently to justify any report of this kind".[32] Harriet's name had obviously been linked in rumour with a person called Ventini and John informed his mother that, though there was a noble house of that name in Florence, the Marquis was married and his wife a great friend of Harriet's.[33] It could not be said, however, that the censorious would have approved of Florentine society in 1793. Two parts of that exotic ménage à trois that was the Devonshire household were there, in the persons of the Duchess, recently delivered of a child that was not the Duke's, and Lady Elizabeth Foster, mother of two children who were the duke's. It was not until August 1794 that the brother and sister journeyed via Innsbruck, Augsburg, Frankfurt, Coblenz and Rotterdam to Harwich, arriving in England on 1 September, almost exactly three years after they had left.

The travels of John and Harriet demonstrate the fortitude of eighteenth century travellers, many of whom were not deterred by crises or wars upon the Continent. If in his letters home, John had spoken more of his sister's courage while in ill health and of her equestrian ability and social success than of her painting and sketching, he was as careful to transport the folios of her work back to England as he was to ensure the safety of his collection of classical and modern Italian books. The motives for travel of eighteenth century tourists were often varied and John and Harriet combined many of them: self-improvement, curiosity, amusement and the cure of ill-health. They must be numbered amongst the elite of tourists who had strong intellectual and cultural interests together with a genuine desire to gain experience of foreign societies.

References

1.   This chapter follows closely my article, "John and Harriet Carr: A brother and sister from the North -East on the Grand Tour" in *Northern History,* Vol XXX 1994.

2.   John Carr to Ralph Carr, 7 June 1788 NRO. 855 .Box 4.

3.   John's expenses for the year 1789 were £800, a moderate sum for a young man on a foreign tour travelling with his own servant and carriage.

4. John Carr to Ralph Carr 15 June 1788.

5. *Ibid*.

6. *Ibid*, 20 Oct. 1788.

7. H. Swinburne, *Travels Through Spain in the years 1775 and 1776* (1779). Few tourists strayed from the beaten track of Italy, France, Switzerland, the Low Countries and Germany. Greece which was part of the Ottoman Empire was visited only by the very adventurous. Sir Charles Monck of Belsay and his bride spent a year of their two year honeymoon there, and returned with their son, Charles Atticus. Business was the only inducement to travel in Scandinavia, though those three rake-hells, Sir Henry Liddell, Mathew Consett and Stoney Bowes, visited Lapland on a three month tour of Sweden, Finland and Denmark. The story goes that that this trip was undertaken as a result of a wager by Liddell that he would bring back two reindeer and two Lap women. He won his bet.

8. *Ibid*, 25 Dec. 1788.

9. Probably Thomas-John Clavering who was to inherit the baronetcy in 1794.

10. Mr Portman was of the family that gave its name to London's Portman Square and his tutor was an experienced traveller who had, John informed his father, escorted some thirteen young men around Europe.

11. J. Carr to Ralph Carr, 30 June 1789. The reference is to Goldsmith's poem, *The Deserted Village*, although the correct quotation is, "loveliest village of the plain".

12. *Ibid,* 16 July 1789.

13. *Ibid,* 17 Oct. 1789.

14. J. Carr to Harriet Carr 25 March 1789.

15. J. Carr to Isabella Carr, 9 Oct. 1791.

16. Quoted in Black, *The British Abroad,* p.168.

17. J. Carr to R. Carr, 2 Sept. 1791.

18. *Ibid,* 10 Sept. 1791.

19. Harriet Carr to Isabella Carr 9 Oct. 1791.

20. J. C. to R. C. 16 Oct. 1791.

21. J. C. to R. C. 17 Oct. 1789.

22. *Ibid , 25 Oct. 1791.*

23. Harriet Carr to Isabella Carr, 21 Nov. 1791.

24. I am indebted for this information to Mrs Carol Blackett-Ord who showed me her entry on Harriet Carr subsequently published in *A Dictionary of British and Irish Travellers in Italy 1701-1800* ed. John Ingamells (1997).

25. J. C. to R. C., 3 Dec. 1791. Prince Augustus was in the following year to meet Lady Augusta Murray in Rome. The following year, 1793, he went through a marriage ceremony with her in defiance of the Royal Marriages Act.

26. The miniature was sold at Sotheby's in 1905. Its present whereabouts are unknown.

27. John Carr to Annabella Carr, 24 March 1792. Such disapproval by Englishmen of men playing women's parts was not uncommon, yet only a century previously all female parts on the English stage had been played by men, while in the 1790s Mrs Jordan, one of the most celebrated actresses of the day, was for ever donning breeches and playing male roles.

28. John Carr to Ralph Carr, 21 July 1792.

29. *Ibid*, 22 June 1792. Lord Orford, the son of Robert Walpole, is better known as Horace Walpole, novelist, politician and indefatigable letter writer. Sir Horace Mann Bt. was the nephew of Sir Horace Mann, the first baronet, who had been Envoy Extraordinary to Florence and was one of Walpole's correspondents.

30. *Ibid,* 11 Oct. 1792.

31. Ex *inf* Carol Blackett-Ord.

32. John Carr to Ralph Carr, 12 Nov. 1793.

33. John Carr to Isabella Carr, 24 Nov. 1793.

Chapter 13

Three Generations

Then Oh my Soul praise ye the Lord
For mercies shown to thee
Who doth both life and health accord
Even to ninety-three.

Ralph Carr

John and Harriet Carr returned to a country at war, France having delared war on Britain in February 1793. In comparison with the wars of the twentieth century, the French Revolutionary and Napoleonic Wars have sometimes been depicted as scarcely affecting the rhythm and pattern of the social life of the upper sections of society. Such a view is misguided: the economic effects of the war were considerable, some beneficial such as the rise in agricultural prices with their complementary effects on incomes derived from land, others less so, such as the steep increase in taxation; invasion was anticipated, which kept the militia active and led to the raising of volunteer regiments, while the dangers of a militant radicalism sympathetic to French Jacobinism were taken seriously in the 1790s; and above all, few families would have been without friends or relatives serving in the army or navy.

Much of the routine of social life did, of course, continue substantially unchanged against this backdrop, for Britain was no society geared for total war by subsequent standards. It was, however, a society prepared to fight to maintain its independence, values and way of life against external and internal threats. Society took on a military hue and the role of the gentry as the leaders and unpaid administrators in their localities and counties became more important than ever.

As the eldest son of what was now a landed family, John Carr had been given a gentleman's education but he had as yet to acquire the experience in estate management and the familiarity with regional politics and administration that were the necessary background for the position he would inherit. His life on his return from Italy was a mixture of the normal routine of a country gentleman combined with the special duties required by the circumstances of the war with France.

He familiarised himself with the family's estates and with the details of the Ponteland and Embleton tithes, working closely with the Carr's agent George Tate. He spent much time at Prendwick where he recorded his game bags which were very modest by the standards of later days; but these were not keepered shoots and John would simply walk for miles with his dog, Bell, shooting what game she put up. Thus, sixteen days shooting in August 1795 accounted for 29 grouse and 15 black game. Much rebuilding and landscaping was taking place at Hedgeley and John made frequent visits to oversee the work, reporting to his father on such matters as the pointing of the outside of the house, "to the want of which a great deal of the rain in the inside is owing". But rural life and its pleasures alternated with spells in London from which he sent his father the latest political and society gossip. In politics he inclined to a moderate Whig position and in Northumberland supported Whigs like Charles Grey and Matthew White Ridley. He was soon firmly established in county circles, his great friends being Sir Charles Monck and Sir John Swinburne, with both of whom he shared the common experience of foreign travel, and Charles Bigge. Monck, Carr and Bigge were all early Vice-Presidents of Newcastle's Society of Antiquaries, founded in 1813 while Swinburne was the first President. This was a period in which societies and clubs were becoming increasingly central to the life of North-East society. As well as the Society of Antiquaries, John was a member of the Literary and Philosophical Society and of the Recorders' Club, a society which still meets today on the premises of the Northern Counties Club, itself founded two decades later in 1829. If he inherited something of his father's good business sense, there was nothing of the merchant about John Carr, his acumen was applied to land rather than trade, and he was a polished gentleman with sophisticated tastes.

Like many landowners, he was much interested in methods of agricultural improvement and in London in May 1800 spent time looking at ingenious implements for cutting straw, grinding wheat and bruising horse corn. He also went with Charles Brandling of Gosforth House to see a device for measuring a given quantity of land which cost 30 guineas and was "Very difficult to operate accurately". He was interested in Sir John Sinclair's experimental agricultural society and in the newly founded National Institute for the Propagation of Science.

John was eager to expand the Hedgeley estate and, when the 570 acre Branton estate of Nicholas Brown was offered for sale in 1802 at £18,000, he was interested in buying it but at a lower price. Brown, confident that land could only become more valuable, refused to lower his price. Seven years later he was still prepared to consider offers but was in no hurry for, "In these perilous times land is better than money".[1]

Despite the existence of a considerable minority of radicals, who continued to both laud the revolutionary regime in France and hope for a similar overthrow of the established order in Britain, British society in its layered but vertically connected orders largely rallied to established authority and cohered against the threat of French invasion in the later 'nineties. The Church and King patriotism of the lower orders and a common rallying of middle and upper orders to the defence of order and property, in which a new kind of monarchism played a significant part, placed loyalty to the constitution and the king above internal differences. This development took various forms from demonstrations and even the riots of anti-radical crowds, to loyal dinners and addresses, patriotic sermons, the formation of the Association for the Preservation of Liberty and Property against Republicans and Levellers and the formation of the Volunteer regiments.

Traditionally, Britain was protected by her navy, had a small professional army, which could be sent anywhere, and militias who were primarily for the protection of their own counties. To these were added supplementary militias, the Volunteers, some 150,000 of them, and in 1803 an Army of the reserve.[2]

John Carr, like most of the county gentry, took an active role in the preparations against a possible French invasion. In 1798 a Supplementary Battalion of the Northumberland Militia was embodied and John became a captain serving at Alnwick and Berwick upon Tweed. This was a year in which there was considerable expectation of French troops landing and the Duke of Northumberland resigned his Lord-Lieutenancy after a dispute with his deputies over his leaving the county.[3] John was himself appointed a Deputy-Lieutenant of Northumberland in 1801. The perceived danger of a French invasion was again intense in 1803, when a General Order was issued as what to do in the event of an enemy landing; a signal was to be given by guns and flags at Tynemouth and Sunderland. A very detailed plan of action was drawn up for County Durham's Chester Ward entitled *In Case of Actual Invasion* and the Derwent Volunteer Legion, a company of the Durham Fencibles, in which John Carr was a captain (he became its Lt. Colonel in 1812) would have had a part to play in resisting such an invasion.[4]

This military activity meant an increase in the number of army camps in Northumberland and Durham with the incidental effect of enlivening the social life of polite society. It was at the social events consequent on this military presence that Harriet Carr met Colonel Cheney of the Grenadier Guards.

Having recovered her health in Italy, Harriet entered enthusiastically into the social round and enjoyed the pleasure of ranging widely on horseback through the Northumberland countryside. It says something both for her stamina and her independence that she thought little of riding from Dunston Hill to Hedgeley with a servant to accompany her. When cautioned by her worried father for not arranging to be escorted by her brother from Morpeth to Hedgeley, she replied that she had often done the journey when her health was much worse and that her invalid sister ran a greater risk when she made the same journey by hack chaise: "Sir, if either she or I could find either hazard or difficulty in journeying twenty miles [from Morpeth to Hedgeley] in a well-known country, how are we ever to get through the long and probably troublesome journey of life".

It was in 1796 that Harriet met Colonel Cheney, who was ADC to Prince William of Gloucester then commanding the troops in the area. It was not, however, until 1798 that they were engaged, the death of her mother, Isabella Carr, accounting for the long delay, and not until January 1799 that they were married.

During John and Harriet's tour abroad their brother, Ralph, had in December 1793 married Caroline Gregg at St Anne's Church in the City of London. Caroline was the daughter of Francis Gregg of Skinners' Hall, London, and Wallington Hall, Surrey, who was a lawyer, a member of the Skinners'Company, agent to the Earl of Carlisle and MP for Morpeth 1789-95.[5] She had first met Mrs Carr, Annabella and Harriet at Harrogate in 1786 and been introduced to Ralph the following year while the family were staying at 141 Bond Street. In subsequent years she was often at Hanover Street when the Carrs were in London for the season. Despite the general popularity of Caroline with the family, the marriage seems to have encountered opposition from both the Carrs and the Greggs. Ralph and Isabella Carr felt that, as their son was just beginning his legal career and a generous marriage settlement from the Greggs was not forthcoming, the marriage was very imprudent. Whether because they disapproved of the marriage or just did not care to part with money, the Greggs seem to have been difficult throughout and Caroline's dowry was only some £8,000.

John, while in Italy, had been informed by his brother of the marriage plans and wrote to his father from Florence in support of the forthcoming union:

> My last letter would inform you of the moment when I first became acquainted with Ralph's connection with Miss Gregg, which was last year at this time since when I have not been at liberty to mention the subject to anybody-I hope upon consideration the seeming imprudence of the intended union will wear off; I cannot help looking upon it as very likely to contribute effectively to his future good conduct and welfare.[6]

In January 1794 he wrote from Rome to try and convince his father to look more kindly upon the marriage, which had now taken place, "in spite of the many unpleasant circumstances that have attended it".[7]

These "unpleasant circumstances" had probably to do with money and the Gregg family's failure to provide Caroline with much of a dowry. Two years after the marriage when the couple had a son, bitter feelings were still evident. Ralph Carr senior was, of course, far too fond of his younger son not to become quickly reconciled to the marriage and soon became the fondest of father-in-laws, while Isabella Carr soon came round, but relations with Francis Gregg and his sons remained hostile. John wrote to his father from London in May 1795 telling him that his brother and Caroline had no communication with the Greggs. The conduct of both the sons (Henry and Francis Gregg) had "been ungentlemanly in the extreme" and later that month he considered that the behaviour of the three Greggs (father and sons) "has been so bad".[8] Caroline Carr, herself, wrote to Harriet of:

> *the unheard of treatment we have received from my family. I had hopes in the beginning that in time they would have felt some remorse and sorrow for what they have done but I now find that they are too hardened in guile ever to be reclaimed to any sense of contrition.....rejoice that all communication is at an end with such a race of selfish mercenary unfeeling beings.*[9]

There was eventually to be some sort of reconciliation of this unpleasant quarrel. By 1801 we find Francis Gregg supporting Ralph's application to succeed him in his post as a Commissioner of Bankruptcy[10] and in the next generation Isabella Carr, Ralph and Caroline's daughter, married her cousin, Charles Gregg.

Ralph Carr was considered a brilliant young lawyer and great things were expected of him; another Stowell or Eldon perhaps; more likely another Brougham, for Ralph was close to that great lawyer and politician and rather shocked his father by his radical sympathies. Although he was successful enough in his profession, being retained on important suits, he never fulfilled his promise. Colonel R.E.Carr argued that: "...he appears to have been prevented from applying himself to his profession, and thus rising to the eminence which his talents warranted, by his self-denying readiness to devote himself to the affairs and interests of numerous relations and friends..."[11] Essentially he didn't have the appetite nor perhaps the incentive to give his all to his profession. The victim of a happy childhood, he journeyed with his wife and children every year during his father's lifetime to spend some three or four months at Dunston Hill. This was not the routine of a fiercely ambitious lawyer but of a contented family man.

He was, in any case, well provided for as his father had told him he would be left about £26,500 and Caroline's dowry, if less than hoped for, had been £8,000. Indeed Ralph might well have ended up richer than his elder brother had an old man not changed his will.

Sir John Dick of Mount Clare, Roehampton, was an old friend of Ralph Carr senior and was extremely rich after a career as a merchant and British Consul at Leghorn, followed by a lucrative spell as Comptroller of Army Accounts and then Auditor of Public Accounts.[12] Newcastle born, he had benefited greatly from the friendship of Ralph Carr who, some eight years older than him, had paid for his education, supplied him with money in his early days and provided him with introductions to foreign merchants. The two remained life long friends and Dick intended to make the second son of his early benefactor his sole heir and made a will to that effect. In Dick's declining years, however, he fell under the influence of those closest to him, his physician, his apothecary and his godson, a clergyman, and made a new will, leaving his estate to be equally divided between these three and young Ralph Carr. Ralph had either neglected his patron or been diffident in maintaining his relationship with him, but even a fourth share of an estate which included the splendid villa, Mount Clare, and its 350 acres beside Richmond, together with a house in Harley Street, must have been substantial.

In 1796 Ralph Carr reached his eighty-fifth year and, although he had another decade to live, his mind turned to what he would leave his children and he wrote a letter to "My Dear Children" outlining what they could expect. He wrote that he had provided them all with "an independent and comfortable income" and continued:

> *I have not acted by you my three youngest childen as too many parents do from the vanity of making what they call a family, by leaving an improper share to your brother John for in my mind and in truth he has the most reason to say I have done wrong tho' I trust he may not, for I never found him liable to the imputation of selfishness - you my Ralpho, have no reason to complain for I have given you a sum which very possibly may be more than one half of what I have given your brother and more than double the sum to both your sisters.[13]*

For a younger son Ralph was indeed to be treated generously and, when his father came to dispose of some of his remaining mercantile assets a few years later, further gifts were forthcoming in the shape of to one eighth shares in two ships, the *Jenny* and the *James*.[14] The father's intention had been that his younger son should become a landowner and he had to this end bought Bygate Hall, an estate of over three hundred acres to the west of the Coquet. Ralph, as we have seen, gave it up ("foolishly" his father said) because he was unable to afford to maintain it, the rental income being small. As we shall see, he was later to become a substantial landowner.

The year 1797 saw the deaths of both Isabella Carr and John Widdrington. The loss of his wife, his companion for more than forty-three years, was a sad loss to Ralph Carr as to her children. He was increasingly dependent on his daughter Harriet for company and solace, for John was often away from home while Annabella spent much time in London and at the spas where she sought respite from her ailments. Ralph and his family could, however, be relied upon to pass several months every year at Dunston Hill.

Widdrington's death was a cause of grief but so was the dreadful mess he left his affairs in and the consequent financial plight of his widow. For long Ralph Carr had railed at the extravagance of his old partner and Mrs Widdrington, whom he nevertheless dearly loved and generously helped in their financial difficulties. John Widdrington had inherited the estate of Hauxley near Amble from Nathaniel Widdrington, his cousin. This inheritance was a mixed blessing. Hauxley was heavily mortgaged and was at the once a drain on Widdrington's resources and a spur to keeping up appearances. Rather than retrench, he immediately set about adding to the house and embellishing it. The Widdringtons were undoubtedly extravagant and burdened with debts but they were fun and all the Carrs were fond of them enjoying both their company at Dunston Hill and Charlotte Square and return visits to the delightful coastal setting of Hauxley. Ralph Carr and his son John were the executors of John Widrington's estate and had to bring the bereaved Mrs Widdrington bad tidings; her husband had left his estate at Hauxley to the sisters of Nathaniel Widdrington, Mrs Cooke[15] and Mrs Tinling, while his wife received only the house in Hanover Square, a small property in Whickham and about £200 a year. Widdrington had left unsigned a draft will leaving all to his wife, Jane, but John Carr, sorting papers at Hanover Square made a discovery he regretted making, a will dated August 6 1783; "Instead of bringing the poor widow comfort I shall now come with a melancholy story".[16]

It seems clear that Nathaniel Widdrington had wished his cousin John to have the estate for his lifetime and then leave it to Nathaniel's sisters. John, no doubt, went along with this in the year of his inheritance, intending to change his will later. His failure to do so condemned his wife to comparative poverty, alleviated only through the generosity of the Carrs, during a long widowhood of twenty-seven years.

The Carrs had a lot of trouble with their relatives. Ralph Carr jnr. considered that "The reckless extravagance of some of my relations (Widdrington and Byne) would almost drive me to the opposite extreme which however is equally to be shunned". Charles Byne, Isabella's brother, led an extravagant life. He was not to be trusted with money[17] and his relations with his mother Anne Byne were cool, while Ralph Carr called him "the bane of my life". An attractive rogue, he married three times. Mrs Isabella Carr would hear nothing against her brother calling him "the most wronged man in the world". His grandson Henry Byne brought a great Chancery suit against his cousin once removed, another Henry Byne, the last member of the family to live at Carshalton. This Henry was ruined by reckless extravagance and by the expence of fighting the lawsuit and, according to Ralph Carr jnr.'s daughter, "he lived much at the house of my father who was a valuable friend to him". John and Ralph shouldered the burden of their relatives manfully. John bought a young Byne a cornetcy when he threatened to enlist if his mother wouldn't buy him a commission, while Ralph, in his legal capacity, successfully appealed to the Commander in Chief against a military sentence passed on another Byne relative, Major General Skerrett.[18]

Ralph Carr could not but feel somewhat sorry for himself at the beginning of 1799 as he contemplated the imminent marriage of his daughter to Colonel Cheney, whose seat, Badger Hall, was in far away Shropshire. He confided his feelings to his old friend, Sir John Dick:

> *I am now going to give away one of my richest jewels-my daughter Harriet - which gives me pleasure but at the same time much grief...My dear Annabella has been from me more than six months and will continue at Bath till the spring. she has been very unwell...My son John I am robbed of by his captainship in the Northumberland Supplementary Militia, which I must own he could not at the present time avoid taking upon himself, tho I two years ago prevented his taking command of five thousand brave smiths of Swallwell Crowleys Works, which he was much pressed to. My dear Ralph is doom'd to thrash on at Westminster Hall- There was a time when I could have recommended him to the first Merchants upon the Change of London, but I have now outlived them all so I must leave him to Providence & his own merit which I trust he possesses- and I am now going to part with my last dear bird, Harriet, which brings me now to the heavy loss of my last two mainstays- my much loved wife and my nephew Widdrington- So that I am now a poor old vessel without masts, cables or anchors-and only fit to be broke up...*

Annabella wrote from Bath to give what comfort she could. The loss of Harriet was "...irreparable. But as she has so good a prospect of happiness and a worthy man we must overcome all selfish considerations". But her letter cannot have given much comfort: "I scarcely dare look forward ever to be able in any degree to supply her place, my health can never be restored-for three years past my life has been a *burden* to myself...".

Poor Annabella, the girl whose youth had been so radiant had become a perpetual invalid moving from spa to spa and doctor to doctor in search of cures. What was wrong with her? Were her ailments imaginary or at least exaggerated? Her doctors couldn't seem to find out and her father obviously thought her something of a hypochondriac:

> *I should not chuse to consult Dr. Darwin again-as he certainly did not happen to discover the nature of my complaint as has been fully proved since...I cannot suppose it possible for a person in the prime of life -thro' choice or whim-to give up the world and lead such a life as I have done- particularly here where I have had every temptation to do otherwise- but it is in vain for me to attempt to convince you. I am really ill...my constant prayer is to be released from my suffering...*

But she still kept an amused eye upon society: "The people are all running after the Prince of Wales as if he was a show and every mark of respect is shown him by the people!! He is so much thinner I would hardly have known him again - he had a concert last night & performed upon the violoncello-admirably".[19]

Harriet's marriage was to be followed within a few years by the marriage which brought our two families together, John's to Hannah Ellison in 1802. The Ellisons and the Carrs had, as it were, shadowed each other since the mid-seventeenth century, both part of the puritan faction in Newcastle during the civil war and both prospering subsequently. For most of this period, the Ellisons, linked closely to their Liddell relatives for the first half of the eighteenth century, had been by far the richer and more prominent family. Even by 1800, although Ralph Carr's business acumen had enabled the Carrs to become substantial landowners, their wealth and standing were modest in comparison to the Ellisons, who had enjoyed gentry status for a century and a half and had produced distinguished soldiers and MPs. Throughout almost the entire period of our study, the Ellisons and the Carrs were known to each other; almost everyone of gentlemanly status was known to his peer group in the relatively small world of North-East society and the two families were near neighbours. There is no evidence, however, that they were particularly close until near the end of the century when references to seeing Miss Ellison at Harrogate and calling upon Miss Elizabeth Ellison in London appear in Annabella Carr's letters. It is a comment upon the Carr's enhanced status that John Carr should have been considered a suitable husband for Hannah, the older sister of Cuthbert Ellison of Hebburn Hall. The Ellisons were pretty careful about marriage. For the most part (and Catherine Airey is the only exception) they either married very well or did not marry at all. There can of course have been no thought that the match would lead to John Carr's son inheriting the bulk of the Ellison estates; Cuthbert Ellison, the head of the family was only eighteen when Hannah and John married and he had two younger brothers.

John and Hannah began their married life at Ponteland Rectory and before his death in 1806 the nonogenarian Ralph Carr had the satisfaction of knowing his eldest son had an heir, Ralph, born at Dunston Hill in November 1805. He was to be the eldest of eight children.

It was, however, the family of his younger son that was to enrich Ralph Carr's last years. Six of the seven children of Ralph Carr junior were born within their grandfather's lifetime and the family's custom of spending much of the summer at Dunston Hill meant that the old merchant had a lively and happy household around him for three or four months of the year.

Caroline, the eldest daughter and third child of Ralph and Caroline Carr, has left an affectionate account of happy holidays at Dunston Hill:

> *...from the first week in July until term time in November when my father's duties as a barrister called him back to London- the travellers filled two chaises and the kind grandfather paid for the journey: which posting 300 miles there and back was no inconsiderable sum- so long a journey with the young children was a formidable undertaking...*[20]

The grandfather fussed over the arrangements, writing to his son before the 1801 journey, "...I beg you would be sure to have the wheels examined at each place".[21]

To the children Dunston Hill was clearly a wonderful and exciting place and as the setting for holidays under the benign rule of an indulgent grandfather far superior to their Bloomsbury home. An elegant house in a parkland setting with spectacular views of the Tyne Valley, Dunston Hill had much to recommend it to adults, but to children it had extra attractions. It was inhabited by more than just people: there was the ghost, the THUD; there was Poll the parrot, an immensely old bird, who was a wicked mimic, especially good at immitating nervous young curates; and many dogs, the favourite being Pan who lived to a ripe age.[22] Their activities and those of the family and servants were meticuously recorded in *Household Gods*, the weekly "publication" written and edited for several summers by Caroline's brother, John, which recounts in lively detail the travels to and from Dunston Hill and the holidays there.

With such company, old Ralph Carr soon got over the depressed state of mind that had briefly overcome him after the deaths of his wife and his nephew and his loneliness at the time of Harriet's marriage. He had lived on into an age where all his contemporaries were dead and his parents belonged to a byegone era-"sixty-four years since the death of my father" he mused in 1803. Yet, he found he still enjoyed life and in the year before his death sat down and wrote the poem which begins this chapter:

> *How few there are, whose days amount*
> *To three score years and ten,*
> *And all beyond that short account*
> *Is sorrow grief and pain.*
>
> *Then Oh my soul praise thou the Lord*
> *For mercies shown to thee*
> *Who doth both Life and Health accord*
> *Even to ninety three.*

Ralph Carr 1805

During his final illness, he was nursed by Harriet. He had always been very particular about what doctors he chose to consult, believing that most of that profession had little to recommend them. In middle age he had gone to London to consult Mr Hawkins rather than rely upon Newcastle doctors. Annabella, who was something of an expert on doctors, was scathing in her condemnation of the treatment her father received. She wrote from Dunston Hill to her brother Ralph that their father had "... been brought into this considerable danger by the ignorance and presumption of Ingham [Mr Ingham and Dr. Trotter were his doctors] in daring to triple the dose of calomel [mercurous chloride, much used as a purgative] ordered by Dr. Trotter. That he should have survived the effects of it is truly astonishing...It is indeed dreadful to think the life of any human creature should be entrusted to such a Blockhead - His extensive practice shows how inadequate the public is to judge of medical skill".[23] Whether his doctors were really at fault or as seems as likely, little could be done to help him, Ralph Carr died a fortnight later.

In his long life he had accomplished a great deal but perhaps not the least of his achievements was to have made a fortune in the hard school of North-East business and remained a kindly, generous and modest man.

References

1. John Dinning [land agent who was handling the sale] to John Carr, 25 Sept. 1809.

2. The rallying of British society casts an ambiguous light upon the strength of the established order. On the one hand, no government which lacks faith in the

loyalty of the mass of the populace arms a significant section of it, while the Loyalist Associations suggest a strong and vigorous popular patriotism, but on the other hand Loyalist Associations and even Volunteers suggest a deepening and widening of the political community, a community which has a voice. See Mark Philp, "Vulgar Conservatism, 1792-3", *The Historical Review*, No. 435, Feb. 1995.

3. Clive Emsley, *British Society and the French Wars 1793-1815* (1979) p.69.

4. Documents contained in folder, "Old Announcements and other interesting papers", Hedgeley Hall.

5. The last position followed from the former as Morpeth was almost a pocket borough of the Earls of Carlisle. Gregg was put in to keep the seat warm for Lord Morpeth, the heir to the earldom.

6. John Carr to Ralph Carr, 9 Sept. 1793.

7. *Ibid,* 11 Jan. 1794.

8. *Ibid,* 16 and 28 May 1795.

9. Caroline Carr to Harriet Carr, 28 May 1795.

10. John Carr to Ralph Carr, 27 May 1801.

11. *Family of Carr*, Vol. I, p.196.

12. He and another junior minister, Charles Townshend, were two of the earliest members of the Association for the Preservation of Liberty and Property against Republicans and Levellers.

13. Ralph Carr to his children, December 1796.

14. Caroline Twistleton, "Family Memoirs".

15. Mrs Cooke's husband the Rev. Joseph Cooke of Newton hall took the name of Widdrington. He died s.p. but his sister married Captain Shallcross Jackson who also took the name of Widdrington despite the most tenuous of connections with that name.

16. John Carr to Ralph Carr, undated but must be 1797.

17. When Charles Byne prevailed upon his mother to loan him three thousand guineas to enable him to purchase a troop of dragoons, he did so with "professions of altering his manner of living; in which if he is not sincere, he is the greatest hypocrit that ever lived". The intermediary in this matter, Edward Lodge, found himself embarrassed: "My crime in this matter was entrusting your son to receive this last money of Troughton and Sir J. Hankey when he took up £50 more than he should have done". Edward Lodge to Mrs Anne Byne, 25 Dec. 1754 and 21 Feb. 1756.

18. Anne Skerrett, daughter of Henry Byne, married John Skerrett, afterwards Lieutenant General Skerrett. Their son Major General John Byne Skerrett was to have a distinguished military career in the Peninsular War and to die of wounds received at the battle of Bergen Op-Zoom in 1814. He defended the Duke of Kent's conduct at Gibraltar when that royal duke was accused of bringing the garrison to a state of mutiny by his martinet's attitude to discipline. Kent wrote to him, Oct. 11, 1804, "I am particularly gratified by your unqualified approbation of my measures and conduct". He went on to congratulate Skerrett on his acquittal after his sentence at a court martial for protecting and favouring some soldiers who had been heavy handed with a riotous crowd at Chichester.

19. Annabella Carr to Ralph Carr, 15 April 1799 NRO. 655. Box 6.

20. Caroine Twistleton, "Family Memoirs", p.34.

21. Ralph Carr to Ralph Carr jnr. 8 July 1801 NRO. 855. Box 7.

22. A clump of Pan's hair is preserved in the pages of Caroline Twistleton's "Family Memoirs", which gives a certain piquancy to reading about this long-dead dog.

23. Annabella Carr to Ralph Carr jnr., 20 April 1806.

Chapter 14

A Gentry Family

We feel...that we have already within our grasp as large a portion of individual and general freedom as social man can possibly exercise; and we will not quit our hold to grasp at specious shadows.

John Carr at a Pitt Club Dinner

The death of a man of ninety-five should not have been unexpected but Ralph Carr had remained an active head of the family till the end and had lived so long that his death did come as a great shock. John Carr was now Mr. Carr of Dunston Hill and the house was no longer "home" in the same sense to his brothers and sisters. Ralph and his family who had spent so much time there felt this loss as did the unmarried Annabella. As she wrote to John some seven years after her father's death: "I understand you have laid out a great deal of money in improvements at DH and made it quite *another place*".

John Carr was to make further improvements to Dunston Hill and his brother Ralph's son, John, revisiting the house in 1822 after a long absence wrote: "I am writing in the library which was the old dining room. The new dining room is towards the old garden, an admirable room-the old drawing room as it was. Another (much larger) made out of the former hall".[1] John also added the present roof, which replaced the old flat roof,[2] and built the stable block at a distance from the house. He extended the size of the parkland buying more than a hundred extra acres of land and diverting the Dunston-Whickham turnpike to the line of the road known as Carr's Bank.

Even before his father's death, John had taken a leading role in county affairs as a JP for both Northumberland and Durham. When the Deputy-Lieutenants and magistrates of Northumberland met to make arrangements for the defence and security of the county in 1803, John Carr was given the responsibility as Deputy-Lieutenant for the defence of the North Division of Coquetdale Ward. After succeeding to his estates, he became an ever more active public figure.

In 1813 he was High Sheriff of Northumberland, an office which occasioned considerable expense and much ceremony. The High Sheriff and his retinue of friends and supporters had to meet the Assize judges on the Durham Road and to do so in state carriages with servants in livery (Carr's was yellow and the dress livery drab, with scarlet facings). The number of county families attending these occasions was a measure of the popularity and standing of the High Sheriff. John Carr came out well, Mrs Hudson sending her carriage all the way from Whitley Bay and Lord Strathmore, who had not attended for years, giving up a day's shooting to appear. It was a colourful occasion: the manes of the horses were adorned with scarlet ribbons, while the pages wore white pantaloons with scarlet jackets trimmed with silver cord and lace together with drab sarsenet sashes that had scarlet and silver lace at the ends. As Miss Rogerson, a friend of the family remarked, "Is it not splendid and what an expense wholly useless after the day".[3]

As we have seen, John Carr was a moderate Whig in his political views, tending to find himself in agreement with such as Lord Grey, Sir Charles Monck, Charles Bigge, Matthew White Ridley and, though he was formally a Tory, Cuthbert Ellison. After the Treaty of Amiens and the renewal of the war with France, there was general opposition to Napoleon and agreement on the necessity of winning the war and divisions between Whig and Tory, always complex and never tidy or very clear, became less bitter. John Carr seems to have admired Lord Grenville above other politicians and Grenville was at once the leading Whig after Fox's death and a man who had served under Pitt. Thus we find John Carr, who declined an invitation to stand for Durham County as a Whig in 1815, presiding at a Pitt dinner in Newcastle the same year. His remarks illuminate his political convictions:

> *We cherish our institutions, as they exist, not because we are friends to arbitrary power, but because we are satisfied with the good we actually possess, and will not risk it for visionary ameliorations ; and we will endeavour to perpetuate this, not because we are the abettors of the monarchical branch of our constitution but because we are the assertors of the just rights of all.*

These words can be interpreted as either Whig or Tory. Burke after all was a Whig.

The inheritance of John Carr was considerable. In addition to Dunston Hill, Hedgeley, Prendwich and Bygate Hall, he had the lease on the valuable Embleton and Ponteland tithes and the land and houses which went with the Ponteland leases. As George Tate looked after the north Northumberland estates, so Robert Kyle was the capable agent at Ponteland. But, as Ralph Carr had been generous to his daughters and to his younger son in his will, John was by no means rich in terms of ready money. Much of the money was in stocks, depressed at the time of Ralph

Carr's death, and the will called upon the younger son and sisters not to ask for their full inheritance for at least five years, so that John would not suffer by selling stock in a poor market. Nevertheless, wartime prices for corn were high, ensuring both healthy rentals and an excellent income from the tithes.

The importance of this tithe income has already been stressed and, not long after Ralph Carr's death, John had to deal with an attempt by Merton College to reduce the Carrs' share. In 1809 the college engaged the Northumberland valuer, John Dinning, to survey Embleton and Ponteland and revalue the tithes. Dinning reported that the tithes were greatly undervalued by the present rental and, when the terms were due for renewal in 1811, the college asked Carr for a fine of £7,777.18s.9d, quoting Dinning's estimate of the clear annual value as £4,443. 18s.9d.[4] Even this greatly increased fine still left room for a good profit with the inflated wheat prices then prevailing but John decided to make a lower offer.

In October 1811 it was recorded in the Merton College Register that:

> *The warden having communicated the contents of a letter from Mr Carr proposing the sum of five thousand pounds instead of seven thousand seven hundred and seventy six pounds twelve shillings and ninepence, the fine fixed by the college for the renewal of the leases of the Tythes of Emildon and Ponteland; it is agreed that such a Proposal is inadmissible, in as much as the Society see no need at present for departing from Mr Dinning's valuation and that the Sub-Warden be desired to acquaint Mr Carr with the result of this meeting: stating at the same time that if Mr Carr should continue to think that Mr Dinning has made an unreasonable Estimate of the Tythes the College in that case will have no objection to submit them to another Valuation by a person of unexceptional character unconnected with the County of Northumberland.[5]*

A valuer connected with the county might well have been expected to give the most accurate estimate but, no doubt, John Carr objected to John Dinning, a man he had dealings with on other matters, just because he had too intimate knowledge of Northumberland and might be prejudiced. He did not in any case press for another valuation but upped his offer to £6,000. The college again declared this offer inadmissible.[6] The way was now open for agreement and at a meeting in the Warden's lodgings it was agreed that the fine be worked out on the basis of two separate valuations Dinning had carried out, the one in 1808 and the other in 1810, instead of the 1810 valuation alone; in addition allowance was made for a five per cent reduction to cover the expence of collecting the tithes. The new sum John was asked to pay was £6,869.9s.[7]

Perhaps unwisely John continued to balk at paying what the college asked and offered to pay 6,000 guineas. It was hardly sensible to risk loosing the tithes for a matter of £500 and his bluff was called. The college not only turned down his offer, but declared the treaty for renewal at an end. John was told he had just over a week in which to accept.[8] By return post the college received a letter in which he agreed to pay their price.[9]

Merton had moved from being negligent about their tithes to becoming eager to exact their full value. This was particularly worrying for John Carr as it is clear that his income was dangerously dependent on the profits from the tithes.

In his dealings with the college, John was able to depend on the professional advice and assistance of his brother, Ralph, now well established as a lawyer. Ralph conducted negotiations with the more recalcitrant of the Ponteland and Embleton tithe payers as well as advising his brother on negotiations with Merton. Ralph had bought the small estate of Barrow Point in Pinner in 1806 but a fondness for his home country made him eager to buy land in Northumberland, where his father had wished to see him established as a landowner.

Land was not easy to come by in the wartime period with its high prices for food and, when an estate at Longhorseley became available, Ralph was eager to purchase it. John, as the man on the spot with a wide knowledge of land values in Northumberland, was at first cautious. He had it surveyed and reported, in December 1806, that it was let at £1,780 a year and "might with prudence be bought at £62,500". A few months later he was more pessimistic. He knew "...of no more bleak or comfortless tract of country" and the present tenants were farming badly and greedily. As a financial proposition its purchase was "a nicely balanced bargain/ in its present exhausted state and the liberties that will be taken with it by the occupiers/ at £60,000".[10] A few days later he had reconsidered and, although still cautious, recommended purchasing along with a partner. He thought Charles Bigge might be interested in a joint purchase and that Ralph could always sell his share later with no loss.[11] By September the transaction was under way; Ralph was to take a 2/5 share of Longhorsley and Bigge the rest.[12] He didn't hold on to his purchase for long and in 1810 sold his share to Bigge and bought an estate of about 1,000 acres at Stannington from Lord Carlisle. The Longhorsley deal seems to have suited both Ralph and Charles Bigge. Bigge immediately started building his house, Linden Hall. John, who still thought the estate to be in "Fawish country" (probably a reference to the bands of gypsies, who still roamed the wilder parts of Northumberland), thought little of the site: "I looked at Bigge's site for his new house and cannot help thinking he might have found a better on so large an estate"; in a reference to the windswept nature of Longhorsley he wondered whether Bigge had planted trees to shelter the house or built a house to shelter his trees.[13] Ralph's new estate at Stannington suited him well though he and his sons used it mainly in the shooting season. He had probably been helped in acquiring it by his wife's family's connections with the Earls of Carlisle to whom Caroline's father Francis Gregg had been agent.

That John and his brother Ralph remained close and knowledgeable of each other's affairs was to prove important. John, early in 1817, was 52, had a large family of eight children and appeared in good health but on 17 January he died of apoplexy. Ralph, with his intimate knowledge of his brother's affairs was able not only to comfort his brother's widow but to look after her and her children's interests.

John's death came just as another renewal of the lease on the Embleton and Ponteland tithes was due. Merton College had had a new valuation made and this time negotiations proceeded face to face in London at meetings attended by the college bursar, John Oglander, the valuer a Mr Crabtree and Ralph. The ensuing agreement, a fine of £8,000, reflected the high prices of 1817 and 1818 (due to poor harvests) which were to drop considerably in subsequent years.

Such a large fine on the brink of an agricultural depression in which grain prices would be halved must have severely diminished the profitability of the Carrs' tithe farming operation. Rents and fines could be reduced as well as raised and this was indeed the case with the renewals of the Carrs agreements with Merton during the depressed eighteen twenties. There was still a good profit to be made from the tithes and Ralph Carr looked after his brother's interests well, but the gold mine his father had shrewdly discerned lay, not in the margin between a professional valuation of the rental and a reasonable allowance to the tithe collector, but in the wide gap between, what the rather indolent college authorities of the eighteenth century were prepared to accept, and the real value of the tithes. The days of two or three hundred per cent profit were gone long before the Tithe Commutation Act of 1836 spelled out the end of the Carrs' lease on the Merton tithes, a lease which eventually expired in 1853.

The diminished returns from the tithes reduced considerably the income of the widowed Mrs John Carr and her young family. The family estates remained extensive, however, and, with the brotherly advice of Ralph Carr available and capable agents looking after the day to day running of the estates, the widow brought up her family in prosperous circumstances. Hannah Carr was unwilling to send her boys away to school at an early age and insisted to their joint guardian, her brother-in-law, Ralph, that they be sent to a small private school at Ovingham-on-Tyne. It was not until he was thirteen that the eldest son, Ralph, went to Harrow before going on to Christ Church, Oxford. He married Elizabeth Werge in 1830 when he was twenty-four. Her father, Major Henry Werge, of a family settled in

Northumberland since the early eighteenth century had been killed at the storming of St. Sebastian in 1813, while her mother was the daughter of the Reverend Henry Ellison of the Newcastle branch of the Ellisons.

Ralph Carr's marriage took place in the same year as his uncle, Cuthbert Ellison, retired from politics. Cuthbert would live for another thirty years and, ten years later, Ralph Carr would inherit the entailed estates of the Ellisons and take the name of Carr-Ellison.

References

1.   John Carr to his sister, Caroline Twistleton, Dec. 1822. "Family Memoirs".

2.   Recent architectural detective work by the Architects, Simpson and Brown, suggests that the development of Dunston Hill into its present form was complex. They suggest that, as the decorative mouldings have a dominant style but with many inconsistencies, the house was, "altered and added to in a piecemeal way over an extended period between the end of the eighteenth century and through the early nineteenth century" and then added to in a sympathetic style in the 1880s. John Carr's Italian sojourn may have provided an Italianate influence. Whether the making of the north door the front door was the work of John Carr in the 1815 rebuilding or of his father, Ralph, the present author thinks it a misconceived alteration: the north front lacks symmetry and the windows to the right of the front door are barrack-like, while the East front is both balanced and charming.

3.   *Family of Carr,* Vol. I, p.108.

4.   Warden of Merton College to John Carr, 3 Aug. 1811. Carr-Ellison Papers, Box 3.

5.   Merton College Register, 30 Oct. 1811.

6.   *Ibid*, 13 Nov. 1811.

7.   *Ibid*, 22 Nov. 1811.

8.   *Ibid*, 11 Dec. 1811.

9.   *Ibid*, 13 Dec. 1811.

10.   John Carr to Ralph Carr, 25 Dec. 1806 and March 1807. NRO. 855. Box 7.

11.   *Ibid*, 23 March 1807.

12.   *Ibid*, 6 Sept. 1807.

13.   *Ibid*, 7 Oct. 1810 and 25 Oct. 1816.

Conclusion

In the 175 years since the young John Carr had set out from Hexham to a Newcastle where Robert Ellison was prospering as a leading merchant and civic dignitary, the fortunes of both Ellisons and Carrs had grown with those of Tyneside. The Ellisons had come to be accounted amongst the richest commoners in England and the Carrs had moved from the status of modest merchants to wealthy landed proprietors.

If the progress of both families had been made possible by a direct line of male heirs, during a period when so many lines failed for the lack of them, and advantageous marriages had played their part, the ability and acumen of men like John Carr (the Patriarch), Henry Ellison (1699-1775) and, above all, that extraordinary merchant, Ralph Carr, had been crucial.

The rise of the Carrs and Ellisons had been interwoven with the development of a region and they had played no little part in that development. The world of a Newcastle still dependent on the strength of its walls and dominated by the Merchant Adventurers Company and the Hostmen was gone and, though the age of an industrialised North East with heavy engineering and great shipyards was still to come, a prosperous and steadily urbanising society had emerged.

As has been emphasised, it is important to consider that society in its own right. Contemporaries could not foresee that steam ships would replace sail, nor steam engines come to power workshops and factories. That parliamentary reform and the end of a confessional state were just around the corner was far from the expectation of the great majority of people. The history of the Carrs and Ellisons casts much light on the way that a unique economy and society worked. The careers of Henry Ellison (1699-1775) and Ralph Carr (1711-1806), in particular, reveal much about how money was made and retained within an economy which expanded and prospered within the constraints of organic power.

Social developments paralleled and, in part, reflected the region's increased prosperity. The two families established themselves amongst the ruling elite. If the Ellisons' wealth and connections placed them on the divide between aristocracy and gentry and the Carrs were by 1830 squarely among the gentry, both could be seen as leaders of that broader category "polite society". As Paul Langford has remarked: "Polite living and commercial consumption with any real degree of choice were for the propertied members of society".[1] That section of society, however, expanded throughout the eighteenth century and, diverse though it was with many gradations within it, polite society provided the context for major social developments. As Langford perceptively discerns, its politeness and its commercial consumption went hand in hand. It set a social standard of manners and behaviour for those within it and it used wealth to purchase, not only the clothes, carriages and houses which distinguished it, but education, entertainment and culture. It was not the aristocracy, the gentry or wealthier bankers and merchants who created the London round of pleasure and shopping, who formed the consumers of what Bath had to offer or created provincial societies with their circulating libraries, assembly rooms and theatres, but all of these categories together as polite society. The development and expansion of that section of society in the North East saw a new refinement in manners, a great increase in the consumption of luxuries, an emphasis upon education and the provision of public forums, open to the paying customer, for the enjoyment of the arts and entertainment. Hughes's discerned a "Caucasian spring" in the building and furnishment of houses like Gateshead Park, Gibside and Seaton Delaval Hall early in the eighteenth century. By the beginning of the nineteenth, comfort and taste were to be found not only in the houses of merchants and gentry but in the public buildings of Newcastle where a provincial society met to dance, to borrow library books, see plays, listen to music or attend lectures. We witness it in the lifestyle of the Carr family at their townhouse in Charlotte Square.

That marital and family relationships could be as affectionate as in any subsequent period is vouched for by the histories of the Carr and Ellison families. The financial provisions made for female members of the family demonstrate that, amongst the wealthier classes of society, women, even after marriage, could be far from propertyless, while the lives of Harriet and Annabella Carr reveal the extent of the education and the degree of independence the mores of the late eighteenth century could permit.

That power and influence in England during the years covered by this volume depended to a significant degree upon connections and, especially, upon vertical connections, has long been held by historians. Whether we consider the long chain of connection which descended from the Duke of Grafton to the Ellisons and from them to quite humble persons, the influence Ralph Carr had with Lords Eldon and Stowell and with Sir John Dick, or the networks which supported Cuthbert Ellison's electioneering, there is evidence enough that such webs of inter-connection bound society together and made it work.

The rise of the Ellisons and the Carrs and, indeed of many other North-East families demonstrate that the elite was an open elite. For several generations both families had straddled merchant and gentry society. There is little in their history to suggest any great gulf between merchants and gentry in North East England, nor that urban wealth was unable to translate itself into broad acres. It was not easy to join the ranks of the region's leading families and few made the leap in one generation, but the steady progress of many families, among them the Carrs and the Ellisons, suggest that the elite was far from closed.

References

1.   Langford, p. 6.

Appendix A

The Ellisons

The ancestry of the Ellisons cannot be traced back further than the sixteenth century with any accuracy. J. Hodgson and R. Surtees, respectively the historians of Northumberland and Durham, concluded that the Ellison pedigree was only certain as far back as Cuthbert Ellison of Newcastle who was Sheriff and then Mayor of Newcastle in the 1550s. The name was previously not unknown in Northumberland: one "Rob. fil Elye" is, according to Welford[1] mentioned in the pipe rolls of the reign of Henry III while a Thomas Elyson is referred to in the "Black Book of Hexham" as a Priory tenant in 1479[2] and a John Ellison was Vicar of Chollerton in 1485.[3] It seems likely, however, that the Ellisons who became prominent in sixteenth century Newcastle came there from nearby Stamfordham where the Elysons had a share in the town fields of Hawkswell.

Ellison Pedigree

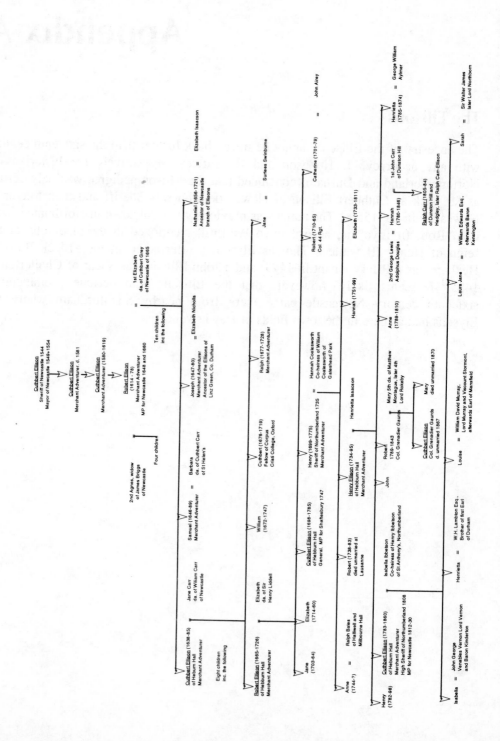

References

1. R. Welford, Men of Mark 'twixt Tyne and Tweed (1895) p.145.

2. Northumberland County History , Vol. III p. 148.

3. *Ibid*, Vol. IV p.267.

Appendix B

The Carrs

The name Carr is a form of Kerr, a long established name on the Scottish side of the Border where the Kerrs were one of the most prominent families in the Scottish Middle March. It seems probable that their arrival in Scotland was part of the process by which the Anglo-Norman feudal ascendancy was established. They were one of the foremost reiving or border-raiding families, though, as they were much given to blood feuds, they expended almost as much energy on internecine warfare with their Scottish neighbours, especially the Scotts sept, as upon raids into Tynedale. As with many border families, branches of the Kerrs were, in more settled times to outgrow their violent antecedents and achieve great wealth and status; the dukes of Roxburgh, the marquises of Lothian and the earls of Antrim have all Kerr ancestry.

Carr was the form that the same sept used on the English side of the border. Trans-border links between families were common, especially during the long peace of the thirteenth century and as <u>Carr</u>, the name is to be found in Northumberland from at least that period. As the two columns of Carrs in the Northumberland telephone directory testify, those who bear the name continue to be common in that county today.

The genealogical research of R. E. Carr and of his brother C. E. Carr[1] established a pedigree for his family going back to a William Carr who held one third of the land at the manor of Bavington Magna near Hexham in the early fifteenth century. Within a few generations, his descendents were established in various parts of Northumberland, owning land at Prudhoe, Ovingham, Hetton, Newton-by-the-Sea, Netherwiton, Holywell, Embleton, Alnwick and Lesbury, while some went were beyond the county in St Helen's Auckland, Craven and Sleaford. Members of the family intermarried with gentry families such as the Claverings of Callaly, the Collingwoods of Eslington, the Erringtons of Walwick and the Greys of Horton Castle.

In the fifth or sixth generation after the William who held land at Great Bavington, a branch of the family came into possession of Woodhall which lies close to Haydon Bridge on the south bank of the River Tyne. Although those two expert genealogists, R. E. Carr and C. E. Carr, disagreed with each other and with the College of Arms as to the exact line of descent, it seems clear that William and John (or James) Carr of the Carrs of Hetton, both of whom are alternatively described as of Woodhall and of Hexham, were respectively the ancestors of the Dunston Hill and the Cars of Eshott and Hetton. From this line also descended the Carrs of Monkwearmouth.

The Woodhall estate remained in the possession of the descendents of John for about a century; his grandson, John of Woodhall, married Catherine Grey of Horton Castle and, in 1615, William Carr of Woodhall, who had married his cousin, Elizabeth, daughter of William Carr of Ford, was listed as one of the eighty-nine heads of gentry families in Northumberland . Shortly after this the family gave up their Woodhall connection and settled at Eshott.

Both the Eshott (ex-Woodhall) Carrs and the Hetton (Ford) Carrs maintained their gentry status into the seventeenth century: Thomas Carr of Ford was, like William Carr of Woodhall, the head of a gentry family and a substantial resident landowner, though he was omitted from the list of gentry drawn up in 1615.[2] The branch of the family which is the subject of this book, that emanating from the first William Carr of Woodhall or Hexham, carried on in a more modest way in the town of Hexham and the surrounding Hexhamshire.

Carr Pedigree

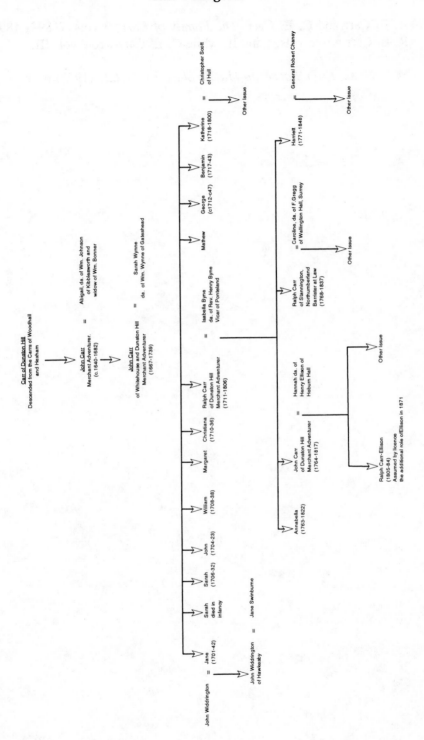

References

1.   R. E. Carr and C. E. Carr, *The Family of Carr*, 3 vols. (1893, 1894, 1899). R. E. Carr wrote vols. I and II, while C. E. Carr wrote vol. III.

2.   S. J. Watts, *From Border to Middle Shire 1588-1625* (1975) p. 59.

Bibliography

Primary Sources

Cotesworth MSS, Gateshead Public Library.

Ellison MSS, Gateshead Public Library.

Carr-Ellison MSS, Northumberland Record Office.

Carr-Ellison and Carr and Ellison MSS, Hedgeley Hall.

Collegii Mertonensis Registrum, Merton College Library.

Newcastle Trinity House Primage Account Boooks, Tyne Wear Archive.

Printed Primary Sources

The Letters of Henry Liddell to William Cotesworth, ed. Joyce Ellis, The Surtees Society, vol. CXCVII, 1987.

The Correspondence of James Clavering, ed. H. T. Dickinson, Surtees Society, Vol. CLXXVIII, (1963).

The Correspondence of Colonel Robert Ellison, ed. Edward Hughes, Archaeologia Aeliana, fourth series, vol. XXXI.

Horace Walpole's Correspondence, The Countesss of upper Ossory, £ Vols. 32-34. Ed. W. S. Lewis (1965).

Memoirs of the Life of Mr. Ambrose Barnes, Surtees Society, vol. L, 1866.

Extracts from The Records of the Merchant Adventurers Society of Newcastle-Upon-Tyne, vol. 1, ed. Rev. J.R.Boyle, Surtees Society, XCIII, 1894, vol. 2, ed. F.W.Dendy, CI, 1899.

Extracts from The Records of the Company of Hostmen of Newcastle-Upon-Tyne, ed. F. W. Dendy, Surtees Society, vol. CV, (1901).

Unpublished Penscripts and Typescripts

Twistleton, Caroline, *Family Memoirs*, Hedgeley Hall.

Ellison, Alfred J., *Ellison Portraits 1510-1936,* (1936) South Tyneside Central Library.

Carr-Harris, Grant, *Ancestry of the Carrs and the Cunninghams,* (1970) Lord Carr of Hadley.

Theses

Barrow, Anthony, *The North-East Whale Industry 1750-1850* (Newcastle Polytechnic Ph.D. 1989).

Ellis, J. M., *A Study of the Business Fortunes of William Cotesworth c.1688-1726* (Oxford University, D.Phil., 1975). Dr Ellis's thesis has been published (New York 1981) but my references are to the thesis.

Banham, John, *Business Development and Banking in North-East England 1755-1839,* Sunderland University Ph.D., 1977.

Stoker, David, *Elections and Voting Behaviour, a study of elections in Northumberland, Durham, Cumberland and Westmoreland,* Manchester Ph.D. 1980.

Books and Articles

Arnold, Ralph, *The unhappy Countess* (1957).

Banham, John, "A very great public convenience: the origins of banking in County Durham", *Durham Local History Bulletin* (1994).

Barton, Peter, "The Alum Ships", *The Dalesman* (March 1969).

Bean, W. W., *The Parliamentary Representation of the Six Northern Counties of England* (1890).

Black, Jeremy, *The British Abroad. The Grand Tour in the Eighteenth Century* (1992).

Bourne, Henry, *History of Newcastle* (1736).

Brett, P. D., "The Newcastle Election of 1830", *Northern History,* Vol. XXIV (1998).

Brewer, J., *The Sinews of Power* (1989).

Burn, W. L., "Newcastle upon Tyne in the Early Nineteenth Century", *Archaeologia Aeliana* (1956).

Carr, R. E. and C. E., *The Family of Carr,* 3 volumes (1893-99).

Carr, R. E. and C. E., *The Family of Werge* (1891).

Clark, J. C. D., *Revolution and Rebellion. State and Society in England in the seventeenth and eighteenth centuries* (1984).

Cooper, J. P., "Social and Economic Policies under the Commonwealth" in *The Interregnum. The Quest for Settlement,* ed. Aylmer G. E. (1972).

Ellis, J. M., *A Study of the Business fortunes of William Cotesworth c. 1668-1726,* (1981).

Ellis, J. M., "The Poisoning of William Cotesworth, 1725", *History Today.*

Ellis, J. M., "The Decline and Fall of the Tyneside Salt Industry, 1660-1790: A Re-examination", *Economic History Review,* Second Series, Vol. XXXIII, (Feb. 1980).

Emsley, Clive, *British Society and the French Wars* (1979).

Ernle, Lord, *English Farming Past and Present* (6th ed. 1961).

Evans, Eric J., *The Contentious Tithe* (1976).

Fairbairn, R. A., *The Mines of Alston Moor* (1993).

Fletcher, A. J., *The Outbreak of the English Civil War* (1981).

Fores, Michael, "The Myth of a British Industrial Revolution", *History,* Vol. 66, No. 217, (June 1981).

Gray, W., *Chorographia or A Survey of Newcastle upon Tyne* (first published 1649, refs. to 1883 edition).

Halliday, S., "Social Mobility, Demographic Change and the Landed Elite of County Durham, 1610-1819: an open or shut case?" *Northern History,* vol. XXX, 1984.

Hayes, James, "Two soldier brothers of the Eighteenth Century", *Army Historical Research* (1964).

Healey, Edna, *Couts and Co. 1692-1992. The Portrait of a Bank (1992).*

Hepple, Leslie W., *A History of Northumberland and Newcastle upon Tyne* (1976).

Hinds, Allen B., Vol. iii of *A History of Northumberland,* Northumberland County History Committee eds. (1896).

Horn, Pamela, *The Rural World* (1980).

Horsley, P. M., *Eighteenth Century Newcastle* (1971)

Howell, Roger Jr., *Puritans and Radicals in North England* (1984).

Howell, Roger Jr., *Newcastle-upon-Tyne and the Puritan Revolution* (1967).

Hughes, Edward, *North Country Life in the Eighteenth Century. The North East 1700-1750,* (1952).

Levine, David and Wrightson, Keith, *The Making of an Industrial Society. Whickham 1560-1745* (1991).

McCord, Norman, *North East England. An Economic and Social History* (1979).

McCord, Norman, "Some Aspects of changes in the Nineteenth Century North East", *Northern History,* Vol. XXXI, (1995).

Mackenzie, E. and Ross, E., *An Historical, Topographical, and Descriptive View of the County Palatinate of Durham,* Vol. 1 (1834).

Mingay, G. E., *The Gentry* (1976).

Manning, Brian, *The Crisis of the English Revolution* (1976).

Middlebrook, Sydney, *Newcastle upon Tyne. Its Growth and Achievement* (1950).

Nef, J. U., *The Rise of the British Coal Industry,* 2 vols. (1932).

Nossiter, T. J., *Influence, Opinion and Political Idioms in Reformed England 1832-74* (1975).

Ormrod, David, *English Grain Exports and the Structure of Agrarian Capitalism* (1985)

Phillips, Maberly, *A History of Banks, Bankers and Banking in Northumberland, Durham and North Yorkshire*(1894).

Philp, Mark, "Vulgar Conservatism, 1792-3", *The Historical Review* No. 435, (Feb. 1995).

Purdue, A. W., "John and Harriet Carr: a Brother and Sister from the North East on the Grand Tour", *Northern History,* vol. XXX (1994).

Purdue, A. W., "An Oxford College, Two Parishes and a Tithe-Farmer: the Modernisation of Tithe Collection", *Rural History* (1997).

Raistrick, Arthur and Jennings, Bernard, *A History of Lead Mining in the Pennines* (1965).

Ridley, Matt, *The Merchant Adventurers of Newcastle upon Tyne* (1998).

Roberts, William I., "Ralph Carr: A Newcastle Merchant and the American Colonial Trade", *Business History Review (1968).*

Russell, C., ed., *The Origins of the English Civil War* (1975).

Sharp, Cuthbert ed., *Memorials of the Rebellion of the Earls of Northumberland and Westmoreland* (1840). Reprinted as the *Rising of the North* (1975).

Speck, W. A., "Northumberland Elections in the Eighteenth Century", *Northern History,* Vol. XXVII (1992).

Stone, Lawrence, *The Family, Sex and Marriage in England 1500-18000* (1977).

Stone, Lawrence and Jeanne C. Fawtier, *An Open Elite? England 1540-1880* (1984).

Tate, W. E., *The Parish Chest. A Study of the Records of Parish Administration in England* (1960).

Watts, S. J., *From Border to Middle Shire* (1975).

Welford, R. T., ed., *Men of Mark 'twixt Tyne and Tweed* (1865).

Wrigley E. A., *People, Cities and Wealth, The Transformation of Traditional Society* (1987).

Wrigley, E. A. and Schofield, R. S., *The Population History of England 1541-1871* (1981).

Index